Dividends
Pros, Cons, Sources and Strategies

By Devin Hobbes

I0483729

Dividends: Pros, Cons, Sources and Strategies. Copyright ©
2012 by Devin Hobbes. All rights reserved.

For Liza, as always.

Table of Contents

Introduction   1

**Part One - Arguments in Favor of Investing in Dividend   3
Paying Stocks**

Chapter 1 - What's the Point of Holding Non-Dividend   4
Paying Shares?

Chapter 2 - Dividends Can Force Share Price Appreciation   12

Chapter 3 - Dividends Can Keep Pace with Inflation   22

Chapter 4 - Dividend Stocks Are Less Volatile   28

Chapter 5 - Other Advantages of Investing in Dividend   36
Paying Stocks

Part Two - Common Arguments Against Dividends   41

Chapter 6 - Important Terms You Should Know   42

Chapter 7 - Arguments Against Dividends   47

Part Three - Dividend Sources: Common Stocks   67

Chapter 8 - Utilities   69

Chapter 9 - Healthcare   72

Chapter 10 - Technology   76

Chapter 11 - Financials   80

Chapter 12 - Basic Materials   85

Chapter 13 - Industrial Goods   90

Chapter 14 - Consumer Goods   93

Chapter 15 - Services   100

**Part Four - Dividends and "Dividends" from Sources   102
Other than Common Stocks**

Chapter 16 - Preferred Stocks   103

Chapter 17 - Real Estate Investment Trusts (REITs)   111

Chapter 18 - Master Limited Partnerships (MLPs) 115

Chapter 19 - Royalty Income Trusts 132

Chapter 20 - Exchange Traded Funds (ETFs) and Exchange Traded Notes (ETNs) 136

Chapter 21 - Closed End Funds (CEFs) 147

Chapter 22 - Bond Funds 158

Part Five - Dividend Reinvestment Plans and Bypassing Your Broker 167

Chapter 23 - Pros and Cons of Dividend Reinvestment 168

Chapter 24 - Pros and Cons of Bypassing Your Broker with Direct Stock Purchase and Transfer Agents 176

Chapter 25 - Buying Funds without a Broker 186

Part Six - Strategies 188

Chapter 26 - Using Options to Get Extra Income and Reduce Portfolio Risk 189

Chapter 27 - Dividend Capture Strategies and Why They Usually Don't Work for Individual Investors 237

Part Seven - Building Your Portfolio 248

Chapter 28 - Mostly Useless Stock Metrics 249

Chapter 29 - Less Useless Stock Metrics 260

Chapter 30 - Save on Costs Whenever Possible 276

Chapter 31 - Have a Plan 283

Chapter 32 - Diversify, Diversify, Diversify! 285

Chapter 33 - My Approach to Dividend Stocks 296

Introduction

This book is not for those hoping to get rich quick from the stock market. Nor is it for those who cannot leave their investments alone, unable to resist constantly buying and selling. If you are of the opinion or are at least open to the idea that the best way to wealth is through slow and steady investment, however, keep reading. If you cringe whenever you hear someone say "buy and hold is dead; this is a trader's market," this book is for you.

The objective of this book is fivefold: First, to present a case for investing in dividend paying stocks. Second, to examine and evaluate arguments against dividend investing. Third, to present the advantages and disadvantages of the various stock market sources of dividends and other distributions. Fourth, to evaluate various income investing strategies. And fifth, to discuss the importance of diversification and having an investment plan.

This book means to provide new investors with the tools they need to begin investing and veteran investors with ideas and strategies that might not have occurred to them previously.

Accordingly, Part One presents the various reasons for owning dividend paying stocks. In Part Two, arguments against dividends are evaluated, both from the corporate payer and individual payee perspectives.

Parts Three and Four examine the various stock market sources of dividend income and the advantages and disadvantages of each. The sources include not only the dividends from common stocks, but also the distributions from preferred stock, real estate investment trusts, master limited partnerships, royalty income trusts, exchange traded funds, exchange traded notes, and closed end funds.

Part five concerns the advantages and disadvantages of dividend reinvestment. Different methods of reinvesting dividends are presented and evaluated. This includes bypassing your broker by enrolling in direct stock purchase and dividend reinvestment programs.

Part six evaluates the various strategies investors use to get the most out of their dividend paying stocks. This includes using options for extra income and insurance. It also includes a chapter on dividend capture strategies and why they are not for individual investors.

The book concludes with Part Seven, which is about building a core dividend portfolio and the importance of diversification and asset allocation.

Part One -Arguments in Favor of Investing in Dividend Paying Stocks

Chapter 1 - What's the Point of Holding Non-Dividend Paying Shares?

To profit from a non-dividend paying stock, you must sell your shares to someone else for more than you paid for them. Once you sell your shares you can no longer participate in the company's growth. If you own a dividend paying stock, on the other hand, you get a return without ever having to part with your shares. You can participate in the future growth of the company indefinitely without decreasing your stake in it. Here is a story to illustrate.

Let's say Bob has a few bucks to invest. An acquaintance of his, who is raising money for a new business venture, offers to sell Bob some stock. Bob looks over the business plan and likes it. He talks it over with his spouse and they agree to buy a few thousand worth of shares. They're sure that in several years the company will have stores not just in their neighborhood, but all over the state.

The acquaintance and his partners control most of the company's shares. They hold management positions and run the day to day business of the company. They also sit on the board of directors. As such, they get paid salaries and receive other benefits. Bob and a few other minority shareholders receive regular reports from them and are invited to the annual shareholder meetings. There they cast votes for the board of directors and ask the board of directors questions.

It turns out that Bob is right. The company grows rapidly. It has several stores now and is looking to expand into neighboring states. As its revenues grow, so do the managers' salaries and perks. The company has no plans to pay a dividend. All its earnings net of expenses and reinvestment go into a bank account.

Ten years after Bob bought his shares, the company operates in several states and has revenues in the tens of millions. His acquaintance and the other managers now live in mansions, drive around in fancy cars, and give lots of money to charity. As the company grew, so did their salaries and bonuses.

Although he has slept soundly in the knowledge that the company is doing well, Bob hasn't seen a cent from his investment yet. At the latest shareholder meeting, management reiterated that the company does not plan to pay a dividend now or in the foreseeable future. His kid is going to college soon, so Bob thinks it's a good time to cash in on his investment.

To whom will he sell his shares? And for what price? Let's say the company isn't interested in buying them back. Management doesn't need them either. They already have control. Bob will tell you, quite honestly, that the company is still growing at a rapid clip. Sales, profits, and cash flows are increasing at a phenomenal rate. The company has no debt and management seems to be making all the right decisions. That is, the company is well run and its future looks just as bright today as it did when Bob first bought the shares.

Would you buy the shares from Bob? You've been given all of the reasons why the company will do well for many more years to come. But do you have any reason to think that it's a good investment? For someone buying a majority stake in the company, absolutely. That is because they will have access to the company's earnings—either by getting themselves a salaried position or making the board of directors declare a dividend. But Bob's stake is a small one. His vote doesn't really count because he holds so few shares. He can attend shareholder meetings and ask the directors questions, but if he doesn't like what they say or do, the only thing he can do about it is sell his shares.

If you were Bob, knowing all that happened during the ten years, would you have bought the shares? Would you buy the shares from Bob now?

If you would, why? There are a few possibilities. (1) You are a masochist. (2) You hope to find a buyer of the shares in the future that will pay more for them than you paid. (3) You hope that the company will eventually pay a dividend. (4) You hope that the company will go public and have its shares trade on a major exchange. Then you might be able to sell your shares to someone else for more than you paid for them. (5) You hope that a big buyer will make a tender offer for all the outstanding shares for a higher price per share than you paid.

Possibilities (2), (4) and (5) (and 1, I suppose) are about the same. You want to buy low and sell high. If you buy the shares with the plan to sell them later at a profit, you are speculating on their price. That they will appreciate in price depends not only on the company's business prospects, but also upon what buyers are willing to pay. That is to say, if potential share buyers are pessimistic, risk averse, skeptical, or broke, neither the company nor you can do anything about it. There are plenty of examples of companies that have grown tremendously while their share prices fell to a fraction of what they once were.

Possibility (3) is different, but it is moot. In our story we've stipulated that the company will not pay dividends.

So, unless you are the buyer in (5), in which case you would have access to the company's cash flows, is there a point in owning the shares? If you're not the buyer in (5), you hope to find someone else to pay you more for them, and that someone else will be buying for the same reason. That is, he will want to sell the shares to a third person for more than he paid. The third person will want to sell the shares for even more to a fourth person, the fourth person will want to sell them for a profit to a fifth person, and so on. First, how is this different from speculating on the price of anything else? How is it different from "investing" in comics, baseball cards, antiques, etc? Second, doesn't it sound like a Ponzi scheme? The early buyers are paid off with funds raised from later ones. The last buyer gets screwed unless the company pays him cash.

Although there is a real asset underlying the shares, their price is very much disconnected from it. Yes, they can rise and fall with the company's prospects, but they don't have to. If Bob offers you the shares, how much will you be willing to pay? It's within the realm of possibility that what you're willing to pay him will be what he originally paid. It might even be less. That revenues and profits increased many times over doesn't matter. It might be that Bob over-paid, in your view. If you buy the shares, you might overpay in a future buyer's view.

Here's a real life example. Research in Motion (RIMM), the famous maker of the Blackberry, made $213 million in the twelve months before February 2005. It traded for around $22 a share at the time. In the twelve months prior to February 2012, RIMM earned over $2.2 billion. That's over 10 times more. Its share price at the end of 2011? $14.50. Someone who bought shares in 2005 and held until

2012 would lose money, even though the company was much bigger than it was seven years prior. Note that the stock was higher in the intervening years, peaking over $140 per share in 2008, but shareholders would have to know that was when to sell—a time when the future looked so bright it was blinding. And those who bought at the peak in 2008 were not wrong in their view that the company would continue to grow. But the buyers after 2008 were no longer willing to pay as much as their predecessors, who were left holding the bag.

It amuses me to no end when a non-dividend paying company's stock jumps after an earnings announcement or press release stating that the company projects higher profits. Who are the people driving up the share price? What do they hope to achieve? It's not like they'll get a slice of the extra profits (as they would if the company paid dividends). The CEO will get a pay bump, but the shareholders will get nothing unless they sell.

They buy with the hope that there will be future earnings announcements that will tempt others to rush to buy the shares from them. But if they're in the stock market for this reason, why aren't they trading other stuff? Any other object, from baseball cards to food to clothes to commodities will suffice. The prices of the latter four have more to do with the economy than the prices of stocks. And if one is good at buying low and selling high, which is the entire point of stock speculation, one can make a lot more money with commodities than with stocks. So why trade stocks?

There's no standard way to value a company that everyone accepts. In fact, as a seller of the shares, you want to find someone who overvalues the company. You want to find the greatest fool possible. But wouldn't you be a fool for buying what is essentially a piece of paper that serves as a subscription to annual reports and an admission ticket to annual meetings? What is this paper good for if you can't find a buyer? Nothing, in my opinion. In our story, while his acquaintance got rich, Bob got nothing.

But suppose Bob does find a buyer for his shares and makes a very nice profit. Good for him. But now what? Let's say the company continues to grow and the buyer of Bob's shares has no trouble finding other buyers willing to pay him more than he paid Bob. Since Bob sold his shares, he no longer has a stake in the company. If it's sold later to a big buyer or goes public, he won't see a cent. He can always try to buy the shares back, but once he sells them, he can make nothing further from the company. That is to say, his gains are fixed once he sells.

But suppose the company did start paying a dividend while Bob was in possession of the shares. First, he would participate financially in the company's growth. As the company grew, Bob would receive ever larger dividend checks.

Second, although the managers would still make more money than him, Bob would see a return on his money without having to sell his stake. And if the company grew enough, maybe Bob would collect enough from dividends to never have to sell his shares. In theory, Bob can live off of the income until he dies and pass the shares on to his children, who can also live off of the income and pass the shares on to their children. (Isn't that what owning a business is all about? Shares represent an ownership stake in a business. How ludicrous is it that you can own a successful business and not see a penny from it until you sell it?) If the company doesn't pay dividends, the shares can also be

9

passed on from generation to generation. But no one will make a dime from them until the shares are sold, and then the shares will be passed on no more. They will be gone.

(Here's another example. Suppose you're broke. A rich friend dies and bequeaths you $1 million worth of stock in a company that doesn't pay dividends. Congratulations. You went from not having a dollar to your name to being a millionaire. But can you now pay for groceries, gas, and rent? Not unless you sell some shares. On the other hand, if your friend bequeathed you $1 million worth of a stock that yields 5% instead, you wouldn't have to sell any shares because you'd collect $50,000 a year in dividends.)

Third, if the company pays dividends and Bob decides to sell his shares, he will find a buyer more easily. The potential buyer will analyze the shares just as he would if the company didn't pay dividends. That is, he'll look at the company's balance sheet, its earnings, sales growth, and so on. In addition, however, he will analyze the dividend stream and calculate how much he will collect while holding the shares. Bob would be more likely to receive a fair price because the price would factor in future dividend payments. Future dividend payments are different from future cash flows because the shareholder gets the dividend and the company gets the cash flow. A shareholder can't get access to the cash flow unless the company pays a dividend. If the company doesn't pay a dividend, cash flow can be a billion dollars or zero. Until the shareholder sells his stake, it doesn't matter.

This is all to ask, which would you rather buy, shares of a company that pays you nothing to hold them, or shares of a company with the same growth rate, business plan, and so on, but that also pays a dividend? Isn't the choice obvious? You can do everything with the shares of a dividend paying company that you can do with the shares of a non-dividend paying company. With a dividend paying company, however, you also make money simply by holding on to the shares. As a dividend investor, you give the company money with the hope that it will grow and give you a cut of its profits. In an ideal world, you don't care about future share buyers at all. It doesn't matter whether others are willing to pay more than you paid, so long as the company continues to send you your cut.

Chapter 2 - Dividends Can Force Share Price Appreciation

Dividends can make a stock's price go up. It may not make sense at first, but it is true. To see why, we have to discuss the dividend yield.

A stock's dividend yield is its annual dividend payout per share divided by its share price and expressed as a percentage. So, for example, let's say company XYZ's stock trades at $40 a share. Let's also say that XYZ pays out an annual dividend of $2 a share. To find XYZ's yield, we divide 2 by 40. The result is 0.05. Expressed as a percentage, it is 5%. XYZ's dividend yield is therefore 5%. In other words, if you buy XYZ at $40 per share and XYZ continues to pay out $2 per share in dividends annually, you will collect 5% of XYZ's share price in dividends every year. For example, if you invest $10,000 into XYZ at $40 per share, you will receive $500 in dividends every year as long as the dividend rate stays the same.

The dividend yield depends on the relationship between two things: the share price and the annual dividend payout. The share price, as long as the dividend remains the same, has an inverse relationship with the yield. This means that the yield goes down if the share price rises. For example, suppose XYZ continues to pay a dividend of $2 per share, but its share price goes up to $50. XYZ's dividend yield will now be 4%. If you invest $10,000 into XYZ at $50 per share, you will receive $400 a year in dividends. It makes perfect sense, of course, as you are able to buy less shares at $50 per share than you are at $40 per share.

Similarly, if XYZ's share price drops to $30 and it continues to pay a dividend of $2 per share, the yield will be 6.67%. If you invest $10,000 into XYZ at $30 per share, you will collect about $667 per year in dividends. This is because your $10,000 buys you more shares at $30 per piece than it does at $40 or $50. Note that once you make your investment, the share price will continue fluctuating daily. Your yield, in contrast, will stay the same as long as your dividend does.

A stock's dividend yield can also change if its dividend payout per share changes. The annual dividend payout per share has a direct relationship to the dividend yield. That is, as long as the share price stays constant, if the dividend increases, the yield increases. And if the dividend decreases, the yield decreases. Let's go back to our example of XYZ, and say once again that it trades for $40 a share and pays $2 per share in dividends per year. Suppose you bought $10,000 worth of the stock. You collect $500 this year. Suppose next year XYZ raises its dividend payout to $2.20 per share. This means that next year, as long as you hold on to your shares, you will receive $550 in dividends. XYZ's dividend hike makes the yield on your investment jump from 5% to 5.5%. Suppose the following year XYZ raises the dividend again, this time to $2.42 per share. This pushes the yield on your original investment up to 6.05%, and you receive $605 in dividends.

When the dividend drops, on the other hand, the yield falls. Let's say that instead of raising the dividend to $2.20 a share in the second year, XYZ's business suffers and it is forced to cut the dividend down to $1 per share. If you invested $10,000 into XYZ at $40 per share, your dividend yield would drop in the second year to 2.5%. You would collect $250 in dividends. Suppose business at XYZ becomes even worse in the third year and the company chooses not to pay a dividend at all. The dividend yield goes down to 0% and you collect $0 in dividends.

To recap, a stock's dividend yield will drop for two reasons: its share price goes up or its dividend payments go down. And a stock's dividend yield will rise for two reasons: its share price goes down or its dividend payments go up.

You're probably thinking something like, "but don't the dividend payout and share price both change?" That's absolutely right, and this is the reason why dividends can contribute to capital gains (and losses). Let's tackle the losses first. In our example above, XYZ cut its dividend in half and the following year eliminated it altogether. What do you think would have happened to its stock price? A falling dividend means that the company is in trouble. This makes investors flee, which makes share prices fall.

On the other hand, rising dividends attract investors, sending share prices higher. Companies usually try to keep their payout ratio within a certain range. The payout ratio is the amount of money the company pays out in dividends divided by its earnings and expressed as a percentage. For example, if a company earns $1 million and pays out $250,000 in dividends, its payout ratio is 25% ($250,000 divided by $1,000,000 and expressed as a percent). If the payout ratio stays constant and profits rise, the dividend will rise too.

Suppose that XYZ's board of directors has a long standing policy to pay out 50% of the company's earnings in dividends. Let's say, as before, the stock trades at $40 per share and this year has paid out $2 per share in dividends, for a yield of 5%. Its earnings this year, let's say, were $4 per share. (Earnings per share are the company's earnings divided by the number of shares outstanding. For example, if a company earns $12 billion and has three billion shares outstanding, it earns $4 per share. That is 12,000,000,000 divided by 3,000,000,000.) Suppose XYZ's earnings next year increase by 10% to $4.40 per share. If the board of directors keeps the payout ratio at 50%, next year the dividend will go up to $2.20 per share, for a yield of 5.5% (as mentioned above). That's a 10% dividend raise. Note that as long as the payout ratio remains the same, dividend increases will mirror earnings increases.

Share prices go up for various reasons. A company's earnings go up, it is recommended by a guru, it is upgraded by an investment bank, etc. The only guaranteed way that a company's share price will go up is if it raises its dividend (as long as the payout ratio remains about the same). That is, while higher earnings, in themselves, can and often do push a stock price up, there is no guarantee that they will.

There are numerous examples. We've already seen Research in Motion. As another example, take Cisco Systems (CSCO), which until March of 2011 did not pay a dividend. While Cisco's earnings have been bumpy in the last few years, they have gone up from $0.25 per share to $1.17 per share from July 2002 through July 2011. If earnings, by themselves, make a stock's price go up or down, one might suppose that since Cisco increased its earnings almost five-fold over the last ten years that its share price has gone up in tandem.

Not quite. See Box 1. In July 2002, Cisco's stock had a low of $11.45 and a high of $15.06. In July of 2011, when Cisco's earnings were 4.68 times higher, its stock had a low of $15.27 and a high of $16.50. Even if one calculates the stock's move from the bottom in July 2002 to the top in July 2011, it is nowhere near the increase in earnings. From the bottom to the top, the stock's price increased 44%. The company's earnings, on the other hand, increased 368%. If the share price mirrored earnings, Cisco would have to trade at $53.59 per share in July 2011.

Box 1: Cisco Systems Share Price from July 2002 to July 2011

As another example, Apple's (AAPL) earnings per share increased from $0.09 in September 2002 to $27.68 in September 2011. That's 30,655.56%! Its share price increased dramatically over the same period, but not nearly as much: 5,235%.

Enough with the tech companies. How about a non-dividend paying conglomerate? Warren Buffet's Berkshire Hathaway (BRK.A) increased its earnings per share from $521 in December of 2001 to $7,928 in December 2010. That's an increase of 1421.69%. Berkshire's share price, on the other hand, only increased by 75.43% over the same period.

These examples show a number of things. They show that neither earnings nor earnings growth have a direct effect on a stock's price. (There are lots of other factors: investors' risk attitudes, upgrades and downgrades, the general economy, the political climate, the sector the stock is in, and so on.) They also show, especially in Cisco's case, that to make money with a non-dividend paying stock, one has to be very nimble. One would have to know to buy at the bottom and sell at the top to realize the maximum gain. In August of 2011, for example, Cisco fell again, to $13.30 a share, erasing most of the gains one would have earned if one bought the stock at the low ten years earlier. As I'm writing, Cisco trades above $18. In the spring of 2010, it traded above $27. A great market timer would have made lots of money trading Cisco. Most people, however, are terrible market timers. Holding Apple over the ten year period would have been worth it, but it too has been very volatile. Not many investors would be able to wait it out to realize the 5,235% gain.

While earnings and earnings increases do not necessarily move a stock, its dividend (when earnings rise and the payout ratio stays the same) always does. It can take some time, but a stock that has increasing dividend payments while the payout ratio stays the same will go up. The reason for this is that if the share price stays constant or falls while the dividend per share goes up, the yield goes up. Investors are attracted by yields, especially those yields that rise because the dividend per share is going up.

Suppose XYZ's share price is stuck around $40 while the company continues to grow its earnings and dividends at a rate of 10% per year. Also suppose, as before, that during the first year XYZ pays $2 per share in dividends (5% yield), earns $4 per share, and its board of directors has a long standing policy to pay out around 50% of the company's earnings in dividends. After a decade, XYZ's earnings per share will be $9.43. With a payout ratio of 50%, XYZ's annual dividend at the end of the tenth year will therefore be around $4.72 per share. See box 2. If XYZ's share price is still at $40 per share, the stock's dividend yield at the end of the tenth year is around 11.8%. While this is certainly possible, it is very unlikely. The company is healthy and is steadily growing its earnings. At some point during the ten years investors will notice the growing dividend yield, notice that the company is not in trouble, and swoop in to buy shares. The stock price will go up as a result. It will have to because if it didn't, the dividend per share will eventually exceed the share price (after 32 years, in this example).

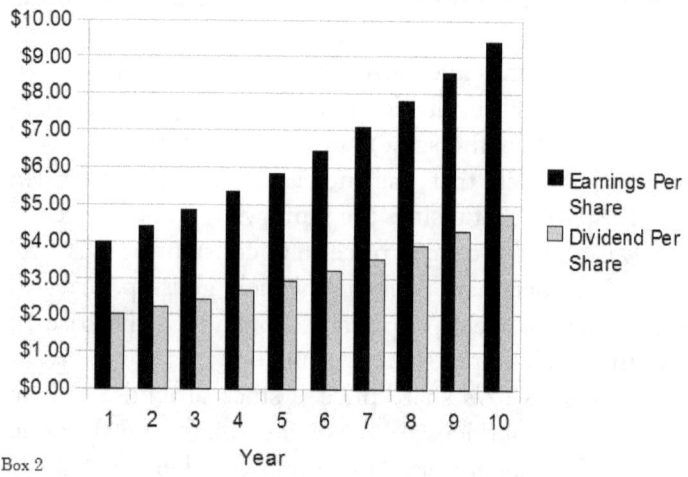

XYZ EPS and Dividends Rising 10% Annually

Box 2

What happens, generally, is a dividend paying stock that averages about the same, more or less, annual earnings and dividend growth, maintains the same yield. Sometimes its share price goes down and the yield is higher than its historical average, and sometimes its share price goes up and the yield is lower than its historical average. But over time, such a stock maintains about the same yield. Now, if its earnings and dividends rise, that means that its share price rises too.

Suppose that XYZ's historic average yield is 5%. As we have seen, if the company averages 10% annual earnings and dividend growth, if it pays a dividend of $2 per share in the first year, it will pay $4.72 per share in the tenth year. If the stock maintains its 5% yield throughout, its share price will have to rise. If at the end of the tenth year XYZ yields 5% and pays out a dividend of $4.72 per share, its share price should be $94.40. That's a decent gain from $40.

This is a theoretical example, and real life is of course much messier. The share price, and therefore the dividend yield, will change over time. At the end of the tenth year XYZ might yield 4% or even 3% because investors are very bullish. It might yield 6% or 7% if the outlook is bearish. But it is almost a certainty that XYZ will yield less than 11.8%, which means that its stock price will be higher at the end of the tenth year than it was at the end of the first year.

Let's look at some real life examples from the end of October 2002 through the end of October 2011. Take dividend stalwart Procter & Gamble (PG). At the end of October 2002, PG traded at a high of $37.21 per share. Its annual dividend was $0.82 per share. That made for a yield of 2.2%. In October 2011, PG traded around $64.50 per share. Its annual dividend was $2.10, making its yield about 3.3%. Dividends increased over 2.5 times. The share price, meanwhile, moved up around 73%. During the period, earnings per share went from $1.55 to $3.93, increasing about 1.5 times. This is certainly worse growth than Cisco's. And yet, PG is up more over the same period (Cisco rose about 64% during the same period) without even including dividends. PG's share price rose less than Berkshire's, but not by much—just a couple of percent (one year's worth of PG's dividends). Including dividends, PG's stock outperformed Berkshire's, even though its earnings didn't increase nearly as much.

Let's take another example: Chevron (CVX). Its high at the end of October 2002 was $46.89. Its annual dividend was $1.40 a share, making for a dividend yield of about 2.99%. In October 2011, CVX traded around $108.70 and paid an annual dividend of $3.12, a yield of around 2.9%. Earnings per share rose from $1.55 to $11.45 during the period. Note how earnings increased over seven times while the stock has gone up 2.32 times. If the stock price followed the company's earnings growth, it should've been trading over $300 per share. Earnings, as I've argued, do not necessarily drive a stock's price. But look at the yield. It was the same in October 2011 as it was ten years prior. Dividends increased 2.2 times, and the stock price has overshot them by a tenth of a percent. I'm not saying that CVX would not be up over the last ten years if it didn't pay dividends, but I think it's more than a coincidence that the stock price has kept pace with its dividend growth instead of its earnings growth.

And just so you know that I'm not cherry picking stocks, check out the following statistics. According to Neil McCarthy and Emanuele Bergagnini of Oppenheimer Funds, from January 1973 to September 2010, stocks in the S&P 500 that paid no dividends had an annual compound return of 1.82%. Stocks that paid a stable dividend had a 7.11% annual compound return. Members of the S&P 500 that raised their dividends, on the other hand, had an annual compound return of 9.27%.

From 1981 through July 2011, over 80% of the stock market returns in the US and more than 90% of the stock market returns in the UK, Germany, and France have come from dividends and dividend growth. Moreover, from 1970 through July 2011, over 80% of European returns have come from dividends and dividend growth (Richard Turnill and Stuart Reeve, "Global Dividends Really Do 'Pay,'" BlackRock, August 2011.)

Chapter 3 - Dividends Can Keep Pace with Inflation

It makes perfect sense if you think about it. The best companies pay dividends from their earnings, and their earnings come from sales of their products. Inflation (whether increasing prices due to more demand, more money in circulation, or a falling currency) drives the cost of raw materials up. Those companies that sell raw materials make more money. As the price of oil goes up, for example, ExxonMobil and Chevron increase their earnings. As their earnings increase, raw materials dividend payers raise their dividends.

Companies that purchase raw materials end up having to pay more for them because of inflation. The rising price of oil, for example, makes plastic more expensive. It also makes the transportation of goods more costly. Those industry dominating companies (I'm talking about businesses like McDonald's, Procter & Gamble, and so on) that buy raw materials sometimes choose to bear the extra costs, for a time. But eventually, they pass the costs on to their customers—other companies and regular people. In other words, they raise their prices. We go to the store and find that everything costs more than it did last year. Because they pass on the costs, these companies are able to grow faster than the rate of inflation. As their earnings grow, so do their dividends.

This is an advantage of dividend paying stocks over fixed income investments. Bonds and bank certificates of deposit (CDs) are called fixed income because their interest payments are fixed. If you buy a bond or CD that pays 3%, it will continue to pay you 3% for its duration. A stock of a dividend raising company, however, will pay out ever increasing amounts. So what might begin as a 3% yield can in a number of years grow into a 6% yield, then 12%, and so on. If you hold a good company long enough, the annual dividend it pays can eventually exceed the total amount you invested.

Recall the example of XYZ increasing its dividend at 10% per year. As mentioned above, if it pays out a dividend of $2 per share the first year, and you buy the stock for $40 a share, you'll have a yield of 5%. Let's say you buy $10,000 worth of XYZ and another investor puts $10,000 into a 10-year CD that pays 5% per year.

The first year, you will have collected $500 from XYZ. During the tenth year, you collect $1,178.97. By the end of the tenth year, the yield on your original $10,000 purchase is 11.7897%. The investor who put his $10,000 into the CD, on the other hand, will collect $500 in income during the tenth year (and every year in between). His yield will still be 5%. See box 3.

Dividend Growing at 10% per Year versus Fixed Income

Year	Dividend from XYZ	XYZ Yield on Cost	Income from 5% CD	CD Yield on Cost
1	$500.00	5.0000%	$500.00	5.00%
2	$550.00	5.5000%	$500.00	5.00%
3	$605.00	6.0500%	$500.00	5.00%
4	$665.50	6.6550%	$500.00	5.00%
5	$732.05	7.3205%	$500.00	5.00%
6	$805.26	8.0526%	$500.00	5.00%
7	$885.78	8.8578%	$500.00	5.00%
8	$974.36	9.7436%	$500.00	5.00%
9	$1,071.79	10.7179%	$500.00	5.00%
10	$1,178.97	11.7897%	$500.00	5.00%

Box 3

24

Suppose that during the 10 year period inflation runs at 3% annually. And let's say your annual expense on cereal is $500. By the end of the 10 year period inflation will make this expense jump to $652.39. The dividends from XYZ will cover your purchase with cash to spare. The investor who chose the fixed income option, however, will either have to buy 3% less cereal every year, or dip into his principal.

This is a theoretical example. Let's look at an example from real life. Suppose you retired in the year 2000, pretty much at the top of the tech bubble and invested $1,000,000 into the top ten highest yielding stocks in the Dow Jones Industrial Average (you put $100,000 into each). At the time, they were Philip Morris (now Altria), JP Morgan (now JP Morgan Chase), Caterpillar, General Motors, Eastman Kodak, 3M, ExxonMobil, DuPont, SBC Communications (now AT&T), and International Paper. The average yield of the stocks was around 3%, meaning that your first year you would expect to collect $30,000 in dividends.

Fast forward to the end of October 2011. As you may know, General Motors was a victim of the financial crisis (and its own mismanagement) and filed for bankruptcy protection in June of 2009. Assume that you lost your entire $100,000 investment in GM. Eastman Kodak failed to adapt to the advent of digital photography. Since 2000, Kodak lost over 97% of its value. Despite this loss of almost $200,000 dollars or 20% of your capital, your portfolio would be worth around $1.4 million at the end of October 2011. More importantly, you would receive over $38,000 in dividend income in 2011. Adjusted for inflation, $30,000 in 2000 is $39,500 in 2011 dollars. You would have lost out to inflation, but not by nearly as much as if you put your money in a similarly yielding fixed income investment —you would still be getting $30,000 in interest in 2011. Note also that your principal (the amount invested) rose about 40% with the dividend stock investment while it would have stayed flat with a fixed income investment like a certificate of deposit.

(A few caveats are in order here. First, the point of the example is to show how dividends keep pace with inflation. Sometimes they underperform, as in the example above, sometimes they outperform. The longer the period, the more likely dividend growth exceeds inflation. For example, investing $1,000 into the Dow Jones Industrial Average in 1944 would have yielded $48.30 in dividends that year. If you held on to the index, by 2009 you would receive $2,100 in dividends—that's twice your original investment amount just in one year! That $48.30 received the first year, adjusted for inflation would be $588.76 in 2009. As you can see, dividend raises handily outperformed inflation during the time frame.

Second, the ten stocks selected for the example were neither the best nor worst. They were what an investor might have decided to buy because they were part of an index mentioned daily on the news and their products were in most people's homes and driveways.

Third, from an investment point of view, stocks were not the best investment during the period. As mentioned, they were near the bubble peak. Treasuries, in hindsight, would have been preferable. For example, a person who put his $1 million into 30 year Treasuries would collect around $65,000 per year in income and would, at the end of October 2011 be sitting on substantial capital gains. Ten year CDs, ten year government bonds, and five year government bonds, also had interest rates around 6% at the time. These too would have been better investments during the period. While inflation would reduce their income's buying power by a larger percentage than the 10 dividend stocks in the example, fixed income investments would have fared better because their total income would be higher.

In sum, the point of the example was not to show that dividend stocks were a better investment during the period. Rather, it was to show that dividend income keeps pace, more or less, with inflation. The more diversified the dividend stock portfolio and the longer the holding period, the more this is true.)

Chapter 4 - Dividend Stocks Are Less Volatile

Studies show that the higher a portfolio's dividend yield, the lower its volatility. A portfolio of S&P 500 stocks that paid increasing dividends, finance professor C. Thomas Howard has found, was about one third less volatile than a portfolio of non-dividend paying stocks from January 1973 through September 2010. Howard also found that

> in a large-cap stock portfolio a 1% dividend yield [DY] increase produces an average gain of 22 basis points [0.22%] in annual compound return, along with a 7bp [0.07%] reduction in annual portfolio standard deviation. For example, if DY increases by 3%, then an investor can expect the large-cap portfolio return to increase by 66bp [0.66%] and portfolio volatility to decrease by 21bp [0.21%]. You can have your cake and eat it too: higher dividend yield led to quantifiably higher returns *and* quantifiably lower volatility. ("The Power of Dividends," C. Thomas Howard, *Advisor Perspectives*, 1/25/2011.)

What is Volatility, and Why Does It Pay to Keep It Low?

Volatility is a statistical measure of the size of the changes in an asset's price. The greater the fluctuations in a stock's price, the more volatile it is. As such, volatility is a measure of a stock's risk, or, in other words, it is the amount of uncertainty about a stock's value. For example, a stock that has 5% moves (up and down) is much more volatile than a stock that moves less than 1% (up and down) over the same period. The more volatile stock is usually more risky, because its value is less certain. Note that while volatility is a measure of risk, it should not be equated with risk. Note also that you need some volatility in your stock investments. Otherwise they will never go up.

One common relative measure (i.e., comparative) of volatility among stocks is the **beta**. The beta is a measure of the volatility of a stock or a portfolio compared to the market as a whole. The market has a beta of 1. If a stock has a beta of 1, that means it moves with the market. For example, if the broad market moves down 1%, the stock will move down about 1%. If the market goes up 2%, a stock with a beta of 1 will make approximately the same move. A stock with a beta greater than 1 moves more than the market. For example, a stock with a beta of 1.1 is 10% more volatile than the market. If the market moves up 1%, the stock will move up around 1.1%. Finally, a stock with a beta less than 1 is less volatile than the market. For example, a stock with a beta of 0.5 will theoretically be 50% less volatile than the market. If the market moves down 2%, this stock will typically move down 1%.

Established, stable, dividend paying businesses typically have betas less than 1. For example, as I'm writing, Procter & Gamble (PG) has a beta of 0.47. This measure indicates that it is half as volatile as the broader market. Look at a chart of PG and the S&P 500. See box 4. Note how much more pronounced the index's moves are compared to PG's. That is because the S&P 500 is twice as volatile as the stock. If you are curious as to the relative price performances of the stock and the index, from 1970 through the end of October 2011, PG is up almost 4,000%. The S&P 500, however, is up a little over 1,000%.

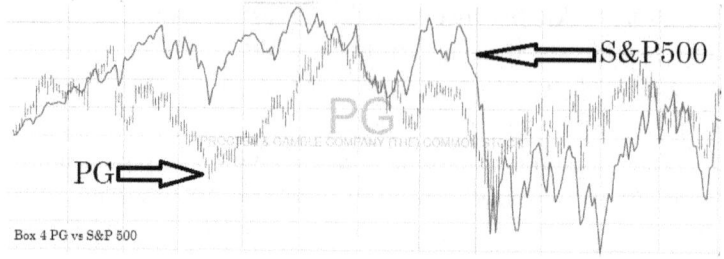

S&P500

PG

Box 4 PG vs S&P 500

It pays to keep a portfolio's volatility low for a number of reasons. Here are three. First, lower portfolio volatility usually results in higher compound returns. Compare two theoretical portfolios.

Suppose that Portfolio 2 is five times more volatile than Portfolio 1. In other words, for every 1% move, up or down, that Portfolio 1 makes, Portfolio 2 moves 5%. Let's say both portfolios start out with $1,000,000. Suppose Portfolio 1 gains 10% the first year, falls 10% the second year, goes up 10% the third year, falls 10% the fourth year, and in the fifth year rises 10%. That means Portfolio 2 gains 50% the first year, falls 50% the second year, goes up 50% the third year, falls 50% the fourth year, and goes up 50% the fifth year. Which portfolio would you rather own?

At the end of the five year period, Portfolio 1 will be worth $1,078,110. Portfolio 2, on the other hand, will be worth $843,750. Portfolio 1 will have a paltry compound annual return of 1.52%, but this beats Portfolio 2's negative 3.34%. See box 5. (The less volatile a stock or portfolio is, the closer to its original value it will be over time. For example, a portfolio with a volatility of 0 will not have moved at all).

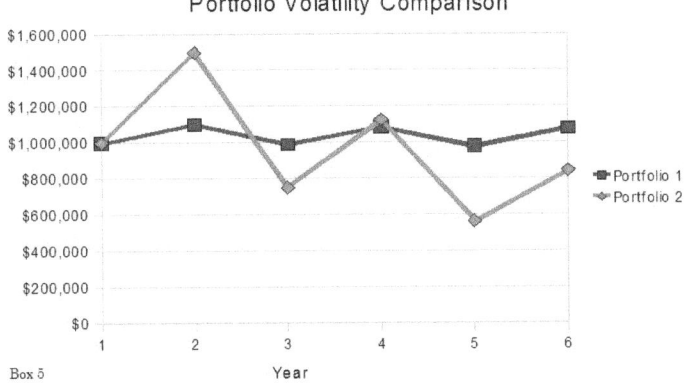

Portfolio Volatility Comparison

Box 5

This is true in theory and it also happens to be true in real life. A recent study of 1,000 stocks over a 41 year period (1968 to 2008) found that portfolios composed of less volatile stocks vastly outperformed portfolios consisting of more volatile stocks. When grouping stocks by trailing beta, the study found that the portfolio with the lowest beta rose 78.66 times (turning every $100 invested into $7,866). The portfolio with the highest beta, in contrast, rose 4.7 times (turning every $100 invested into $470). When grouping stocks using trailing total volatility, the least volatile portfolio rose 53.81 times (turning every $100 invested into $5,381) while the most volatile portfolio rose only 7.35 times (turning every $100 invested into $735). (Malcolm Baker, Brendan Bradley, and Jeffrey Wurgler, "Benchmarks as Limits to Arbitrage: Understanding the Low-Volatility Anomaly," *Financial Analysts Journal,* January/February 2011, Vol. 67, No. 1, pp. 40-54.)

Second, you never know when you might have to sell your investments (because you lose your job, you need money for something, etc). The more volatile your portfolio, the more likely your investments will be down when you sell them. They may be up, of course. It all depends on the time frame. The greater the volatility, the greater the risk. The greater the risk, the greater the possible rewards—and losses. For example, a portfolio full of high beta non-dividend paying stocks can be giving you great returns (remember, it's all unrealized capital gains until you sell). You are about ready to retire when the market crashes and the portfolio loses half its value. There goes your retirement. The longer the period in question, the more likely that there is a market crash. There was the market crash from October 2007 through March 2009, when the NASDAQ, S&P 500, and the Dow Jones Industrial Average lost 54.9%, 56.6%, and 53.9% respectively. There was the dotcom bust starting in March of 2000 and lasting about two years, over which the NASDAQ lost around 78% of its value (it still hasn't recovered by October 2011) while the Dow lost over 30%.

Third, a lower volatility portfolio helps you sleep better at night. It's a frightening sight to see one's investments make big moves daily. Sure, it can feel good on an up day. Not so much when you lose thousands of dollars on a down day. High volatility leads to stress, which leads to all sorts of ailments. High volatility is only great for the traders that can catch the bottoms and tops. It's not very good for the rest of us. And many stock traders, even successful ones, eventually burn out.

So how do you lower your portfolio volatility? By investing in stable, high quality, dividend paying stocks. These stocks, on average, have lower volatility than non-dividend paying stocks. There are a number of reasons for this (two of which are explained in the next chapter).

One reason is that companies that pay regular dividends tend to have established, stable businesses. Their earnings are more predictable than their non-dividend paying counterparts. Their investors' returns are also more predictable. That is because when a company pays dividends, its investors are fairly sure that they will get $x amount in dividends for the year. Investors in a non-dividend paying company have much less certainty about what their return will be in the future. This uncertainty makes non-dividend paying stocks bounce around much more (as the market attempts to price them) than dividend paying stocks.

My dad worked in an office with a number of older people. Although they never received very high salaries, a few of them had steadily amassed multimillion dollar stock portfolios and collected tens of thousands of dollars in dividends every quarter. They owned nice homes and even had summer houses in the country. My dad was surprised to learn that they never sold their shares, even when the future looked bleak. While he was sweating bullets, watching his stocks get pummeled when the dotcom bubble bust, these investors were happy. They welcomed the opportunity the downturn provided them to buy more shares of quality companies for less money. Why? Because they knew that companies like Boeing (BA), Coca-Cola (KO), Lockheed Martin (LMT), and Procter & Gamble (PG) weren't going out of business. If their shares didn't rise, they would receive higher dividends by taking advantage of the share price drop. The bear market gave them a reason to celebrate. They slept just fine at night while my dad paced around in the basement, worrying about the future. He had been buying shares of companies like Exodus Communications and InfoSpace (INSP) in the late 1990s. By 2000 he was a paper millionaire. After March 2000, his wealth went up in flames and he lost almost all of the money he had invested. Exodus went bankrupt. InfoSpace survived, its share price topping out at over $1,300 before plunging to under $4. Most of the other companies he put money in did about as poorly. And of course, when my dad finally decided to sell it was at the market bottom, not that any of his high flying tech stocks (those that survived, anyway) ever broke even.

It's not like my dad didn't do enough research. He could have told you all the figures from the companies' quarterly and annual reports, from what they spent on salaries to how much they had borrowed to what their projected sales were. His co-workers, on the other hand, couldn't even tell you the name of the CEO of their beloved Johnson & Johnson (JNJ) or Chevron (CVX). All they had to know to be satisfied was that people used these companies' products every day, and the companies were able to pay ever increasing dividends. The lower their share prices went, the happier my dad's co-workers were.

My dad's mistake was being caught up in a mania. His thinking was, why should he buy shares of something that would give him 3% in dividends in a *year* when he could buy a stock that would move up 30% in a *day*? He subscribed to the notion, repeated daily in the financial press that it was the new economy. The rules of investing had changed, and this time it was different. (Don't they always say that? And doesn't it always turn out to be the same as before? There's a bubble. Everyone thinks the good times will last forever. Then there's a crash. Everyone thinks the bad times will last forever. And then there's another bubble, somewhere else.)

But of course it wasn't. Boring old Johnson & Johnson easily outperformed InfoSpace and Exodus over a five year time frame. My dad laughed at his co-workers for two years, but they got the last laugh. Most of the dotcom darlings have gone out of business. The stable dividend payers, on the other hand, are still going strong. They have for decades, and there is no reason to think that they won't for decades more.

This is not to say that you can't make money with the more volatile, non-dividend paying stocks. You can make hundreds, thousands of times more money with them. But few people ever will. No amount of research will enable you to find such needles in a haystack. You have better odds at a casino. Indeed, casino odds are more pure in the sense that you know exactly what your chances are of winning before you enter the building.

Chapter 5 - Other Advantages of Investing in
Dividend Paying Stocks
Dividends Make Management More Responsible

When a company starts paying dividends, investors react very poorly when the dividend is cut. Therefore, a dividend paying company does everything in its power to keep its dividend rate stable or rising. Management is more diligent with its use of corporate funds, knowing that a portion must be paid out to shareholders. It does not, at least comparatively, waste money on useless projects. The company therefore experiences less fluctuations in its business. And investors seeking its regular cash flow support its stock price when the market turns down.

For the same reason, dividends can also prevent excessive executive compensation and expensive acquisitions. The more money a corporation keeps in its bank account, the more likely it is to overpay for things. The more likely there is to be waste and inefficiency.

Once a Dividend is Paid, It Cannot Be Taken Back

Earnings can be restated, and often are. Companies that restate their earnings (sometimes because of mistakes and sometimes because they were cooking the books a little and decided they might get in trouble with regulators) can have their stock prices fall. Companies that have been cooking the books can have their stock prices decline to zero.

Dividends, on the other hand, can't be restated. Once you are paid a dividend by an exchange traded corporation, it is yours. No matter what happens to the company in the future, the dividend is yours forever (that portion of it that the taxman doesn't take, that is).

Suppose there are two companies, A and B. They're the same in every way except that A pays a dividend and B does not. Let's say that after growing at a healthy rate for a couple of decades the companies fall on hard times and go out of business. Investors in B lose everything, unless they have been selling their shares. Investors in A, in contrast, might even have a gain because they've been collecting cash payments for decades.

Dividends Are More Predictable than Capital Gains

Although nothing in the world of investing is 100% certain, dividends are a surer thing than capital gains. When a company tells us what the dividend rate will be in the coming year, we tend to believe it. Analysts and stock quoting services cite the forward dividend yield as they do any other valuation metric. Those of us collecting dividend checks make plans for the money and those of us thinking about buying the stock take what the company says into consideration.

Sometimes companies don't fulfill their promise to pay a dividend, but most of the time they do. Dividends are deposited into investors' accounts in the exact amount that management stated. This is usually the case because the dividend is in the company's control. It doesn't control everything, of course, but it controls enough for us not to doubt most dividend announcements.

We would laugh, on the other hand, if management were to announce that we will receive a capital gain of a certain amount by a certain day. That's because for the most part a company's share price is wholly out of its control. The price is up to the market, and changes from second to second during trading hours. It is subject to many factors that have nothing at all to do with the company. For instance, the share price can go down because investors need to raise cash because they are losing money on some other asset.

That dividends are more certain than capital gains is one of the more contentious claims that can be made on the subject. As such, in Part Two I will examine arguments against this claim.

Qualified Dividend Income is Taxed at a Lower Rate than Ordinary Income

Through 2012, qualified dividends are taxed at a maximum rate of 15%. That means that taxpayers in the highest tax brackets get to keep 85% of their dividend payments. Investors in the two lowest tax brackets (15% and under) pay no taxes on their qualified dividends.

To be qualified, a dividend must come from a domestic corporation or a qualifying foreign corporation and you must hold the stock "for more than 60 days during the 121-day period that begins 60 days before the ex-dividend date." (See IRS Publication 550.)

Bonds and certificates of deposit, by way of contrast, have their interest taxed at the ordinary income rate. That is, someone in the 35% bracket will pay a 15% tax on his qualified dividend income, but he'll have to pay the ordinary income tax rate on the interest he receives from his CDs. As another example, a person in the 15% tax bracket will have to pay a 15% tax on his bond income, but his qualified dividends will be tax free.

(The qualified dividend tax rate is scheduled to expire on December 31, 2012. It may be renewed. If it is not, dividends will be taxed as ordinary income, on par with bank and bond interest.)

Dividends Can Make You a More Disciplined Investor

It seems like every year someone comes out with a

study that shows that while the stock market returned x% over some period, individual investors' returns were only a fraction of it. This is because our emotions make us terrible market timers. We are greedy when the market is about to fall and fearful when the market has finished falling. We are comfortable buying shares not when everything looks bleak but when everything is looks rosy and the future looks brighter than ever. This kills returns.

A steady stream of dividends, however, may put a damper on our emotions. When you hold a dividend paying stock, you know that as long as the company's business remains stable or growing, you are guaranteed to earn a return in the form of dividend checks. No matter what happens with the stock market, as long as business remains steady, the dividend checks will continue to arrive. Whereas owners of non-dividend paying shares might panic and sell their stocks just as the market bottoms, owners of dividend paying shares might not even notice the market downturn.

And if you are still accumulating shares or are reinvesting your dividends, instead of causing panic and fear market downturns might make you smile. The lower the share price, after all, the more shares you buy and the greater your potential future gains. Recall my dad's co-workers. They did not worry as long as the dividends continued to be deposited in their brokerage accounts.

Dividends Don't Lie (Most of the Time)

In their seminal book *Dividends Don't Lie*, one of Geraldine Weiss's and Janet Lowe's central arguments for investing in dividend paying stocks was that companies that pay dividends are forced to be more honest about their accounting. A company that does not pay dividends can resort to all sorts of accounting tricks to make it appear profitable. We all know about Enron. A company that pays a cash dividend, on the other hand, must have that cash in a bank account. If it doesn't, its checks will bounce. A dividend paying company's earnings statement, therefore, is more trustworthy than a non-dividend paying company's because the ability to pay dividends is a sign of financial health.

(The argument makes perfect sense and I agree. But there is a caveat. While it's true that a company must have cash in the bank to pay a cash dividend, it's not necessarily true that that cash comes from earnings. Rather than cut the dividend, the company might pay the dividend from borrowed money. It might also pay out of cash reserves or by selling off assets. Although neither method is sustainable (because dividends cannot lie forever), a dividend paying company may appear healthier than it actually is.

Take the drug maker Pfizer [PFE] as an example. It continued raising its dividends despite earnings declines. When earnings didn't cover the dividend payment, PFE started to dip into cash. Eventually, Pfizer cut its dividend in half so it could afford to acquire another drug maker to boost its earnings. So remember: a steady or even rising dividend can indicate that a company is healthy and growing, but it is not always the case.)

Part Two - Common Arguments Against Dividends

Chapter 6 - Important Terms You Should Know

Before we get to the arguments against dividends, we should be familiar with some terminology. If you already know what dividends, the ex-dates, record dates, etc are, feel free to skip this chapter. If a term comes up later with which you are unfamiliar, return to this chapter. Otherwise, continue reading.

We'll start out with an obvious one. A **dividend** is a distribution, usually out of earnings, by a company to a class of its shareholders. Dividends most commonly are in the form of cash, but they can also be stock or other property (e.g., you can get a house as a dividend). If a company has more than one class of shares (e.g., Class A, Class B, preferred Series A, etc), it can pay a dividend on one, two, etc, or all of its share classes.

A dividend is declared by the company's **board of directors** (or board, for short). The board of directors is a group of individuals elected by the company's shareholders. In addition to declaring dividends, the directors establish corporate policies, hire the company's management, and decide other major issues relating to the corporation. Corporate **management**, on the other hand, is responsible for the day to day business of the company and reports to the board of directors.

The day on which the board of directors announces the next dividend, when it is payable, how much and in what form, and the ex-date is called the **declaration date**. Once the board has authorized the dividend, it becomes the company's legal obligation to pay it.

The **ex-date** is the date on which the corporation's stock trades **ex-dividend**. That is to say, on and after the ex-date, the company's stock trades without the declared dividend. By contrast, after a dividend is declared but before the ex-date, a stock trades **cum dividend**. In other words, it trades with the dividend. If you own a stock the day before the ex-dividend date, even if you sell it on ex-dividend day you will receive the dividend.

When the stock opens for trading on the ex-date, the amount of the dividend is subtracted from its price. For example, suppose stock XYZ closes at $40 a share on March 1st. About a month ago, XYZ's board declared a dividend of $0.50 a share, with an ex-dividend date of March 2nd. If XYZ opens unchanged on March 2nd, it will open at $39.50 a share. Stock market quoting services will report no change in the stock's price. As another illustration, suppose that everything in the example above stays the same except that the stock opens up 10 cents. If so, it will open at $39.60, and all stock quoting services will report a change of $0.10 a share.

The **payment date** is when the company pays the dividend. It is when the checks are mailed (or property is sent), and when you receive the dividend in your brokerage account. (Some brokers pay the dividend right away. Others take a few days. The latter are making interest off of your money and are therefore probably not very good brokers.)

The **record date** is the date established by the company to determine the **holders of record**—who is entitled to receive the dividend (and in other cases, who is entitled to attend and vote at a shareholders' meeting, receive a stock split, receive a spinoff, and so on.) Basically, the record date is used to determine who owns the shares. That is, the record date is when the company looks at its records to see who the shareholders are. For example, if I sell my shares to you but I am the holder of record for purposes of the dividend, even though you now hold the shares, I will get the dividend check. This may be confusing, so I will explain in greater detail with a real life example below.

First, however, there are two more terms you need to know: **transaction date** and **settlement date**. The **transaction date** is the day on which you buy or sell your stock. The settlement date is when the transaction is **settled**. It is when the buyer must pay for the stock and when the seller must deliver it to the buyer. In today's stock market, it takes three business days to settle a transaction. In other words, settlement date is three business days from the transaction date. This is known as the **T plus 3 rule**. Here's how the Securities and Exchange Commission puts it:

> when you buy securities, the brokerage firm must receive your payment no later than three business days after the trade is executed. When you sell a security, you must deliver to your brokerage firm your securities certificate no later than three business days after the sale. (See the SEC website at sec.gov for more information.)

And now for the example, taken from a real life press release:

> GREENSBORO, N.C., Nov. 9, 2011 -- /PRNewswire/ -- Lorillard, Inc. (NYSE: LO), the third largest manufacturer of cigarettes in the United States, announced today the declaration of a quarterly dividend on its common stock in the amount of $1.30 per share, payable on December 12, 2011 to stockholders of record as of December 1, 2011.

In this example, the **declaration date** is November 9, 2011. The size and form of the dividend is $1.30 per share in cash. The **payment date** is December 12, 2011, and the **record date** is December 1, 2011. December 1 is when Lorillard will look at its records to determine who its shareholders are—to determine where it should send the dividend checks on December 12.

Because of the T plus 3 rule, this means that if you want to receive the dividend you must buy LO stock at least three business days before December 1, 2011. So the last day that the stock trades **cum dividend** is November 28, 2011. On November 29, 2011, LO will trade **ex-dividend**, and its share price will be reduced from the previous close by $1.30 (because of the T plus 3 rule, the ex-dividend date is normally two business days before the record date). In other words, those investors that buy LO before November 29 and hold it at least until November 29 will receive the dividend. Those investors that buy LO on or after November 29 will not receive the dividend. This means that if you own LO at market close on November 28, 2011, you will receive the dividend—even if you sell it the next day (on ex-date).

(I've simplified things above. On the record date the corporation does not find your name listed in its records, unless you bought its shares directly from it. Instead, the corporation's records will list financial institutions like banks, brokers, clearinghouses, and transfer agents. These financial institutions will have their own records, which might list other banks, brokers, and transfer agents, or actual shareholders. Brokers and transfer agents hold shares on their customers' behalf. They receive a bulk dividend payment, which they then dole out to their clients. For example, say many customers at Broker Corporation own shares of LO. Most customers have different quantities of shares. Some have less than ten, others have hundreds. Some have thousands. Let's say the total number of shares of LO that Broker Corporation's customers own is 12 million. On payment day, LO sends $1.30 per share to the broker, or $15.6 million. Broker Corporation then divides this $15.6 million for its customers. Those with one share get $1.30 deposited into their account. Those with 100 shares get a $130 deposit, and so on.

Note that this is a simplification too. Most transactions that take place on the stock market, like when you buy or sell shares of stock, involve one or more financial institutions changing a couple of digits in their records. Moreover, rarely, if ever, does a retail investor's [that's you] order actually make it to the NYSE, NASDAQ, or other stock exchange. Most of the time the orders are sent to wholesale market makers, like Knight Capital, Citadel Securities, UBS, Citigroup, and E*Trade, who fill the order and pay your broker a small fee for the privilege of dealing with "dumb" money.)

Chapter 7 - Arguments Against Dividends

As you read the arguments against dividends below, keep in mind that there are two general types. One type is concerned with whether the company, apart from its shareholders, is better or worse off for paying dividends. This type of argument works best if we pretend that the company is a separate entity with no owners, or if we assume that what is best for the company is best for its owners. The other type of argument is concerned with whether the shareholder is better off. This necessarily concerns both the company and its owners, for if the company isn't doing well it's probably not a good investment for its owners. Some arguments are against investing in dividend paying stocks, while other arguments are against paying dividends. An argument can, however, be both against investing in dividend paying stocks and against the payment of dividends.

Another thing to keep in mind is that some of these arguments seem to neglect the life cycle of a company. That is, they ignore the fact that at the beginning stages of a company's life dividends are not appropriate because the company needs all of its earnings to expand. A company's life may be divided as follows: start up, high growth, medium growth, low growth, and decline. How long each stage lasts and what growth rates are required for each stage depends on what business the company engages in and other factors. Some companies never reach the final stages (these are the ones you want to invest in, whether for capital gains or dividends). As a result, people who favor dividends sometimes mistakenly think that all companies should pay dividends.

The best arguments against dividends concern those companies in life stages where dividend payments can be made. For example, arguing that companies in the start up stage should not pay dividends is like arguing that water is wet. It's obvious and unnecessary. Arguments that companies in the medium and low growth stages shouldn't pay dividends, on the other hand, merit attention. Keep these things in mind in the following.

Double Taxation

That dividends are taxed twice is probably the most powerful argument against them. When people say that dividends are subject to double taxation, what they mean is: first, the company is taxed on its earnings, paying the corporate tax rate; second, when the company pays you a dividend, you are taxed on the dividend. But by the time you get that money, it has already been taxed! The money is subject to double taxation because both you and the corporation have to pay taxes on it.

Here's an example. Suppose you own all the stock of a small business, which after expenses and salaries earned $50,000. It is subject to a 15% tax, and must therefore pay the government $7,500 (15% of $50,000). That leaves the company with $42,500 from which it can pay dividends. Let's say the company's policy is to pay out 50% of earnings in dividends. So the company sends you a check for $21,250. Remember, this money has already been taxed. But, because it was paid as a dividend, it is once again taxable. Assuming that you are in the highest tax bracket and the dividend is considered qualified, you have to pay a tax of 15% on the dividend, or $3,187.50. That leaves you with $18,062.50.

So, had there been no taxation at all, the company would have had $50,000 from which to pay dividends, and your share would be $25,000. Had there been only one level

48

of taxation, the company would have $42,500 from which to pay dividends and your share would be $21,250. But because there are two levels of taxation, even though the company pays you 50% of its earnings, you end up receiving only 36.13% (versus having no taxes at all) or 42.5% (versus having one level of taxation).

This is a large chunk of money that is simply wasted. Neither the company nor you receive it. The common reaction is that you and the company would have been better off if the company had not paid a dividend at all. The company would be better off because it would have more money to expand. And you would be better off because you are the company's shareholder. The reinvestment of earnings, so long as it's put to good use, will make the business grow at a faster rate.

I disagree with the conclusion that most people draw from this argument, which is "don't pay dividends." Rather than being an argument against dividends, isn't it an argument against taxation?

And if we put the conclusion as "don't pay dividends because they are subject to double taxation, my question is, if the company doesn't pay dividends how are you going to realize any gains on your investment? What's the point of owning the shares if they don't pay you? Sure, I can sell my shares to someone else, but then I won't own the business anymore. I'd rather get paid something, preferably for the rest of my life, and pay taxes on it than sell my stake to realize a gain.

A better takeaway from the double taxation of dividends is: don't let your dividends get taxed twice. Own your dividend paying stocks in a tax deferred account. This works for investors who have some time before retirement.

It does not work for those who need current income. These investors might invest in companies that do not pay taxes. Yes, there are major firms that earn billions in profits and pay no taxes. Some of these are real estate investment trusts, master limited partnerships, and other "pass through" entities. I will discuss them in later chapters. There are also regular corporations that would normally pay taxes, but, thanks to their accounting departments, do not. Sometimes they even get tax credits. One example is General Electric (GE). The firm usually gets a tax credit despite earning billions of dollars. That its accounting department employes former government officials and files tax returns that number in the tens of thousands of pages might have something to do with it. (GE is an example. Whether it is a good investment or not is another question entirely.)

Here's a final thing to think about on the issue of double taxation. Aren't capital gains also subject to double taxation? A company pays taxes on its earnings. The after tax earnings increase the value of the firm. In an ideal world, this increase in value translates into share price appreciation. The investor sells his shares for a higher price than he originally bought them. The investor is then taxed on his gain. If this gain, the result of share price appreciation, comes about because of an increase in the company's value through the use of its after tax profits, the after tax profits have been taxed once again. Isn't this the same thing as paying a tax on dividends?

Arguments from a "Companies Have Better Things to Do with Their Money" Perspective

People who are against the payment of dividends typically suggest that there are better uses for this money. These better uses include reinvestment in the company and share buybacks. They are both meant to make a company's shares more valuable. The first is supposed to make earnings grow faster, which should increase each share's price. The second is supposed to make each share of the company more valuable because it decreases the number of shares outstanding.

Faster Growth Through Reinvestment of Earnings

A company should not pay dividends, many dividend objectors insist, because it can grow faster by reinvesting all of its profits. And faster growth is ultimately beneficial for shareholders.

For example, suppose there are two companies, A and B, that are identical in every way (they sell the same stuff, management makes the same investment decisions, employees are equally efficient, and so on) except that company A decides to pay out half of its earnings in dividends while B chooses not to pay a dividend. Let's say both companies earn $1 million at the end of the first year. Company A pays its shareholders $500,000 and keeps $500,000 while company B keeps the entire million. Both companies reinvest all their cash into the same new project. Let's say the project has a rate of return of 20%.

Since company A invested $500,000 in the new project, it makes an extra $100,000 (20% of $500,000) in the second year. Company B, meanwhile, makes $200,000 (20% of one million) on the same project. So, in the second year, company A makes $1,100,000 in total while company B makes $1,200,000. As company A pays out half of its earnings in dividends, it pays shareholders $550,000 and keeps the remaining $550,000 for itself. Company B, on the other hand, keeps the entire $1,200,000.

During the third year, both companies once again invest all their retained earnings in a new project. Let's say this project also has a rate of return of 20%. Company A invests $550,000 and therefore makes an extra $110,000 (20% of $550,000). Company B invests $1,200,000 and therefore makes an extra $240,000. At the end of the year company A pays its shareholders half of the profits, and both companies invest their retained earnings in another project that yields 20%. And so on, every year.

Notice that although both companies have the same rate of return, because company A invests less money it makes less money. Paying dividends slows down its growth as compared to company B. It's only a matter of time before company B's earnings are several times greater than company A's. In an ideal world, company B's market capitalization will also be several times higher than company A's. As not paying dividends leads to faster growth, the argument goes, it is better not to pay dividends.

The argument relies on common sense and is therefore appealing for many people. And yet real life does not always bear this out. According to Robert D. Arnott of Research Affiliates and Clifford S. Asness of AQR Capital Management,

> The historical evidence strongly suggests that expected future earnings growth is fastest when current payout ratios are high and slowest when payout ratios are low. This relationship is not subsumed by other factors, such as simple mean reversion in earnings. Our evidence thus contradicts the views of many who believe that substantial reinvestment of retained

earnings will fuel faster future earnings growth. Rather, it is consistent
with anecdotal tales about managers
signaling their earnings expectations
through dividends or engaging, at
times, in inefficient empire building.
("Surprise! Higher Dividends = Higher
Earnings Growth," *Financial Analysts
Journal*, Vol. 59, No. 1 January/Febru-
ary 2003.)

Arnott and Asness are saying that the data shows that companies paying out a higher percentage of their earnings through dividends grow faster than companies paying out a lower percentage of their earnings through dividends. This seems to defy common sense, but it doesn't when you look at it more closely. As I argued in Part One, companies that retain more of their earnings are more likely to invest in bad projects, overpay for acquisitions, and be inefficient (overpaying for supplies, overpaying managers and employees, paying too much in taxes, having their workers sit around not doing anything, and so on). These, in turn, lead to lower earnings growth. It takes a very disciplined management team not to misuse company funds when the company is flush with cash. When the company does not have a lot of cash, on the other hand, it takes no special skill not to overspend on things. The company simply doesn't have enough cash to overspend with.

Here's an analogy. Suppose you want to eat a hotdog. The hotdog vender closest to you sells them for $1.10. The vender a few blocks away sells them for $1. If you only have a dollar, you will have to go to the vender a few blocks away. If you have $2, you might go to the closer hotdog stand or you might go to the one farther away. Among the things that will factor in your decision will be whether you want to buy something else and how much it costs. Whatever you decide, you will at least take a moment to think about it. If you have a few hundred dollars, on the other hand, how likely is it that you'll schlep a few blocks instead of buying the hotdog at the nearer vender? The more money you have in your pocket, unless you are a cheap bastard, the more likely you are to buy the hotdog from the closer vender. So, the more money you have in your pocket, the more likely you are to overspend on the item (in this case, you'd be spending 10% more than you have to). Apply this to corporations. The more money they have, the likelier they are to spend more than they should.

There's another thing to consider. Successful companies can grow to the point where there aren't any worthwhile projects left. Their retained earnings end up sitting in a bank account, collecting measly interest. Having so much cash on hand encourages the company to be fiscally irresponsible (this is not to say that it makes the company so, only that it encourages it), which can lead to bad things down the road. The company that gives a percentage of its earnings to its owners, on the other hand, is less likely to face this problem.

Buying Back Shares is a Better Way to Return Value to Shareholders

Because dividends are subject to double taxation, a better way to reward a company's shareholders is for the company to buy back its own stock. Many people are very adamant on this point. The idea is the following. Suppose a company has 1 million shares outstanding. It earned $100 million after taxes this year. Its shares trade for $200 apiece. Let's say management determines that it needs $60 million to continue its operations and to invest in new projects. That leaves $40 million. The board of directors must decide what to do with this money. They can keep it in the bank, pay it out as a dividend, buy back some of the company's shares, or a combination of these.

Let's say the choice is between using all of the money for a dividend or a share buyback. Let's say the company's shareholders must pay a 15% tax on the dividends they receive. So, if the company pays them $40 million, the government will get $6 million. The dividend payment will therefore net the company's shareholders $34 million.

If the company buys back its own shares, on the other hand, no one will have to pay a tax. At $200 apiece, the company can buy 200,000 shares with the $40 million. This will reduce its share count by 20% to 800,000. As long as demand for the shares remains the same, their price should go up because the supply will have decreased by 20%. In an ideal world, the buyback should increase the value of the shares more than the after tax dividend that the shareholders would receive. So, fans of buybacks argue, instead of paying dividends companies should buy back their own shares.

The argument makes sense, but it has a few problems. The first is that the real world is not ideal. In the 18 months prior to June 2007, S&P 500 companies spent over $700 billion on stock repurchases. A study by S&P Equity Research Services found that during this period stock prices didn't go up because of the buybacks, more buybacks were not better than fewer buybacks, and announced share buybacks did not significantly reduce the number of shares outstanding (Todd Rosenbluth and Stewart Glickman, "The Failure of Stock Buybacks," Bloomberg Businessweek,

November 7, 2007). An earlier study conducted by John P. Evans and James A. Gentry concluded that

```
in  the  long-run  firms  create  more
value  with  a  strategy  of  not  repur-
chasing  [their]  shares....the  findings
do  not  support  the  theory  that  share
repurchase  programs  are  related  to
management  signaling  an  increase  in  a
firm's  long-run  performance  in  the
market.  Nor  does  the  study  show  that  a
strategy  to  repurchase  shares  signals
that  shares  are  undervalued.  ("Do
Strategic  Share  Repurchase  Programs
Create  Long-Run  Firm  Value?"  Univer-
sity  of  Illinois  Working  Paper  #99-
0119.)
```

Lawrence C. Strauss of *Barron's* has a similar opinion: "Buybacks...may not be all they're cracked up to be. There's scant evidence they do much for stock prices, other than produce small short-term pops." ("Beware the Buyback Craze," *Barron's*, January 22, 2011.)

Second, the problem with share buybacks is that they're often very poorly timed. Think about it this way. Companies generally have cash to spare during good times, not bad. That is, if a company has enough money to initiate or continue a share repurchase program, that means business is good. If business is good, the company's stock is likely not falling. It may be stable, but it's probably rising. So, in general, businesses tend to buy back their stock during good times when share prices are high.

On the other hand, share prices are low when times are bad and business is not booming. Tim Koller, partner at consulting firm McKinsey, said, "We have trouble finding companies that have systemically been able to buy back undervalued shares." ("Beware the Buyback Craze," *Barron's*.) And it is during the bad times that companies, in need of funds, initiate secondary offerings. They sell shares when they need money. Remember all of the banks selling new shares at deep discounts during the height of the 2007 to 2009 financial crisis? These same banks were buying their shares back at much higher prices during the prior years. So, in general (and excepting initial public offerings and secondary offerings to expand their business), companies tend to sell their stock during bad times when share prices are low. They end up buying high and selling low. It's no surprise that share buybacks reached record levels in the first half of 2007, just before the crash.

Third, share counts usually do not decrease after buybacks. This is because companies issue new shares through stock options to their executives and employees and for acquisitions. So share repurchases are often just a means of stealthily financing transactions rather than increasing shareholder value.

Fourth, even if share buybacks increase the stock price, the only investors that are rewarded are the ones that sell their shares. Investors that continue holding the shares receive no tangible benefit. Sure, their account value is higher, but they can't do anything with these gains until they sell. This seems like bad policy to me. Shouldn't a company reward those of its shareholders that choose to stay? It seems perverse that in a share buyback the company is paying its investors to leave.

In sum, while they look promising in theory, there is little evidence that share repurchase programs increase shareholder value. (Even if it turns out that the stocks of companies that repurchase shares outperform those that do not, it may well have nothing to do with the share repurchases. Companies that have the ability to repurchase shares may outperform, regardless of whether or not they actually go through with the repurchase. That is because the ability comes from having strong sales and solid earnings—things that would probably drive the stock price higher anyway.) Investors would probably be better off if the company used the money for new projects or dividend payments. Finally, if share buybacks actually work as intended, they reward the wrong stockholder.

If for some strange reason you are interested in investing in companies that have long histories of share repurchases, you might consider buying the PowerShares Buyback Achievers ETF (PKW) or choosing among its holdings. In the five years ending at the end of October 2011, PKW's share price has outperformed the broader market and, by a slim margin, the dividend focused ETFs. But with dividends included, the dividend focused ETFs provided greater total returns.

Paying a Dividend Signals a Slowdown in Growth

Some people say that they hate dividend paying stocks. Dividend payments, they claim, signal that the company has fewer growth possibilities than in the past.

Taken as an argument against paying dividends, this is utter nonsense. Suppose it is true that the company has fewer growth opportunities. Why should it be a secret? If the company doesn't have anywhere to invest its money, why should it get to keep the cash and not its investors?

Taken as against investing in dividend paying stocks, on the other hand, this argument has some merit. It makes perfect sense that companies that retain more of their earnings for reinvestment will grow faster and investments in them will outperform other, slower growing companies. And we have no shortage of examples. Microsoft's (MSFT) stock, before it paid dividends, went up hundreds of times. So did Cisco's (CSCO). Everyone wishes they'd have bought shares of Apple (AAPL), or Amazon (AMZN), or Baidu (BIDU).

But these are all home runs. When you're going for a home run you're much more likely to strike out. Many more companies fail than succeed, especially among the fast growing companies at the initial stages of their life cycles. Over the last 40 years non-dividend payers as a whole only performed better than dividend cutters. Stable dividend payers and dividend raisers performed best. Adjusted for inflation, investing solely in non-dividend payers would have lost you money. So not only would you have to pick the right stocks (and it was far from obvious that they would succeed—everyone laughed at Jeff Bezos, the founder of Amazon, for example), you would have to hold them through all the gut churning volatility for a long time to realize their gains. Very few investors can do this. The best non-dividend paying stocks will always crush the best dividend payers, but it's a lot easier to find and hold good dividend payers than it is non-dividend payers.

Arguments from a "Dividends are Irrelevant" Perspective
The "Bird in the Hand" Fallacy

A common argument for dividends is that a bird in the hand is better than two in the bush. In other words, dividends paid now are more certain than future capital gains. Therefore, dividends are more valuable or better than capital gains. I argued something to this effect in the first part of this book. For capital gains, you need a willing buyer of your shares. With dividends, in contrast, the company just has to make money. Moreover, once a dividend is paid, it can't be taken away from you. But capital gains, if you don't sell your stock, can vanish and turn into capital losses.

One argument against dividend investing is that this "bird in the hand" notion is a fallacy. The fallacy comes about, proponents of this argument say, from a false comparison. We shouldn't compare dividends today with capital gains tomorrow. Instead, we should compare dividends today with capital gains today. In this comparison, all other things being equal, there is no difference between dividends today and capital gains today because when a stock goes ex-dividend its price is reduced by the dividend amount. Then, if you factor in taxes and tax rates, it may be that on this comparison dividends are worse than price appreciation (for example, if the tax rate on dividends is higher than the tax rate on capital gains).

With respect to public firms (those that trade on the exchanges) this is true. The share price cum dividend is usually higher than the share price ex-dividend. The argument assumes, however, that dividends and capital gains are "guaranteed" in the same way. Capital gains depend on the market, which is mostly outside of the company's control. Dividends, in contrast, are very much in the company's control. It decides whether to pay them, how much, and when. Furthermore, does this argument really matter in the case of non-public firms? Non-public firms do not have a share price as such, especially when no one is looking to buy or sell. If you hold shares in such a company and it declares a dividend, do your shares really lose value the day following record date as they would on a stock exchange?

Moreover, is a firm then most valuable, in terms of share price, before the ex-date of the first dividend it ever pays? What I mean is, let's say over a number of years a firm pays dividends that total $100 per share. If it didn't pay dividends, would potential buyers be willing to pay $100 more per share? I doubt it.

Let's say a firm pays a dividend of $6,250 four times a year. Its business is stable and earnings are flat. Let's say there is no inflation. If it's true that someone wanting to buy the company would be willing to pay $6,250 more before ex-dividend day than on ex-dividend day, it is also true that he would want to pay $6,250 less on ex-dividend day than the day before. The first ex-dividend day, the company's shares are worth $6,250 less than the day before, the second ex-dividend day, the company's shares are worth $6,250 less than the day before, and so on—it seems that the share price will drop by $25,000 a year. But does this mean that if the buyer waits long enough he can buy the company for free? Surely not.

The argument that the bird in the hand notion is a fallacy assumes that dividend payments have no effect on the share price other than lowering it on ex-dividend day. But as I argued in Part One, dividends support a firm's share price and can force capital gains. If they didn't, all dividend paying firms' stocks would be priced at zero, even though the firms would continue to own assets, employ workers, sell things, and generate profits.

See box 6. This example assumes that a company makes enough money to support its dividend payments. It also stipulates that the share price starts out at $60 and the company pays $6 per share per year in dividends. If dividends do not force share price appreciation, the share price will be $0 in the tenth year, despite the fact that the company's business has not changed at all. It is still profitable and is still paying dividends.

The argument that dividends are irrelevant would be absolutely correct if securities traded at net asset value (NAV), the total market value of all the company's assets net of debt divided by its shares outstanding (book value per share). Paying shareholders a dividend decreases the NAV, and so would decrease the share price. The value of the investor's position is exactly the same as if the dividend hasn't been paid: the market value of the stock plus the dividend in his pocket is the same as the market value of the stock before the dividend. And we see that this is the case with exchange traded funds and mutual funds—which are always priced at NAV (or near NAV). If funds did not pay dividends and instead kept the cash on their books, the NAV would be that much higher.

For example, suppose a fund that trades at NAV pays a quarterly dividend of $0.25 per share. This means that in a year's time, if the fund kept the cash on its books instead of giving it to shareholders, its share price would be $1 higher. In three years' time its share price would be $3 higher.

Individual stocks, however, do not trade at NAV. Their share prices often have no apparent relation at all to the value of their underlying assets (because investors and traders think about the future value of the company as well as its current value). We have the same company, same business, same everything, but over a short period of time its

Dividends Can Force Capital Gains

Year	Share Price	Dividend	Dividend Yield	Total Cash Received per Share	Total Value per Share
0	60.00	6.00	10.00%	$0.00	$60.00
1	54.00	6.00	11.11%	$6.00	$60.00
2	48.00	6.00	12.50%	$12.00	$60.00
3	42.00	6.00	14.29%	$18.00	$60.00
4	36.00	6.00	16.67%	$24.00	$60.00
5	30.00	6.00	20.00%	$30.00	$60.00
6	24.00	6.00	25.00%	$36.00	$60.00
7	18.00	6.00	33.33%	$42.00	$60.00
8	12.00	6.00	50.00%	$48.00	$60.00
9	6.00	6.00	100.00%	$54.00	$60.00
10	0.00	6.00	N/A	$60.00	$60.00
11	-6.00	6.00	-100.00%	$66.00	$60.00

Box 6

63

share price can be up 10%, down 10%, down 50%, up 100%, and so on. A company's share price fluctuates whether it pays a dividend or not. If it traded at NAV, dividends and capital gains would be equally predictable and, as long as taxes weren't an issue, it would be irrelevant for its shareholders whether the dividends were paid or not. But companies' shares don't trade at NAV.

Dividends Do Not Make a Company More Valuable

A related argument against dividends being better than capital gains is that if a company's business policies and therefore sales, earnings, cash flows, etc, remain the same, the value of the company can't change with dividend policy. Assuming taxes don't matter (say in a tax deferred account), shareholders should be indifferent between receiving dividends or capital gains. That is to say, if we ignore taxes, whether a company pays dividends or not does nothing to its value because the company's value derives from the results (sales, profits, etc) of its investment policies.

The argument relies on a number of assumptions. First it assumes that stocks are fairly valued (trade at net asset value). That is, the share price of a non-dividend paying company should increase by the same amount as an identical dividend paying company's dividend.

Second and related to the first assumption, the argument assumes that the transaction costs between receiving a dividend and selling shares for capital gains are the same. Just as an investor will receive his dividend check, he should be able to receive the same amount in capital gains net of costs by selling shares of the non-dividend paying stock.

Third, the argument assumes that companies that do not pay dividends will not misuse the extra cash by making bad investments (or increasing management's compensation). Conversely, the argument also assumes that the dividend paying company, if it pays out too much, is able to issue more stock at no cost.

If the three assumptions are true, investors should not care whether their gains come in the form of dividends or capital gains. Therefore, dividend investing is no better (or worse) than investing for capital gains. If tax policies change and one of the gains (capital gains or dividends) is taxed more than the other, then the other would be preferable. For example, if the tax on dividends is more than the tax on capital gains, investors should prefer capital gains.

If the assumptions are not true (and they seem not to be in the real world, where stock prices can be very volatile), investors who need current income should prefer dividends over capital gains.

Real life is more complicated than what happens in the lab, a fact these academics don't seem to get. Again, take two companies, identical in every way except that one pays dividends and one doesn't. Say both companies grow at a steady annual rate. Suppose also that the dividend payer has a policy to keep its payout ratio the same from year to year.

From these facts we know that investors in the dividend payer will receive a steadily increasing gain every year. We also know that the share prices of both companies will be up some years, down in others, and flat the rest of the time. We can't say anything else, except maybe that the dividend paying stock will be less volatile. But that's it.

Fast forward a dozen years. The share prices might be the same then as they are today. They might be lower, and they might be much higher. No one knows. But it bears repeating, on these facts we do know that the investors in the dividend paying company will reap ever increasing returns.

It is money that they can spend, save, or reinvest—all without doing anything to their stock position. Investors in the non-dividend paying company, in contrast, will have no cash to spend, save, or reinvest until they sell some or all of their shares and the size of their gain (or loss) will depend on when they sell.

Part Three - Dividend Sources: Common Stocks

Almost all of the stocks you read and hear about are common stocks. Thus, most of the dividend paying stocks that investors are familiar with are common stocks.

Common (or ordinary) stock is a class of shares that represents ownership of a corporation. In other words, each common share gives you a part stake (a share, a slice) in a corporation. It entitles you to a portion of the corporation's profits and to a portion of the voting power in all corporate elections. Common shareholders elect a corporation's board of directors. They also vote on other important corporate matters, including changes to the corporation's charter, mergers, acquisitions, and other major changes to the corporation.

These powers come at a price. Common shareholders have the lowest priority in the capital structure. The bond holders must be paid first (the recent law-defying precedents of the Obama administration [with GM and Chrysler] suggest, however, that the company's employee union might be highest on the pecking order). Then the preferred stockholders must be compensated. Only then, if there is anything left, do the common shareholders get a piece of the pie.

Every common stock trading on a major exchange falls within one of eight sectors. Accordingly, the next eight chapters are each on one of these sectors: utilities, healthcare, technology, financial, basic materials, industrial goods, consumer goods, and services. The chapters are ordered by average dividend yield (at the time of writing), from highest to lowest. (This does not mean, however, that all stocks within a sector have higher or lower dividend yields than the stocks in another sector.)

Chapter 8 - Utilities

With a market capitalization of around $1.67 trillion (at the time of writing), utilities make up approximately 3% of the stock market. They have traditionally been called "widows and orphans" stocks because they usually pay higher than average dividends and are considered safer than other stocks. This is because they are less prone to economic cycles. Whether the economy is booming or in recession, people still need the utilities' services. They might use less during tough times, but light, heat, and water are the last things people will give up.

There are four types of utilities: natural gas, electric, water, and those that deliver a combination of these. Although there are some companies that are geographically diverse (for example, National Grid [NGG] operates in the northeastern United States and the United Kingdom), most utilities are regionally based. As a result, their earnings growth is usually toward the lower end of the spectrum, keeping their stock prices from rising too quickly. Because their shares are not as in demand as those of higher growth companies, utilities typically have higher dividend yields than other common stocks. At the time of writing, utilities averaged a 3.91% yield, compared to the 1.65% from the less generous and faster growing services sector.

Utilities are safer than other common stock investments, but no one expects to become super rich overnight by holding their shares. What they are good for, however, is slow and steady growth. As a city expands, as its population grows, there is a higher demand for its utilities' services. Pretty much monopolies in their respective regions, utilities are usually subject to federal and state regulation, which in general keeps them from raising their rates too much. Nevertheless, state and federal regulators often allow utilities to boost their rates, usually by the rate of inflation. Even if you use the same amount of water, electricity, and gas, you are almost certainly paying more today than you did a few years ago. That is the advantage of utilities stocks—they are monopolies that are allowed to steadily increase the rates they charge customers for their services. As their earnings grow, so do their dividends.

Investing in utilities comes with certain risks. These risks include higher interest rates, higher fuel costs, union strikes, population declines, more burdensome regulations, accidents, and new energy efficiency standards. Utility stock prices may fall if there is high economic growth and investors are drawn to other sectors where they think they can make higher returns (it is a good time to invest in utilities after this occurs, as the yields will be higher). For those utilities that generate electricity, another thing to consider is how they do it. The main sources are nuclear, coal, natural gas, hydro-electric, wind, solar, and biofuels. Although the United States has vast supplies of coal, politicians are against using it. There's a big stink about global warming and carbon emissions. Whether you believe in the connection or not, it can affect a utility's business. Nuclear power plants are said to be clean (if you ignore all the radioactive waste that has to be buried somewhere) because they don't release politically incorrect gasses into the atmosphere (because carbon dioxide is far scarier than the occasional radioactive cloud), but there is political pressure to get rid of them too. Germany, for instance, is phasing out its nuclear power plants. Most utilities have a number of different power plants. Consider what portion of their total production is made up by each when you're thinking about investing. For example, a utility that derives half its electricity from coal may have a far tougher time paying its dividend if coal is outlawed than a utility that produces 5% of its energy from coal.

If you are interested in utilities and would rather buy the entire sector instead of looking for individual companies, there are a number of exchange traded funds (ETFs—more on these in the next part of the book) available. All of the major ETF issuers (iShares, PowerShares, SPDR, Vanguard, etc) have one or more utility ETFs. There are even foreign utilities ETFs. You can find these ETFs by visiting their issuers' websites or by looking at lists on such sites as SeekingAlpha.com or Yahoo! Finance.

Chapter 9 - Healthcare

With a market capitalization of around $5 trillion (at the time of writing), the healthcare sector makes up almost 9% of the total stock market. This category of stocks encompasses companies that provide medical services as well as healthcare goods. The industry includes hospitals, drug makers, biotechnology firms, medical research firms and laboratories, medical insurers, as well as medical appliance manufacturers and suppliers of medical instruments.

One reason people invest in the healthcare sector is because they believe (and how can they not?) that we will always need healthcare. As the population grows and ages, the sector should make more money. Given that the sector is very diverse, however, not every healthcare stock is created equal.

Drug Makers

The major drug makers make up most of the sector's market capitalization. They also pay the most in dividends. This industry is dominated by old, large firms that have in most cases been paying out dividends for decades. You've probably heard of the biggest ones: Pfizer (PFE), Merck (MRK), Johnson & Johnson (JNJ), GlaxoSmithKline (GSK), Novartis (NVS), Bristol-Myers Squibb (BMY), Eli Lilly (LLY), Abbott Laboratories (ABT) and Sanofi-Aventis (SNY). Chances are that if you are taking any kind of medication, whether prescription or over the counter, it was made by one of these companies. If you are searching for healthcare dividends, this is the place to look.

The advantages of investing in the giant drug makers include, as stated, the fact that people will always need healthcare and this need will increase as the population grows and ages. For this reason, the major drug manufacturers (and they produce more than just drugs—many of these companies are diversified giants, making everything from bandages to diagnostic equipment) have been relatively consistent performers. Their dividends are more or less stable and rising, as are their share prices.

The risks of investing in drug makers include class action law suits, product recalls, tougher regulations, and, probably most important, patent expiration and research stagnation. Drug patents last for 20 years. But because drugs are usually patented when clinical trials begin, the typical drug enjoys patent protection on the market for between seven and twelve years. During this time, the company that patented the drug is the drug's exclusive seller (unless it sells some or all of its rights under the patent to some other party). That is to say, while the drug enjoys patent protection, only the company that patented it can sell it. It's like having a monopoly on the drug. So, if it's something that most doctors prescribe for a prevalent condition, the drug company can make a lot of money. When the patent expires, however, the drug maker stands to lose sales and profits because any other company can come along and sell the drug as a generic at a steep discount. What the drug maker once sold for $100 a pill might now sell for $4 per 100 pills. Pfizer's (PFE) woes, for example, were in part due to a series of expiring patents.

Because drug patents expire, drug companies are always trying to develop new medicines. This comes at considerable expense. Many drugs never make it to the market because they fail in clinical trials or because the FDA bans them. Of the drugs that are deemed safe and are approved, many end up market failures because there is no demand for them (because some other drug better treats the condition, there aren't very many people afflicted with the condition, or doctors aren't prescribing the drug or consumers do not want to buy it for some other reason). Billions of dollars can be spent on research and marketing with no profitable outcome. When a drug company's product pipeline is not very promising, it often turns to acquisitions to fuel its growth. Acquisitions come with their own risks, including overpayment and taking on the liabilities of the acquired company (lawsuits, recalls, expiring patents, debt, etc).

Biotech

Biotechnology makes up most of the rest of the market cap of the healthcare sector. The vast majority of these firms do not pay dividends and unless you work in the industry you've probably never heard of any of them. Biotech companies develop, discover, and manufacture various products like recombinant proteins, cell production stimulants, tumor inhibitors, and so on. This industry is, basically, the application of technology to biology. It is probably very interesting and investors might make a lot of money here, but as stated, there are few dividends to be found. (There's also the possibility that biotech companies will unleash flesh eating zombies on the world, which might be good for profits if they sell the vaccine, but think of the lawsuits!)

Medical Equipment and Supplies

You can find some dividends, however, in the medical appliances, equipment, and supplies industries. You may even have heard of some of the companies, which include Baxter International (BAX), Becton, Dickinson and Company (BDX), and Medtronic (MDT). That last one has been paying ever increasing dividends since at least 1982. Companies in these industries make pacemakers, defibrillators, diagnostic and monitoring equipment, artificial limbs, intravenous tools, premixed drugs, vaccines, and sterile packaging, among many other products.

The advantages of investing in such companies include potentially fast earnings and dividend growth. Risks include lawsuits, product recalls, tougher regulations, and the possibility that competitors will be more innovative. These companies also have lower dividend yields than the major drug makers, while their share performance in the last five years has been about the same.

No other industries in the healthcare sector are worth noting in terms of dividends.

At the time of writing, there are over a dozen healthcare ETFs, the majority of whose holdings are the major drug makers. There are ETFs dedicated to global companies and to particular industries (e.g., medical devices). So if you are interested in buying a bunch of healthcare stocks in one shot, visit sites like SeekingAlpha.com to find a list, or go to the websites of the ETF issuers (SPDR, PowerShares, iShares, and so on).

Chapter 10 - Technology

Tech companies manufacture the various gadgets we use daily, along with the components these gadgets are assembled out of. They also provide a variety of services, from communications, to data storage, to information services. As most of the technology sector's dividends come from one particular industry, the chapter is divided into telecommunications companies and all the rest.

Telecoms

A large part of the technology sector's dividends come from the telecommunications industry. This industry is home to such high dividend payers as AT&T (T), Verizon (VZ), Vodafone (VOD), and many regional companies. Most of these have lots of infrastructure and a regional monopoly in the declining landline business. Most of their growth (and this is very slow, if there is any) comes from rate hikes and subscribing new customers to high speed internet and other services. Similarly to utilities, telecoms can pay out most of their free cashflow as dividends. This, combined with slow growth results in high dividend yields. Some telecoms have had double digit dividend yields (because the market thinks that the dividends are unsustainable) for years. Industry leaders like T and VZ yield about half as much, but at the time of writing that is still over 5%.

Future growth in the industry will come from wireless communications, as people dump their landlines in favor of cellphones and mobile internet devices. AT&T and Verizon dominate this part of the industry in the United States, while Vodafone, which shares a stake in Verizon's wireless business, dominates Europe. Vodafone has a number of landline competitors on the continent, and these too have high dividend yields. Latin America and Asia seem to have lower yields.

The advantages of investing in landline businesses include regional monopolization, relatively stable stock prices, and high dividend yields. Risks include rising interest rates (like utilities, telecoms tend to have a lot of debt), expensive rollout and upkeep of equipment, government regulations, labor disputes, and a declining customer base as people switch to wireless and internet based communication.

The advantages of investing in wireless businesses (which generally have lower dividend yields) include the fact that it's where the growth is. If the current trend persists, it's hard to imagine very many people paying for landlines. It's also hard to imagine that people will stop communicating, going on the internet, and so on. The potential risks are the same as with landlines. An additional risk is shortages of spectrum (to handle data loads, as more people switch to 4G, 5G, etc smart phones—Verizon and AT&T have lately been buying spectrum from cable companies. The auctioning of wireless spectrum in the 700 MHz range was held in 2008 by the FCC. Another, smaller auction was held in 2011. Over one hundred companies bought at least one license to operate in the 700 MHz range.)

There are a number of exchange traded products dedicated to domestic and international telecoms. iShares seems to have the largest collection at present time, but the other usual suspects (Vanguard, PowerShares, SPDR) have offerings as well.

Other Technology Companies

Consistent tech dividends are hard to find outside the telecom industry, but there are a few giant corporations, leaders in their respective industries, that have been sending their investors ever increasing dividends for years. These include Automatic Data Processing (ADP), Microsoft (MSFT), Intel (INTC), Texas Instruments (TXN), and International Business Machines (IBM). The latter usually has a paltry yield, under 2%, but don't discount it for that reason. It has paid dividends to its shareholders for 100 years, and has raised the payouts in each of the last 16. IBM's dividend payout has more than tripled since 2005. If the dividend rate hikes continue on the same pace, what is paltry yield today can be a fat one in a few years.

The advantages of investing in the industry dominant dividend paying tech stocks outside the telecom industry include faster earnings and dividend growth than in other sectors, more exposure to the economy (which is a good thing when the economy is growing), and solid balance sheets with little to no debt and lots of cash in the corporate treasury. Risks include tougher regulations (industry dominant companies face more scrutiny from regulators because they are so large and often exert monopoly-like power over their competitors), slow or contracting economic growth, declines in business spending, and, what I think is most important, the constant need to innovate. Technology changes quickly. Companies that are slow to adapt will die.

As cable companies are increasingly offering their customers high speed data and communications services, they can be classified as technology companies (they are normally placed in the services sector). Some of these, like Cablevision (CVC), Time Warner Cable (TWC), and Comcast (CMCSA) have paid decent dividends in the past. To the extent that cable companies engage in similar activities as telecoms, the advantages and risks of investing in them are similar. Cable companies also tend to be content providers. To the extent that they are, they are also subject to such risks as ratings declines, advertising spending declines (because of a weak economy or weak content—at some point viewers get fed up with remakes of terrible shows from twenty years ago), subscriber losses (if they own premium channels), and more stringent FCC regulations.

There are a number of technology sector ETFs from the usual issuers. Apart from the telecom specific ones, however, most of their holdings are companies that do not pay a dividend. If you are after dividends and are interested in tech stocks, it is better to either buy them separately or through dividend focused funds (there will be a chapter on this further in the book).

Chapter 11 - Financials

Most of the juicy dividends in the financial sector come from real estate investment trusts (REITs). There will be a chapter dedicated to REITs in Part Four of this book.

Banks

The money center and regional banks dominate the financial sector by market capitalization. This industry includes most of the famous and infamous names you hear on the television and read about in newspapers, including JPMorgan Chase (JPM), ING (ING), Toronto Dominion (TD), WellsFargo (WFC), US Bancorp, and a host of others that you probably use or at least drive past daily, but which, because of the financial crisis, do not pay much by way of dividends. Investors used to own the major banks for the dividends. The advantages were a constant stream of income, stable stock performance, and direct exposure to the economy (as the economy expanded, banks lent more money, thereby increasing their earnings and dividends). The risks, it has turned out, have not been worth it. Apart from the risk of recession and poorly performing loans, in the last several years we have found out about the fraud and almost complete lack of transparency in the banking industry. While CEOs were telling the public how everything was great, they were borrowing billions from the Federal Reserve just to keep their doors open. There is no question that there are good, stable, and growing banking corporations. The problem is finding them and differentiating them from the bad ones. Dividends that once seemed invulnerable have been reduced to one cent per share or eliminated.

There are a few safer ways to invest in banks. For example, preferred share dividends and bond interest payments are generally safer (with regard to the payments, but not with respect to inflation) than common stock dividends. As another example, and this applies to small banks, you can open savings accounts in mutual savings banks. These banks do not have shares of stock, and are instead owned by their members. They have historically been very conservative with their investments and have weathered financial crises much better than their commercial bank counterparts. Mutual savings banks stood strong while bigger institutions collapsed around them during the Great Depression, for example. Advantages of putting your money into mutual savings banks include higher yields than the bigger commercial banks, and FDIC protection for amounts up to $250,000 (or $100,000 after 2012, unless the $250,000 limit is extended).

But wait, isn't this book about dividends from the stock market? And isn't this chapter about common stock dividends? Yep. Another advantage of mutual savings banks is that should they decide to go public and convert to a banking corporation with shares of stock that trade on the major exchanges, or if a publicly traded bank buys them, you, as a depositor, will receive shares of stock based on how much you keep on deposit. You will still have your cash readily accessible, but in addition you'll get common stock—which you can sell or keep (and hopefully collect dividends on). Such conversions are rare, but they do happen.

The risks of putting your money into mutual savings banks include inflation, currency collapse, account fees, loss of principal (if you put in more than the FDIC ceiling and the bank fails), and bank failure (you should be reimbursed for any amounts covered by the FDIC, but it can take a long time to access your money).

Insurers

The next biggest financial industry by market capitalization is insurance. This includes companies like Prudential (PRU), MetLife (MET), ACE Limited (ACE), Allstate (ALL), Travelers (TRV), Chubb (CB), and AFLAC (AFL). The latter three have increased their dividend payments every year since the 1980s. (In this industry you might want to include the health insurers [those companies that pay for your doctor and hospital visits and cover the cost of prescription drugs], but they are usually classed in the health-care sector. I did not mention them earlier because none of them have consistent dividends, high enough yields, or high enough dividend growth.)

The principal business of insurers is to collect more in premiums than they expect to pay out when events their clients want to insure against occur and to invest the difference as safely and as profitably as possible. The advantages of investing in insurance dividend payers include steady business that can grow when the economy expands, but does not contract too much when the economy slows down, and inflation protection (insurers take every opportunity to raise their rates). The risks include more stringent regulations and risk mismanagement. Insurers can make poor decisions about what and whom to insure and they can make poor investment choices. The financial crisis brought the former into the public spotlight. American International Group (AIG), a great company to invest in for many years, and a number of other insurers decided to sell mortgage bond protection during the housing bubble. In most cases, the companies insured more money in bonds than their market capitalization—in the event the mortgages and other bonds would default, it would be impossible for AIG and the other insurers getting into this business to pay their clients. Mortgages did go sour. As a result, a number of insurance companies went out of business, and AIG had to sell off assets and be bailed out by the government. One division was able to ruin the entire company, even though AIG's other divisions were doing quite well. It always pays to know from where an insurer's profits are coming.

Note that if you have life, property and casualty, and other forms of insurance, you are increasing your exposure and therefore risk by buying your insurer's stock. That is because if the company goes out of business, your premiums will have been for naught, your shares will tank, and the dividend will be eliminated.

As with mutual savings banks, another way to invest in insurers is to buy whole or universal life insurance from a mutual insurance company. Such companies don't have shareholders and are instead owned by their policyholders. Mutual insurance companies' profits are either distributed to policyholders through dividends or are used to lower the policyholders' premiums. Policyholders often have a number of options as to what to do with their dividends: they can take them as cash and spend them however they want, reduce their premiums, leave on deposit to compound at interest, repay policy loans (if they have any), buy term insurance, or buy additional paid up insurance that will itself be eligible for dividends. If the company ever decides to demutualize and go public, its policyholders are given shares.

Note that unlike putting money into mutual savings banks, you can lose your principal with life insurance (if the company goes bankrupt). Also, life insurance is a lot more complicated than the very brief outline here. In many cases whole and universal life insurance is far worse than buying term life insurance and investing the difference (e.g., paying a $200 premium versus paying a $14 premium for the same death benefit). Buying insurance involves either a lot of homework or getting the help of someone trustworthy and knowledgeable.

Investment Banks, Brokers, and Diversified Investment Houses

This category includes brokers (retail and institutional), exchanges, underwriters, so on. Among the more consistent dividend payers (Goldman Sachs [GS], Morgan Stanley [MS], etc), the yields aren't very high. There are a few exceptions. For example, NYSE Euronext (NYX), the company that runs the NY Stock Exchange, pays a 4.5% yield at the time of writing. As with the money center banks, the advantages and risks relate to the economy and transparency. Goldman Sachs, for example, makes a lot of money from trading and underwriting stocks and bonds. The better the economy, the better the markets are doing, and, in theory, the more money Goldman Sachs will make. Nevertheless, as the financial crisis continues to reveal, no one really knows what is going on at the banks and brokers. Are they really doing well, or is management lying through its teeth? Are they using customer funds to cover their losses? They're not supposed to, but MF Global appears to have done just that. Given the paucity of high dividend payers and given the large potential for fraud and surprise risks, it is best to stay away from these industries if you're looking for stable dividend paying stocks.

Chapter 12 - Basic Materials

You may be surprised to learn (no, not really) that the basic materials sector is composed of companies that provide basic materials—the stuff that manufactured goods are made out of—to other companies and consumers. Basic materials include oil, gas, chemicals, metals, and minerals.

Oil and Gas

The oil and gas industry dominates the basic materials sector by market capitalization. It has also been a great place for dividends. You have heard of the major corporations in this industry and probably use their products everyday. They include BP (BP), Royal Dutch Shell (RDS-A & RDS-B), Exxon Mobil (XOM), Chevron (CVX), and ConocoPhillips (COP). Most of these have been excellent dividend payers for decades with an impressive history of dividend raises.

Companies in this industry engage in drilling, refining, or marketing oil and gas, or some combination of these. Most of the companies that you have heard of do all three and are therefore sometimes referred to as "integrated oil and gas" companies. They find oil and gas fields, drill, extract, refine and treat the raw materials, and then market it. They also transport these natural resources, but more specialized companies do most of the moving work. There will be a separate chapter on these (master limited partnerships) in the next part of this book because most of them have partnership units instead of common shares. There are a few exceptions, however: the companies with common shares that derive income from these partnerships. One of the most notable is Kinder Morgan (KMI). The company makes its money by operating pipelines—what are essentially toll roads in the oil and gas industry. It doesn't matter so much what price fossil fuels sell for. It's these resources' flow through the pipelines that make such companies and their investors money. More on this in the chapter on MLPs.

The advantages of investing in oil and gas companies include inflation hedging (higher inflation equals higher oil and gas prices equals higher profits equals higher stock prices and dividend raises), participation in economic growth, having a stake in a resource that literally runs the world, growing world demand for oil while supply shrinks (oil and gas aren't renewable resources), stable dividends, and relatively stable companies (oil and gas companies are some of the largest in the world both by profits and market capitalization—Exxon Mobil, depending on the day, is the largest company by market cap).

Risks include environmental disasters (recall the BP oil spill), tougher regulations, "excessive profit" taxes that politicians call for every time the price of oil goes over a certain threshold, war (this can be a boon, as it drives oil prices higher, but if tankers, pipelines, and oil fields are destroyed, no one makes money from that oil), terrorism, sabotage, excessive drops in the prices of oil and gas (from oversupply, weak economy, deflation, etc), nationalization of oil fields and facilities by governments, and technological innovations that make oil and gas obsolete (but note that the major companies in this sector don't really consider themselves "oil and gas" companies; rather, they are "energy" companies. As such they are working on other fuel sources and buy up patents on a variety of competing technologies. When the time comes to abandon fossil fuels, the major companies will probably be ready for the change).

There are a number of exchange traded products dedicated to the oil and gas industries, but because many of the smaller companies pay no dividend, their dividend yields tend to be low. A better way to buy these companies all in one shot is through one of the dividend focused ETFs.

Metals and Minerals

The metals and minerals industries consist of companies that mine and refine (surprise, surprise) metals and minerals, including copper, silver, lead, zinc, gold, diamonds, coal, nickel, bauxite, titanium, and so on. Major companies in these industries include BHP Billiton (BHP), Rio Tinto (RIO), Alcoa (AA), Barrick Gold (ABX), Newmont Mining (NEM), Southern Copper (SCCO), and Freeport-McMoRan (FCX). The dividends tend to be very unstable (high payouts one year, and little the next) and the yields tend to be low. This should not be surprising, as commodity prices are very volatile.

The advantages of investing in the companies in the metals and minerals industries are similar to those of owning oil companies: inflation hedging, participating in economic growth, and having a stake in the materials needed to manufacture goods. The risks are also similar to those of oil company investing, including commodity price swings, war, accidents (mine collapses), environmental issues, nationalization, weak economic conditions, innovations or regulations that decrease demand for the resource (for example, US policy has recently been very much against coal, with the President calling for the closure of coal fired power plants). Mining companies also seem to be very prone to labor disputes (mining is a tough, unhealthy job, after all) and the nationalization of their mines. Given the risks, the wild swings in stock prices, and the low dividends, dividend investors should wade very carefully in the mining industries.

Chemicals

Chemicals are used in pretty much all manufacturing and refining processes. Companies in this industry supply manufacturers of consumer products (pretty much anything you can think of, from cosmetics to medicine to food to electronics) with raw materials. They also sell farmers fertilizer, pesticides, specialized seeds, and so on. Major companies include Dow Chemical (DOW), DuPont (DD), and Monsanto (MON). As with the miners, the dividends here are not very stable and the yields tend to be low. Dividend raises are rare and the stock prices tend to be quite volatile. This industry is not a very good place to look for income.

The advantages of investing in chemicals companies include exposure to the economy (as their products are in everything that we use daily) and the fact that they have very valuable patent portfolios. Monsanto, for example, is often treated as merely a fertilizer and pesticide company, but its future revenues are highly dependent on innovations in seed technology. It has the potential to obtain a monopoly on the world's food supply (a scary thought).

The risks include economic weakness, rising prices for raw materials (like oil), class action law suits and fines (chemicals tend not to be very good for these companies' workers or the towns where their plants operate, and sometimes even consumers become ill), and consumer and government backlash. Europe, for example, is generally not very fond of genetically modified crops. You may also lose your soul if you invest in these companies, but that's just my opinion.

If you are interested in buying the chemicals and mining companies all in one shot, one ETF to consider is the iShares Dow Jones US Basic Materials ETF (IYM). Its yield is usually under 2%, but it allows you to buy companies like DuPont, Dow, Freeport-McMoRan, and others all in one purchase.

Chapter 13 - Industrial Goods

The industrial goods sector is the second largest segment of the stock market by capitalization. Companies in this sector supply the world with tools, components, tractors, passenger and fighter jets, aircraft carriers, engines, turbines, building materials, and so on. The sector includes conglomerates like General Electric (GE), Siemens (SI), 3M (MMM), and United Technologies (UTX), notable defense contractors like Raytheon (RTN), Northrop Grumman (NOC), Lockheed Martin (LMT), Honeywell International (HON), and Boeing (BA), farm and building equipment makers like Caterpillar (CAT) and Deere (DE), power and automation equipment makers like ABB (ABB), industrial equipment makers like Emerson Electric (EMR), machine tool manufacturers like Stanley Black & Decker (SWK), component makers like Illinois Tool Works (ITW), and waste managers like Waste Management (WM). Pretty much all of the companies in this lengthy list have long histories of stable and rising dividend payments, along with decent yields. In fact, of those companies that pay a stable dividend, only one cut its dividend during the financial crisis: GE, mostly because of its financial division—it's sometimes said that GE is a bank that also happens to make stuff. Most of the rest continued their annual dividend raises.

The advantages of investing in industrial goods companies depend on what each company produces and for whom, but in general they include solid growth, stable dividends, entrenchment in the military industrial complex, and some insulation from economic slowdowns. While a few industrial goods companies have consumer segments, their customers are usually other corporations, such as utilities, farms, builders, contractors, airlines, shippers, and so on, or governments, as in the case of the weapons makers. Much of this equipment has to be replaced as it becomes worn from use, outdated, or destroyed. Moreover, most of the major dividend payers in this sector are multinationals. Despite the weakened economies of the developed nations, the world economy is growing. People are building cities, factories, airports, roads, and so on. This ensures steady business for these companies.

Risks include higher costs for raw materials, tougher regulations, higher tax rates, a slower growing (or declining) global economy, currency fluctuations, hostile foreign governments, and serious governmental budget cuts (this especially affects defense contractors).

If you are interested in industrial goods businesses and are looking for ETFs, there are a few choices. A couple are dedicated to defense contractors: the iShares Dow Jones US Aerospace and Defense ETF (ITA) and the PowerShares Aerospace & Defense ETF (PPA). There are also broader ETFs such as the iShares S&P Global Industrials ETF (EXI), the iShares Dow Jones US Industrials (IYJ), and the Vanguard Industrials (VIS). Furthermore, most of the large industrial companies are components of the S&P 500, and are therefore included in the holdings of all index funds tracking that index (e.g., SPY, IVV, VOO). A few of the larger industrial goods companies listed above (GE, UTX, BA, CAT, and MMM) are in the Dow Jones Industrial Average (along with some of the major companies mentioned in the previous chapters and in the next one). As such, you can skip all the individual stocks and sector ETFs and just grab the SPDR Dow Jones Industrial Average (DIA) instead. It pays a monthly dividend and yields a little more than most of the individual sector ETFs.

Chapter 14 - Consumer Goods

Consumer goods is the largest sector by market capitalization. It includes all of the major companies that we do business with daily. The sector is often divided into consumer staples, composed of companies that sell the daily necessities of life, and consumer discretionary, composed of cyclical companies like clothing stores, luxury goods, toy makers, recreational goods, and so on. As the consumer discretionary sector does not pay much by way of dividends, the focus here will be on the staples.

These include industries such as tobacco, food, beverages, and personal products. Among the major dividend payers, you'll find tobacco companies like Altria (MO), Reynolds American (RAI), Lorillard (LO), beverage companies like Coca-Cola (KO), junk food companies like Pepsico (PEP) and Hershey (HSY), personal products companies like Procter & Gamble (PG) and Kimberly-Clark (KMB), food companies like Kraft (KFT), Unilever (UL & UN), HJ Heinz (HNZ), Nestle (NSRGY), General Mills (GIS), Campbell Soup (CPB), Kellogg (K), ConAgra (CAG), Sysco (SYY), and Archer Daniels Midland (ADM), household goods companies like Clorox (CLX) and Colgate-Palmolive (CL), and alcoholic beverage companies like Diageo (DEO), Brown-Forman (BF-B), Anheuser-Busch Inbev (BUD), and fast food restaurants like McDonald's (MCD). Most of the companies listed have been solid dividend payers and raisers for decades.

There may be some debate as to why companies like MCD, BUD, BF-B, DEO, KO, PEP, MO, RAI, and LO are on the staples list. After all, restaurants, alcoholic and non-alcoholic beverage makers, junk food producers, and tobacco companies do not necessarily make products that we need daily, unlike toilet paper and food. But many people do *need* them. They must have a cigarette or a drink, and they can't live without their Diet Coke. They must have their potato chips and beer during the game, and they need their burger and fries. What? You expect them to cook? McDonald's is in a sense the quintessential consumer staples stock. There are few places where one can eat as cheaply or deliciously. In general, the worse the economy gets, the more customers McDonald's has. And as for the alcoholic beverage industry, it seems that people always have enough money for booze. They drink more when things are good because they're celebrating, and they drink more when times are bad because times are bad.

For these reasons, consumer staples stocks are often called "defensive." They pay good dividends and either go up or don't decline as much as other stocks during recessions. They can underperform during good times, but that is to be expected. If they had a motto, it would be "slow and steady."

Tobacco

The tobacco industry may be divided into two parts: the developed world where the number of smokers is declining, and the developing world, where the number of smokers is increasing. Companies operating in the developed world are similar to landline telecoms in that they have a declining customer base. Smoker numbers are decreasing at around 2% per year. As a result, tobacco companies in the developed world have slow earnings growth, which comes from acquisitions and price increases. They are fighting each other for a bigger slice of a shrinking pie. This does not mean, however, that they are poor investments. Maybe they are, but it's not a necessary fact. The dividend yields are quite high, often ranging between 4 and 7%, and the payout amounts usually increase annually. Over the last few decades they have been some of the best investments ever (Altria in particular), and can continue to be good ones for years to come.

Tobacco companies like Philip Morris International (PM) that sell their products in the developing world, on the other hand, stand to be like their developed world counterparts decades ago. Not only are the markets where they sell their products growing, there are also markets that they haven't even entered yet.

The advantages of investing in tobacco companies include their steady dividend increases, the addictive nature of their products, and their strong name brand recognition. Other advantages include a sort of dependency of governments, which derive lots of tax revenues from tobacco.

The industry has always been fraught with risk, however. Tobacco causes all sorts of health problems. Even though everyone who is not mentally retarded knows this, the lawsuits keep coming, especially in the developed world. Governments impose more stringent regulations and higher taxes on both the companies and their customers whenever they have the chance. Whenever a politician wants to distract his constituents from real problems or wants to show how hard he is working, he takes aim at tobacco companies. There is less of this in the developing world, but it can become a problem at any time. Moreover, unlike the more diversified companies in other industries, tobacco companies make most of their money from one product (sold in different forms): tobacco (duh!). If tobacco is outlawed, there is little other business on which to fall back.

Alcohol

Investing in brewers and distillers has advantages similar to those of tobacco investing. The product, which can be addictive, is always in demand and is often called "recession-immune." People always seem to manage to scrounge up enough cash to buy another drink. The alcoholic beverage industry is also similar to the tobacco industry in that it can be divided into the relatively stagnant developed world and the growing developing world.

The risks include increased government regulations and higher taxes, which can drive down sales. While prohibition is unlikely in the major markets, it has happened in the past. There is also the risk that the economy is so terrible that people don't have enough money to drown their sorrows on brand names and take to making moonshine. Finally, currency fluctuations and raw materials costs can adversely affect companies' profits and dividend distributions.

Food

The investment thesis here is simple. Barring some new innovation or dramatic evolutionary change, everyone must eat. The food industry's growth in the developed world depends largely on population growth (more mouths to feed equals more revenues), and to a certain extent, waistline growth. In the developing world it depends on people's income growth. Most of Kraft's (KFT) future growth, for example, is expected to come from the developing world. To this end, the company plans to split itself in two: one a fast growing, global snack company, and the other a slow growing grocery giant. The main risks in this industry are higher raw materials costs, product recalls, and unhealthy food bans.

Non-Alcoholic Beverage Producers

The beverage industry is largely dominated by a few companies: Coca-Cola (KO), Pepsico (PEP), and Nestle (NSRGY) (which also happens to be the world's largest food company). These companies produce soda, juices, athletic beverages, energy drinks, and plain water. Chances are that whatever non-alcoholic beverage you buy at the store, it is made by one of these companies. Pretty much everything drinkable on the supermarket store shelves is a brand owned by one of the three (they have competitors of course, ranging from Kraft to FEMSA to Dean Foods and Dr. Pepper Snapple—a great website to find out more about beverage makers is beverageworld.com). When a new, popular product comes to market, like Vitamin Water, for example, one of these companies swoops in and buys it. So it can be pretty amusing, if you ever go to something like an organic, healthy beverage trade show, that behind all the green and environmentally friendly logos you'll find the familiar corporate parents Coke, Pepsi, and Nestle.

Because their products are so ubiquitous, the major beverage makers grow by stealing market share from each other, by buying smaller competitors, and by introducing new products. The developed world is quite saturated, but the developing world, experiencing income growth, is developing a taste for brand name beverages to go with their new western snacks and fast food.

Industry domination, and the propensity of people to ingest fluids in order to live are some of the advantages of investing in the major beverage producers. Risks include major economic upheavals, product recalls, stricter labor laws, and more stringent pollution controls. Other risks include stagnation and inefficiency. The larger a company

97

gets, the more moving parts it has, the more likely it is that there is waste.

Personal and Household Products

Women wear makeup, style their hair, put on lotions and paint their nails. Most men shave regularly. Everyone showers, from time to time, and pretty much everyone wears deodorant. We brush our teeth and wipe our behinds (hopefully not simultaneously or with the same instrument). We clean up our messes with sponges and paper towels. When this doesn't work, we use bleach and other cleaners. We use detergent when we do laundry, and fabric softener when we dry our wet clothes. Our babies and old timers wear diapers. We take pills for gas, indigestion, heartburn, and other minor aches and pains. And so on. Jot down the mundane details of a typical Western life and you'll have a long list of products that we don't need in the strictest sense (as in Henry David Thoreau's), but that we use all the time and would be very cranky without. Personal and household products are therefore as recession proof as alcohol, food, and tobacco. If there's not enough money for toilet paper, there's not enough money for anything else.

Strong dividend payers like Procter & Gamble (PG), Kimberly Clark (KMB), Clorox (CLX), Church & Dwight (CHD), and Colgate (CL) make their money from the mandatory comforts of daily life. They raise their dividends like clockwork, all because most of the disposable items in your house are made by them. These companies' growth in the developed world comes from population growth, product innovations, acquisitions of smaller rivals, theft of market share from competitors and price increases. The developing world, on the other hand, is a brand new market. The emerging middle class there is just starting to develop a taste for

98

products that are essentially superfluous to life until their use is so widespread that they are necessary. Think of your reaction to someone that isn't wearing deodorant or hasn't brushed his teeth. The more people use such products, the more likely society will drive the holdouts to follow.

The main risks include currency fluctuations, rising raw materials costs, labor regulations, product recalls, and competition from cheaper, generic brands.

There are a number ETF offerings in the consumer goods sector, often divided between staples and cyclicals. All of the major ETF issuers have one or more funds dedicated to these stocks. Another way to pick them up is through the dividend focused ETFs.

Chapter 15 - Services

The services sector includes grocers, publishers, restaurants, wholesalers, all sorts of stores, broadcasters, casinos, resorts, airlines, shippers, and railroads. Dividends are by and large scant and inconsistent, but some of the major companies in each industry pay their shareholders generously. These include Home Depot (HD), Lowe's (LOW), Viacom (VIA & VIAB), Time Warner Cable (TWC), Time Warner (TWX), Shaw Communications (SJR) (a monthly dividend payer), Target (TGT), Best Buy (BBY), Walmart (WMT) (about as close to a consumer staples stocks as one can get and still be a store), Costco (COST), United Parcel Service (UPS), Northfolk Southern (NSC), Union Pacific (UNP), and CSX Corp (CSX).

All of these operate in very different businesses, but the advantages of investing in them are similar. They all benefit from a growing economy: the broadcasters get more ad revenues, the stores sell more stuff, and the shippers ship more goods. Their risks are similar too. Slow economic growth, joblessness, and rising basic materials costs all affect their bottom lines. Airlines go bankrupt every few years, it seems. Department stores have their heyday and then disappear as a new generation of customers begins to favor a competitor. (Remember Caldor, Woolworth's, Filene's Basement, Gold Circle and hundreds of others? Where are they now?) Railroads seem to be more resilient, but if you look through history, they used to make up a much larger part of the economy. Many of the Dow Jones Industrial Average stocks used to be railroads. Now none are.

Many of the stores in the services sector are found in consumer discretionary and retail ETFs. The railroads and

100

other shippers can be bought through about half a dozen ETFs focused on transports. Neither group of exchange traded products has yields worth buying because most of their holdings do not pay dividends.

When investing in services stocks, therefore, be extra careful.

Part Four - Dividends and "Dividends" from Sources Other than Common Stocks

Dividends and other distributions can come from stock market sources other than common stocks. These include preferred stocks, real estate investment trusts, master limited partnerships, royalty trusts, mutual funds, and various exchange traded products. The following chapters will be about these.

Chapter 16 - Preferred Stocks

Although it's easy enough to find common stocks, information relating to preferred stocks is usually hard to come by. Most stock screeners don't include them, and it's often hard to even get a quote on widely used financial websites. Furthermore, some companies have many different preferred shares while others have none at all.

There are different classes of shares. So far we've looked at the most familiar, common stocks, which are the lowest on the pecking order in a corporation's capital structure. A corporation's bond holders have the highest priority to its earnings and assets, next come the preferred stockholders. Note that different preferred share classes can have different priorities. For example, some of corporation XYZ's preferred shares are classified as junior while others are classified as senior. Owners of the senior preferred shares will have priority over the junior preferred shares.

As preferred shares are between bonds and common stock on the priority ladder, it is unsurprising that they share characteristics of both. The rights that come with a preferred share's ownership (stated in the "Certificate of Designation" and in the prospectus) vary by company and series, but we can say a few general things about them. Most preferred shares pay a fixed dividend, like bonds (except we call it "interest" or "coupon" when we talk about bonds). It is also usually the case that the company reserves the right to buy the shares back at any time for a certain price (most commonly for $25 a share). Some preferred share dividends are classed as ordinary income (like bonds) while other preferred share dividends are classed as qualified (like common stocks), most often depending on how the company treats the payments (are they debt or dividends?).

Some preferred shares come with voting rights (e.g., for a class of directors), while most come with none. The major difference between preferred shares and bonds is that bond interest must be paid whereas in general preferred dividends must be declared and the board of directors has the discretion not to do so. That is, the board of directors, in most cases, can decide to stop paying dividends on the preferred shares. While this is so, it is usually the case that if the board of directors wants to pay a common stock dividend, it must pay the preferred stock dividend first. Preferred share dividends are thus seen as safer than common stock dividends. In other words, there is less danger that a preferred stock dividend will be cut than there is the elimination of the common stock dividend. You may recall that during the heart of the 2007 through 2009 crisis, most banks cut their dividends, as did a number of other corporations (GE comes to mind). But most continued to pay out their fixed preferred share dividends.

As far as dividend priority goes, there are two kinds of preferred shares, **cumulative** and **non-cumulative**. A **cumulative preferred** stock is one that has a fixed dividend schedule (usually quarterly). The board of directors decides whether to declare and pay the dividend. If it decides not to pay, the company owes this dividend to its preferred shareholders. As with most preferred stock, if the company does not pay a dividend on its preferred stock, it cannot pay a dividend on its common stock. If a company misses a cumulative preferred stock payment, it must repay it before being able to declare a dividend on its common shares. In other words, if any dividend payments on the cumulative preferred shares are missed, these missed dividends must be paid out to preferred shareholders before common shareholders can receive dividends. Missed cumulative dividends must also be paid if the company decides to buy the preferred shares back (it might want to do this, for example, if it wants to issue new preferred shares or bonds that pay a lower rate).

For example suppose company XYZ, in addition to its common stock, has a cumulative preferred stock XYZ-CP. XYZ-CP is supposed to pay $0.25 per share per quarter. Let's say the company experiences some financial trouble and the board of directors decides not to declare a dividend. First, as with most preferred shares, since XYZ isn't paying scheduled dividends on its preferred shares, it cannot pay dividends on its common stock. Second, the missed payments on XYZ-CP add up. Suppose that the company misses five XYZ-CP payments. If the company ever wants to pay dividends on its common stock or buy XYZ-CP back, it will have to resume dividend payments on XYZ-CP and pay the preferred stock's holders $1.25 per share in missed payments ($0.25 dividend per share x 5 missed payments).

Non-cumulative preferred shares, on the other hand, are not entitled to any missed dividend payments. Suppose that in the example above, corporation XYZ also has a non-cumulative preferred stock XYZ-NC. If it is to pay dividends on its common stock, the corporation must pay dividends on all its preferred shares. Nevertheless, the corporation has no obligation to pay back holders of XYZ-NC for any missed payments. You will find, therefore, that if a company has cumulative and non-cumulative preferred shares, the non-cumulative shares will usually have a higher yield—because they are riskier.

Among these two broad kinds of preferred shares, there are various different types. Here are several. Some preferred shares expire just like bonds. Their expiration date (also known as the maturity date) is listed in their prospectus and Certificate of Designation. It is up to the company to set the date. When the shares mature, the company buys them back for a set price (the most common, as mentioned, is $25). If the dividend on this type of preferred share is fixed, this type of preferred share is called a **fixed rate hard retractable**. If the dividend is not fixed (that is, it can vary) this type of preferred share is called a **floating rate retractable**.

Another type of preferred share is the **fixed rate soft retractable**. These shares have a fixed dividend but at maturity the company pays for them in cash or stock equivalent to 95% of their market value. If this type of preferred share does not have a fixed dividend, it is called a **floating rate soft retractable**.

Fixed rate perpetual preferred shares have a fixed dividend rate and no expiration date. Sometimes the company that issued them reserves the right to buy them back for a certain price after a certain time. If the dividend rate is not fixed, these preferred shares are the **floating rate perpetual** type.

Finally, there are **fixed floater** preferred shares. These have a fixed dividend for a certain period of time with a change to a floating rate thereafter.

Most of these types of preferred shares can be cumulative or non-cumulative. Moreover, they can be convertible. **Convertible preferred** shares can be exchanged (sometimes after a certain date, sometimes right away) by their holder into another class of stock. For example, one convertible preferred share might be exchangeable for 20 shares of common stock. Be aware that some convertible preferreds (and convertible bonds) can be converted into common stock (or whatever security they are convertible into) at the holder's option while others convert automatically on a certain date or after the occurrence of a certain event.

Trust Preferreds

Trust preferred shares are mostly issued by banks and make up around 20% of the preferred share market. They are debt (debentures) that is not secured by any kind of physical asset or collateral, making them lower in the capital structure than other debt. Note that if you own a trust preferred stock, you may have to pay taxes on the dividends even if the dividends are deferred until the redemption date. Note also that because of the new financial regulations that will take effect in 2013, companies have less incentive to issue new trust preferred shares. They also have incentive to call back the trust preferreds that are outstanding. The upshot is that most trust preferreds will disappear. They are likely to be replaced by riskier types of shares that will hopefully pay higher dividends.

Exchange Traded Debt Securities

Although they are bonds, exchange traded debt securities (ETDS) are very similar to preferred shares. Some investors call them "preferred equity traded bonds" as a result. They are, basically, bonds that are usually issued in $25 denominations (in contrast to the usual bonds, issued in $1,000 denominations) and trade on the stock exchanges like stocks. They have three letter ticker symbols, pay interest quarterly (sometimes monthly), and so may be confused with preferred shares or common stock. Typically, ETDS have a maturity of 30 years but can be called five years after issuance.

Because they are bonds, their "dividends" are taxed as ordinary income. Yields at issuance are fairly high, ranging from 4% to 10%. In the capital structure, ETDS are above preferred stock, on par with the company's unsecured debt, and below the company's secured debt. In other words, if the company goes out of business, first its secured debt holders will be paid, then the unsecured debt holders (including holders of ETDS), then the preferred shareholders, and then the common stockholders. So, for example, if you are choosing between an ETDS and a preferred stock issued by the same company, so long as the yields are the same and the securities trade below par (under liquidation value), the exchange traded security is the safer choice. It will be a rare occurrence, however, that an ETDS will yield the same or higher than a preferred share issued by the same company. Less risk means a lower yield. If you're confused about what kind of a security an issue is and where it is in the capital structure, read the prospectus, which may be found on QuantumOnline.com and in the investor relations section of the particular company's website.

Other Considerations

The company's credit rating, dividend rate, whether a share is cumulative or non-cumulative, whether it is perpetual or retractable and when, and whether it is convertible will all play a role in determining a preferred share's price. If you want to buy individual preferred shares, read their prospectuses with a fine toothed comb. Be very careful. For example, during good times or when investors are stretching for yield, preferred shares can trade above the price at which the corporation can call them back. One of my law school professors (an expert in corporate law) once lamented that he thought he had found a great deal on Ford preferred stock for his elderly father. He invested a substantial portion of his father's assets in the stock, only to have it called away months later for less than he put in, losing thousands of dollars.

If you are wondering where to find preferred stocks, the most widely held ones are listed in major newspapers' stock tables. Some newspapers list them with common stocks while others have a separate section for them. You can also find them listed on corporations' websites and on websites dedicated to preferred stocks. A great website is QuantomOnline.com. It requires registration, but at the time of writing it is free. Financials typically have the greatest number and variety of preferred stocks and ETDS.

It bears repeating, please be very careful with preferred stocks. Consulting an investment professional is advisable.

But as most people have neither the time nor the inclination to do diligent research not only into a certain company but its various preferred shares (and no time, inclination, or money to spend on an adviser), there are preferred stock funds (ETFs, CEFs, and Mutual Funds). Lists of these can be found on websites dedicated to fund lists. (Seekingalpha.com has an easy to find list of the major ETFs. Your broker might have a fund screener, and services like Lipper and Morningstar can offer ratings on these funds based on their past performance and costs.) ETFs usually attempt to replicate an index. Their holdings therefore do not change very much, and this results in low fees. Note that the majority and in some cases all of the holdings of an ETF dedicated to preferred shares come from the financial sector. At the time of writing, the most popular preferred share ETFs were PowerShares Financial Preferred (PGF), PowerShares Preferred (PGX), SPDR Wells Fargo Preferred Stock (PSK), and iShares S&P US Preferred Stock (PFF). By the time you read this there will probably be one or more ETFs dedicated to international preferred shares. There is already one dedicated to Canadian preferred stocks (CNPF).

Chapter 17 - Real Estate Investment Trusts (REITs)

Would you like to be part owner of apartment buildings, offices, malls, hospitals, and industrial properties? Would you like to be a landlord and collect rents from many buildings in a wide geographic area? If so, you might be interested in REIT investing. A real estate investment trust (REIT) is a company that owns, operates, or finances real estate. What makes a REIT different from other companies, aside from its real estate focus, depends on the laws of the country where it conducts its business. In other words, a company must comply with certain laws to be classified as a REIT.

One of the most common (and important for dividend investors) requirements is that the company must pay out at least 90% of its taxable earnings to shareholders in dividends. The REIT itself pays no taxes—it is a "pass through" entity. Different countries have different requirements for a company to qualify as a REIT. In the United States the requirements include (in addition to paying out 90% of its income): the corporation must have at least 75% of its gross income come from rent or mortgage interest, 95% of its income come from interest, property income, or dividends, have transferable shares, be managed by a board of directors, and be structured as an association, corporation, or trust.

There are several types of REITs. Residential REITs invest in apartments and houses. Office REITs rent out office and industrial space. Retail REITs operate malls and shopping centers. Lodging REITs operate hotels and resorts, while healthcare REITs make their money from hospitals and clinics. Other REITs invest in mortgages, operate self storage businesses, college dorms, and even timberland. Of course, nothing prevents a REIT from diversifying its businesses into several categories. If you look at owning a company's stock not as a trading vehicle but as an ownership stake in the business, owning REIT stocks is like owning fractional stakes in office buildings, residential buildings, malls, forests and so on. It is an easy way to invest in income producing land without having to set foot outside your house.

Since REITs pay out 90% of their earnings in dividends, one might expect to see their stocks have super high dividend yields. For the most part this is not the case. At the time of writing, most REIT dividend yields range from 2 to 7% and average between 3 and 4%.

Mortgage REITs (companies that attempt to borrow money at a low interest rate, buy mortgages that pay a higher interest rate, and make money on the difference), which may or may not exist in the future (at the time of writing the SEC is contemplating a rule change that would make it hard for them to remain REITs), often pay the largest dividends as a percentage of stock price. Annaly Capital Management (NLY), for instance, typically pays out more than 10% of its stock price annually. From December 2010 to the end of September 2011 it paid $2.51 per share in dividends while its stock price ranged from $16 to $18.70 a share. Taking the higher price, NLY has paid out 13.42% of its share price in dividends. Note that while they are good dividend payers, mortgage REITs are quite risky. They have no control over things that substantially affect their business: access to the capital markets, interest rates, conditions in the house market, and whether mortgage borrowers default on or prepay their mortgages (both of which lower mortgage REITs' returns). Many mortgage REITs went out of business during the financial crisis.

Unlike regular dividend paying companies, REITs often do not have a stable dividend. That is, the dividend can rise and fall from quarter to quarter with a much greater frequency than regular corporations'. REIT dividends tend not to be "sticky" (if the dividend a company pays every quarter is the same or larger than the previous payment, it is said to be "sticky." Earnings, on the other hand, are "bumpy," rising or falling at different rates every quarter.) When looking at a REIT's dividend yield, therefore, keep in mind that it is subject to change and is usually based (on the stock quoting services) on dividends paid out during the last 12 months. Most REITs pay out quarterly dividends. A small number pay their dividends monthly. The most famous monthly payer is probably Realty Income Corp (O). It has paid an ever rising monthly dividend since 1994.

If you are thinking about investing in REITs, keep in mind that there are various things that affect their businesses. This includes interest rates, the health of the overall economy, the health of regional economies, the economic conditions in particular sectors, and changes in income and property tax rates. Also keep in mind that traditional value measures like payout ratio and earnings per share do not give you a very good picture of a REIT's profitability, financial health, or ability to pay dividends. What you want to look at instead are funds from operations, adjusted funds from operations, cash available for distribution, and net asset value.

Funds from operations shows you the REIT's cash flows. This figure is arrived at by adding earnings, amortization (debt payments), and depreciation (a method of alloc-

113

ating the cost of an asset over its useful life—e.g., if you buy a physical asset, like a truck, building, or computer that is supposed to last x years, every accounting year you can expense 1/x of its cost) together. **Adjusted funds from operations** is a figure that usually adjusts a REIT's funds from operations by recurring expenses used to maintain the underlying assets. **Cash or funds available for distribution** is a figure that tells you how much cash the REIT has on hand that can be paid out as dividends to shareholders. The **net asset value** of a REIT is the market value of all its assets net of debt.

If you want to buy a number of REITs in one shot, there are a number of ETFs dedicated to real estate investment trusts. At the time of writing there were around 20, in various broad and narrow indexes, including international, domestic, world, regional, and sector (residential, office, etc). SeekingAlpha.com has a good list. A quick internet search will no doubt yield an even greater number. Lipper, Morningstar, and possibly your broker can tell you which one is best for your needs. You can almost always view an ETF's holdings at its website, along with the expense ratio, past performance, the prospectus, and other useful information.

Chapter 18 - Master Limited Partnerships (MLPs)

Master limited partnerships (MLPs) have, as an asset class, outperformed the broad stock market in every time period except the 1998 through 1999 tech stock mania. See boxes 7 and 8 for recent performance. Instead of shares of stock, MLPs have "units," and instead of shareholders, they have "unit holders." But you can buy and sell their units through the stock market just as you would any stock. To be an MLP, 90% of the business' earnings must come from activities, dividends, or interest payments relating to natural resources, commodities, or real estate. Although there are a few MLPs that are in other industries (e.g., Blackstone Group [BX], a private equity firm, and Stonemor Partners [STON], an operator of cemeteries), most MLPs' businesses have to do with natural resources. The majority of MLPs, both in number and in market capitalization, are companies that discover, produce, treat, or transport oil, gasoline, or natural gas.

MLPs versus S&P 500 and Russell 2000 (1996 – 2011)

Asset	Growth	Value of $10,000 investment in 2011
MLPs	937.00%	$103,700.00
S&P 500	183.00%	$28,300.00
Russell 2000	186.00%	$28,600.00

Source: Credit Suisse

Box 7

MLPs are managed by general partners while limited partners supply the capital. In other words, the limited partner is a person or group that, by purchasing the investment units, provides capital to the master limited partnership. The general partner, on the other hand, is the person or group that manages the business. Limited partners, in exchange for their capital, receive distributions (which we can think of as dividends) out of the partnership's cash flow. You, the investor, become a limited partner when you buy units of the MLP. The general partner, on the other hand, is paid for managing the MLP. General partners can be structured in a number of ways, usually as a regular corporation or partnership, and in some cases their shares or investment units are publicly held and trade on the exchanges.

Annual Returns from 2000 through 11/30/11

	S&P 500	MLP Index
2011	1.10%	7.70%
2010	15.10%	35.90%
2009	28.50%	76.40%
2008	-37.00%	-36.90%
2007	5.50%	12.70%
2006	15.80%	26.10%
2005	4.90%	6.30%
2004	10.90%	16.70%
2003	28.70%	44.50%
2002	-22.10%	-3.40%
2001	-11.90%	43.70%
2000	-9.10%	45.70%

Box 8
Source: MLP Guy Blog

The general partner's compensation is linked to the performance of the MLP through something called incentive distribution rights. These distribution rights incentivize the general partner to grow distributions to the limited partners. The general partner's take increases incrementally as certain distribution tiers are reached.

Most MLPs have a minimum quarterly distribution (MQD) and three distribution tiers. The MQD is the minimum distribution the partnership plans to pay its unit holders, as long as the business generates enough cash flow from operations to do so. The distribution tiers entitle the general partner to collect incrementally greater portions of the MLP's cash flow—as certain predetermined levels of distributions to the limited partners are met, the general partner receives a greater portion. The MQD and distribution tiers are outlined in the partnership agreement between the general partner and limited partner when the MLP is created.

Here's an example. Let's say an MLP has an MQD of $1.80 per unit and three distribution tiers. Tier 1 includes all distributions less than or equal to $2 per unit, tier 2 includes distributions greater than $2 per unit but less than or equal to $2.50 per unit, and tier 3 includes distributions greater than $2.50 per unit but less than or equal to $3 per unit. And let's say the general partner is entitled to 2% of distributions up to tier 1, 15% of the distributions up to tier 2, 25% of the distributions up to tier 3, and 50% of the distributions above tier 3.

Suppose that the MLP pays its limited partners $4 per unit. Under the above scheme, the general partner will receive $0.04 per unit under the first tier, $0.09 per unit under the second tier, $0.17 per unit under the third tier, and $1 per unit above the third tier, for a total of $1.30 per unit. (In this example, then, the MLP will have paid out a total distribution of $5.30 per unit--$4 to the limited partners and $1.30 to the general partner.) (Source: Wells Fargo Securities.)

As you can see, the general partner has an incentive to grow distributions above the third tier, because it receives half of everything above that level. Although they retain a smaller portion of the partnership's cash flows as each tier is reached, the scheme is beneficial to the limited partners too because it motivates the general partner to grow the business. As a result of incentive distribution rights, the publicly traded general partners usually command a premium over the businesses they manage—their distribution or dividend yields are usually lower. Kinder Morgan's (KMI) yield, for example, is typically over 150 basis points lower than Kinder Morgan Energy Partners' (KMP), the limited partner KMI manages.

Advantages of MLPs

MLPs have certain advantages over common dividend paying stocks. For one thing, the partnership structure means that MLPs pay no taxes at the entity level. All the taxes are passed on to unit holders. Thus, just as with RE-ITs, there is no double taxation of distributions. If you recall, double taxation of dividends is one of the strongest arguments against owning dividend paying stocks.

Another tax advantage of MLPs is that most of the income they distribute to unit holders is tax deferred. The cash distributions that unit holders receive often have little to do with the MLP's earnings. Rather, the "dividends" that MLPs pay come out of the entity's distributable cash flow (basically, the money that the partnership generates after expenses). In general, the periodic distributions that unit holders receive are much higher than their share of the taxable income (typically, about 20 cents of every dollar of the distribution is taxable). The rest of the distribution is tax deferred. It is treated as return of capital. As you receive these tax deferred distributions, they are subtracted from your cost basis. You pay taxes on the tax deferred portion of the distributions when you sell the units or when your adjusted cost basis becomes 0.

For example, suppose you buy 100 units of a master limited partnership whose ticker is ABC. Let's say you pay $30 per unit, for a total of $3,000. That is your cost basis. Let's say you hold the MLP for four years, and during this time it pays an annual distribution of $2 per unit, $0.40 of which is taxable. Over the four years, you will receive $8 in distributions per unit (or $800). Of this $8 per unit, $1.60 ($0.40 taxable income per year x 4 years) will be taxable at the ordinary income rate and $6.40 ($1.60 deferred income per year per unit x 4 years) will be return of capital, which is tax deferred. You will pay ordinary income tax on the $1.60 per unit ($160), while your cost basis in ABC will drop by $6.40 per unit, or $640 since in our example you have 100 units. Thus, your cost basis at the end of the four years will be $23.60 per unit or $2,360.

Suppose that at the end of the four years, you sell ABC for $33 a unit. Your capital gain will be $3 per unit ($33 sell price minus $30 original purchase price), and you will pay taxes on it at the regular capital gains rate. In this example, since you hold ABC longer than one year, you will be taxed at the long term capital gains rate. You will also have to pay taxes on the $6.40 per unit ($640) in tax deferred income. This amount will be taxed as regular income, and the amount of tax you pay will depend on your income bracket. So here's the advantage of MLPs: if you don't want to pay taxes on the bulk of your distribution income, you don't have to—as long as you don't sell your units! In our example, if you don't sell ABC, $640 of your income is tax free. Another benefit of holding MLPs for the long haul is that when the units are transferred to your heirs, their cost basis is reset to the market price. In this scenario, you never have to pay taxes on the tax deferred portion of your income.

As MLPs have these tax advantages, it does not make sense to hold them in a tax deferred account (it is inadvisable to hold MLP units in a tax deferred account for other reasons, which will be outlined below). Many investors stay clear of or fret over MLPs because these firms do not issue 1099 forms like regular dividend paying stocks. Instead, they send you K-1 forms. For some reason these forms really freak people out. But they shouldn't. If you already have an accountant do your taxes, he'll handle it. If you do your taxes yourself, dealing with a K-1 form is almost like dealing with a 1099 thanks to updates to popular tax programs like TurboTax. There are just a few more boxes to fill out. If you use a tax program like TurboTax, it really is as simple as inputting your 1099 or W-2 information.

Another advantage of investing in MLPs is that they are usually very resilient businesses that provide steady income even during economic downturns. For example, during the financial crisis 23% of MLPs cut their distributions. As a comparison, 85% of REITs cut their dividends during the same period.

And, as mentioned, MLPs have as a group outperformed the stock market. All this with less volatility and tax deferred dividends. As a point of comparison with a long time dividend payer, compare the performance of one of the oldest MLPs, Buckeye Partners (BPL), with that of AT&T (T). Suppose you put $10,000 each in BPL and T in January of 1987 and reinvested all after tax dividends (based on the highest tax bracket). By the end of November, 2011, your AT&T position would be worth around $66,000. Your Buckeye position, in contrast, would be worth over $348,000! ("Got MLPs? BPL vs. T and the Extreme Power of Compounding Over the Long Haul," MLPProtocol.com.)

<u>Some Important Considerations</u>

There are a few things to watch out for with MLPs. One is that if or when the cost basis on your units drops to $0, all cash distributions thereafter are no longer tax deferred. In our example above, once you receive $30 per unit in tax deferred distributions from ABC, all future distributions will be taxable right away.

Another thing to watch out for is that you may have to pay taxes in the states, localities, and foreign countries where your MLP income is generated. This can be a hassle. Moreover, don't think that you can get away with not paying any taxes by sticking the MLP into a retirement account. You might still owe taxes. Some MLP distributions are considered unrelated business taxable income (UBTI). If your total UBTI is $1,000 or more in any year (be aware that laws may change), your IRA may owe taxes. Consult a tax adviser if you intend to put MLPs in a tax sheltered account. If you absolutely must own MLPs in an IRA, you will save yourself a lot of grief by owning institutional shares or funds rather than the individual partnerships.

Institutional, or I-shares (not to be confused with iShares, the ETF issuer) have the same economic interest in the underlying assets of an MLP but they pay their distributions in the form of more shares (instead of cash) in paid-in-kind distributions, which are not taxable until they are sold (at which point you will receive a 1099 instead of a K-

1). All sales are taxed at capital gains rates. At the time of writing, there are only two I-share securities available. These are Kinder Morgan Management (KMR), which has the same underlying assets as Kinder Morgan Energy Partners (KMP) and Enbridge Energy Management (EEQ), which has the same underlying assets as Enbridge Energy Partners (EEP). KMR pays about the same distribution as KMP, but instead of cash it is additional shares of KMR. EEQ pays about the same distribution as EEP, but instead of cash it is additional shares of EEQ. Pay attention to how these trade if you wish to buy them. Sometimes the I-shares trade at a premium to their underlying assets, and sometimes at a discount. If you intend to reinvest your distributions from KMP and EEP, it may make more sense to own KMR and EEQ instead. Moreover, KMR and EEQ can be held in an IRA without any of the potential UBTI problems that KMP and EEP may cause. Holding MLPs through funds (exchange traded, mutual, closed end) also gets rid of the K-1 and UBTI IRA problem.

Different MLP Businesses

The oil and gas business is generally divided into three different activities. Energy companies engage in one, two, or all three of the different activities, which are upstream, midstream, and downstream. As mentioned, those companies that engage in all three are often referred to as "integrated" oil and gas companies.

Upstream

The upstream business consists of finding or acquiring oil and gas fields and taking the resources out of the ground. Upstream MLPs are therefore very exposed to commodity prices. As such, they tend to be more volatile and have a higher distribution yield because investors want to be better compensated for the extra risk.

Some advantages of investing in upstream MLPs include inflation hedging, participation in rising energy prices, and participation in economic growth. Risks include depletion of assets, a drop in oil and gas prices, high maintenance expenses, rising labor costs, accidents, environmental disasters, warm weather (less natural gas consumed equals lower prices), mismanagement, and competition from other upstream companies. Some of these risks can be managed or hedged. For example, upstream MLPs usually lock in prices for most of their anticipated production in long term contracts. Another important risk to consider is that upstream companies' growth depends to a large extent on acquisitions. To make acquisitions, these companies must tap the debt or equity markets. Rising interest rates or lack of access to the debt market is therefore a risk. Unit holders also face the risk of unit dilution, if the MLP decides to issue new units to finance its activities.

Midstream

Midstream companies gather, process, compress, treat, store, and transport petroleum (and other, e.g., biofuels) products after the products have been taken out of the ground by upstream companies but before they are distributed and marketed by downstream companies to end users (consumers, institutions, factories, etc). This part of the business is called midstream because it is in the middle of the process—between the upstream drilling and the downstream marketing and selling.

Midstream companies are relatively immune to commodity prices because their revenues are largely fee based. The fees they charge are outlined in long term contracts that usually have inflation clauses. As a result, midstream MLPs tend to have more stable cash flows than upstream companies. Their cash flows are also inflation hedged.

The risks of investing in midstream MLPs include declining oil and gas prices or a weakening economy (there is less production when prices fall and when the economy is weak, so less oil and gas flow through the midstream MLPs' pipes), rising labor costs, rising maintenance costs, tougher regulations, and too many competitors (an overbuild of the US energy infrastructure), lower fees when new contracts are signed, rising interest rates, accidents, environmental disasters, and mismanagement.

Owning midstream companies can help hedge the risk of owning upstream companies. For example, natural gas prices tend to drop during warm winters because less gas is used to heat homes and businesses. Upstream companies therefore make less money. But the unused gas has to be stored somewhere—so midstream companies make more money from storage fees.

Downstream and Other

Downstream companies refine, market, and distribute products to the end user. They are the last link in the chain from getting the resource out of the ground to selling it to the parties requiring the resource. They are usually not structured as MLPs.

MLPs that are involved in the propane industry are generally involved in the midstream and downstream aspects of the distribution chain. They gather and process propane, transport it, market it, and distribute it to end users. They typically charge their end users a fixed percentage above their supply costs. The propane MLPs' margins and the volume of propane sold is usually fixed in one year contracts with wholesale suppliers. Retail propane distributors (think Hank Hill) buy from the wholesale suppliers under similar schemes. Declining propane prices thus increase profits, because retail prices usually lag costs. Rising propane prices can decrease profits, but in the past propane companies have been able to increase their margins despite increasing prices. Most propane sales (around 70%) are made during the colder weather months (October through March).

Risks include energy conservation on the part of end users, warmer weather, switchover to competing products like natural gas, and propane price swings.

Other companies structured as MLPs in the energy industry include tankers, which ship crude oil, diesel, gasoline, heating oil, liquified natural gas, asphalt, and other petroleum products. Investing in tankers is usually much riskier than investing in other MLPs. Reasons for this include stringent regulations, commodity price volatility, competition from other shippers (glut of oil tankers), declines in demand for petroleum products, piracy, spills, and changes in the law.

As mentioned, companies in industries other than petro-energy sometimes also choose the MLP structure. These include bulk shippers, ports, toll roads, utilities, financial firms, cemeteries, coal miners, and timber companies. They have the same advantages and disadvantages with regard to taxation as energy companies, but their business risks and advantages have to do with their activities.

Other Things to Consider When Looking to Buy Energy MLPs

As with REITs, common valuation ratios like earnings per share (in this case earnings per unit) or payout ratio do not really tell you much. This is because amortization and depreciation distort earnings (it is not uncommon for an MLP to post negative earnings even though it is making money). Instead, you should look at what the MLP does, and where. For example, you should ask, does it produce oil or gas, or just treat and transport them? If the former, how much of the resource is estimated to be left? Are there any environmental regulations coming that might close the field early? If the latter, where are the MLP's pipelines? Where do they go? Is the flow through them expected to increase or decrease in the future? By how much? Are there any pipelines that will be opened in the future? And so on.

These types of questions can give you a better idea of how risky the distributions are. Midstream companies tend to have much more stable distributions than upstream companies. A few MLPs have what is considered a "rock solid" distribution because most of their cash lows are derived from fees. These MLPs have almost no direct exposure to commodity prices: Buckeye Partners (BPL), Boardwalk Pipeline (BWP), El Paso Pipeline (EPB), Magellan Midstream (MMP), PAA Gas Storage (PNG), Spectra Energy Partners (SEP), Sunoco Logistics Partners (SXL), and Teekay LNG Partners (TGP). Their median yield is around 5.7%.

A riskier group of MLPs has some exposure to commodity prices and engages in certain non-fee based activities like marketing. Their distributions are considered "secure," and their median yield is around 6.4%. These companies include AmeriGas Partners (APU), Chesapeake Midstream (CHKM), Crestwood Midstream (CMLP), Enbridge Energy Partners (EEP), Enterprise Products (EPD), Energy Transfer Partners (ETP), Exterran Partners (EXLP),

Genesis Energy (GEL), Kinder Morgan Energy Partners (KMP), Niska Gas Storage Partners (NKA), Inergy (NRGY), NuStar Energy (NS), Oneok Partners (OKS), Plains All American Pipeline (PAA), Regency Energy Partners (RGP), Suburban Propane Partners (SPH), TC Pipelines (TCP), Transmontaigne Partners (TLP), Teekay Offshore Partners (TOO), Western Gas Partners (WES), and Williams Partners (WPZ).

The riskiest group of MLPs has a median yield of around 7.4%. This group has greater exposure to commodity prices and derives more revenues from non-fee activities. These include Atlas Pipeline Partners (APL), Alliance Resource Partners (ARLP), Breitburn Energy Partners (BBEP), Blueknight Energy Partners (BKEP), Copano Energy (CPNO), DCP Midstream Partners (DPM), Eagle Rock Energy Partners (EROC), EV Energy Partners (EVEP), Ferrellgas Partners (FGP), Holly Energy Partners (HEP), Legacy Reserves (LGCY), Linn Energy (LINE), Martin Midstream Partners (MMLP), MarkWest Energy Partners (MWE), Targa Resources Partners (NGLS), Natural Resource Partners (NRP), Oxford Resource Partners (OXF), Pioneer Southwest Energy (PSE), Penn Virginia Resource Partners (PVR), Vanguard Natural Resources (VNR), and Crosstex Energy (XTEX). (Source: Wells Fargo Securities. The categorizations by riskiness of business should not imply that one group of MLPs is better than another and should in no way be deemed an endorsement of one group over another or any individual company.)

For all MLPs, as with all other firms you invest in, you should look at the management team. How have they fared in the past? Do they have a history of overpaying for acquisitions? Did they spend money on projects that did not increase distributable cash flow?

After these more subjective appraisals, you should look at the numbers. Look at the operating expenses. Are they stable? Can they be predicted? Is revenue stable or growing from year to year? To what extent is it vulnerable to changes in demand or commodity prices? Does the majority of the MLP's cash flow come from only a few customers? If so, what are the health and prospects of the customers?

Research how much capital is required to maintain the MLP's assets. Do the assets produce enough income to pay for expenses and distributions? Do cash flows support interest payments on the partnership's debt? Is the distribution coverage ratio greater than 1.3? (Distribution coverage is a ratio that is calculated by dividing cash available for distribution by distributions paid. The dividing line between health and concern is usually around 1.3, greater than this number denotes health, while less than this number raises a red flag.) Are earnings before interest, taxes, depreciation, and amortization (EBITDA) growing? Is the partnership's debt to EBITDA ratio growing (bad, unless the debt is used to expand capacity and will be paid for by future profit growth) or shrinking? How does it compare to the industry average?

If the thought of all this research makes your head spin, you might be considering just buying a fund instead. Although this is a suitable option for REIT investing, I don't think it's a good idea with MLPs. With funds, your choices are ETFs, ETNs, CEFs, and mutual funds. I will discuss these in greater detail later in the book. What I want to say here is, all these funds have expenses. If they are passively managed, their objective is to follow an index. Passively managed funds have low enough expense ratios to make them worthy of consideration. Actively managed funds have higher expense ratios, and these will cut into your returns. Moreover, with an active fund manager you have the additional risk that the manager is not very good at his job (that is, with an active fund, you are not only investing in MLPs, you are also betting on the fund manager's ability to do a good job). Active fund managers are, in a sense, professional gamblers who charge you a fee to gamble with your money. This is a strike against mutual funds, CEFs, and actively managed ETFs and ETNs (there aren't any at the time of writing that are dedicated to MLPs). This leaves the passively managed ETFs and ETNs. Because of tax considerations, an MLP ETF (if it is organized as a corporation) will always underperform its index. This is because the ETF will have to pay taxes at the entity level. ETF holders will receive qualified dividends from the fund instead of tax deferred income, thus subjecting your investment to double taxation and negating a major benefit of MLPs. An ETN will more closely follow its index. But ETNs come with issuer risk. If the bank that issued the ETN goes out of business or investors think it will, the ETN can drop in value even if the underlying index is rising. For these reasons, I am not a fan of MLP fund investing.

This doesn't mean that you have to research individual firms. Instead, you can buy all or a portion of the fund's holdings individually. Unlike broad market and sector funds, MLP funds typically have around 30 holdings, and the top ten usually make up at least 50% of the fund's portfolio. For example, the Alerian MLP ETF (AMLP) at the time of writing has 26 holdings, and its top ten account for around 66% of the fund.

If you buy the top ten holdings (in proportion to their weighting) for the same money that you will have spent on the fund, you will replicate the index's performance. At the same time, you will avoid the expense ratio and the double taxation of distributions. Here's an example:

Box 9 shows AMLP's top ten holdings at the time of writing. Let's say you wanted to put $6,000 into AMLP. To replicate the investment, you can instead put $903.84 into Enterprise Products Partners (EPD), $893 into Kinder Morgan Energy Partners (KMP), and so on.

Note that you would have to pay your broker commissions on all ten purchases, and this will be more costly than if you simply purchased the ETF (10 separate purchases versus one purchase). Nevertheless, as long as you keep your total commissions at 1% or less of your total purchase, it is not too much to pay. And, if you do not sell your units right away, the cost savings you will produce by avoiding fund fees, double taxation, and index underperformance will more than make up for this one time expense.

Ticker	Name	AMLP Top 10 Holdings Weight in Fund	Amount to invest for $6,000 in total
EPD	Enterprise Products Partners LP	10.01%	$903.84
KMP	Kinder Morgan Energy Partners LP	9.89%	$893.00
PAA	Plains All American Pipeline LP	7.12%	$642.89
MMP	Magellan Midstream Partners LP	7.08%	$639.28
ETP	Energy Transfer Partners LP	6.65%	$600.45
BPL	Buckeye Partners LP	6.28%	$567.04
OKS	Oneok Partners LP	5.12%	$462.30
WPZ	Williams Partners LP	4.83%	$436.12
MWE	MarkWest Energy Partners LP	4.77%	$430.70
EEP	Enbridge Energy Partners LP	4.70%	$424.38
	Total:	**66.45%**	**$6,000.00**

Box 9

131

Chapter 19 - Royalty Income Trusts

If you are interested in REITs because the idea of being a landlord without having to leave your home appeals to you, you'll love royalty income trusts. Instead of rents and mortgage interest, royalty trusts give you a stake in oil and gas fields and other resource producing land. Similarly to MLPs, American royalty trusts invest in assets that generate income from natural resources. The difference between royalty trusts and MLPs is that while MLPs generate income from discovering, drilling for, or transporting natural resources, royalty trusts generate all their income from the land itself.

A royalty trust owns a stake in the land or the land's minerals. While it trades like any common stock on an exchange, a royalty trust has no employees, managers, or physical operations of any kind. It is run by a trustee, usually a bank. As resources are extracted from the land, the trust receives royalties. The net income from these royalties is distributed to the trust's unit holders (ownership stakes in the trust, as with MLPs, are called units instead of shares). The trust itself pays no taxes. Like an MLP or REIT, it is a pass through entity.

The trusts usually offer a high yield, often over 10%. A few distribute income quarterly while the rest do so monthly. For example, San Juan Basin Royalty Trust (SJT), which owns royalty interests in New Mexico, has seen its unit price increase around 140% from 2001 through October 2011. At the same time, it has generated more than twice its unit price through monthly cash distributions. In other words, if you invested $10,000 into SJT in 2001, the trust's market worth at the end of October 2011 would be around $24,000. And you would have collected another $20,000 in income.

One advantage of owning royalty tursts is that, as with MLPs, their distributions are tax deferred. They are not considered income by the IRS. Instead, the distributions reduce your cost basis, and you don't pay the majority of the taxes on the income until you sell.

Also like MLPs and REITs, because royalty trusts are pass through entities, distributions are only taxed once. This is an advantage over common stock dividends. Trust unit holders have another advantage in that they may qualify for various tax credits that have to do with fuel production.

Finally, royalty trust income can be an inflation hedge. As all of the income is derived from natural resource extraction, when commodity prices go up, all other things being equal, your royalty income should increase as well, and this should increase the unit price.

But there are costs, of course. That last advantage becomes a disadvantage when commodity prices fall. If the price of the underlying commodity drops, not only might the unit price plummet, but the distributions will also. A related disadvantage is that, since income depends on market rates (as well as changing levels of production, among other factors), the distributions aren't stable. It is not uncommon that a royalty trust pays out $2 per unit one year, and $0.30 per unit the subsequent year. The unit price also is also subject to a lot of volatility.

Another disadvantage of royalty trusts is that they own rights to limited resources. In the United States, royalty trusts generally cannot expand. They cannot acquire more rights once they are established. So, as natural resources are finite, royalty trusts cannot last forever. Various events can close the trust down. These include but are not limited to depletion, further resource extraction being uneconomical, costs rising above a certain royalty level, or a vote by a set percentage of unit holders.

A further disadvantage is that unit holders are responsible for their portion of the trust's income when it comes to paying taxes. Royalty trusts do not typically issue K-1s. Instead, investors have to figure out their own cost basis, expenses, and so on. Worse still, depending on the tax thresholds in the states where the trusts generate royalties, unit holders may have to pay taxes in several states. It pays to keep careful records, especially when investing in royalty trusts.

Besides these disadvantages, other risks include general and regional economic health, environmental laws, environmental disasters, endangered species laws, changes in the tax code, pipeline breakages and other things that can slow down production (you can't pump oil or gas if there's nowhere to store it), and ineptitude on the part of the operators of the resource producing property.

At the time of writing, I am not aware of any funds, whether ETFs, ETNs, CEFs, or mutual funds, that are dedicated to American royalty trust investing. If you are interested in finding royalty trusts, a great website is, as mentioned, QuantumOnline.com.

The above was about US royalty trusts. Another variety is Canadian royalty trusts. Around two dozen trade on US stock exchanges. Many more trade in Toronto. The biggest differences between US and Canadian royalty trusts include Canadian trusts being able to acquire additional property after formation, hire employees, issue new shares, borrow money, and manage their property themselves. Originally pass through entities like their US counterparts, Canadian royalty trusts are now taxed as regular corporations. This means that a crucial advantage (no double taxation) has been taken away from the Canadian trusts. They still earn their income from natural resources, but less cash is available for investors. Once having double digit yields, many Canadian trusts now sport single digit ones and their unit prices are lower than they were before the tax change.

Even though they might still be worthwhile investments, what happened to Canadian trusts should serve as a warning to US royalty trust, MLP, and REIT investors. Governments often think of the nonexistence of a certain tax as costing them money. There is no reason to assume that the government will stop extorting its citizens in its efforts to fund wasteful spending in the future—the risk that US tax code will change for the worse is therefore very real and MLP, REIT, and royalty trust investors should be mindful of it.

Chapter 20 - Exchange Traded Funds (ETFs) and Exchange Traded Notes (ETNs)

Commonly known as ETFs, exchange traded funds are a very popular, often efficient way to replicate an index's performance. There are stock, bond, commodity, and other indexes. For example, the Dow Jones Industrial Average (DJIA) is an index of 30 stocks. To replicate the DJIA's performance, you can buy all 30 stocks. Alternatively, you can buy the SPDR Dow Jones Industrial Average (DIA), which holds the 30 stocks.

Oftentimes the term ETF encompasses a variety of exchange traded products (ETPs). They are classified by asset class, which is usually one of stocks, bonds, commodities, currencies, or alternatives. All these products come in one of five structures: open end funds, limited partnerships, grantor trusts, unit investment trusts, and exchange traded notes. An example of an open end fund is the Vanguard Large-Cap ETF (VV). (Note that all mutual funds are open end funds.) An example of a limited partnership is the Powershares DB Commodity Index Tracking Fund (DBC). The Merrill Lynch & Co. Oil Service HOLDRS (OIH) is an example of a grantor trust while the SPDR S&P 500 (SPY) is an example of a unit investment trust. Finally, the ELEMENTS Rogers International Commodity Agri ETN (RJA) is an example of an exchange traded note.

As all of these except exchange traded notes are sufficiently similar for our purposes, I will refer to them as ETFs. Exchange traded notes, which I would like to distinguish, I will call ETNs.

ETFs

Whether passively or actively managed, ETFs trade like stocks. Their prices change throughout the day as they are bought and sold. If their holdings generate cash (e.g., bond interest, dividends, other distributions, or capital gains on holdings that are sold), ETFs pay dividends. Some pay once a year, others twice. Most dividend paying ETFs make quarterly distributions, and a number do so monthly (especially those that hold bonds or preferred shares; an example of a common stock ETF that pays a monthly dividend is DIA).

Dividend Stock ETFs Pros and Cons

There are dozens of ETFs dedicated to dividend paying stocks, with more on the way. They are sliced and diced in every conceivable way, from domestic small caps to international large caps, and everything in between. There are even ETFs tracking stocks that have a history of raising their dividends. A couple of examples of the latter are the PowerShares Dividend Achievers Portfolio (PFM) and the Vanguard Dividend Appreciation Index Fund (VIG). All of the major ETF sponsors have at least one product dedicated to dividend paying stocks. Most of WisdomTree's offerings are based on dividend indexes.

ETFs dedicated to dividend paying stocks have a few things in common. They usually follow similar indexes, making their holdings about the same. What is different is the weight each holding takes up in the portfolio. For example, both PFM and VIG hold IBM. At the time of writing, IBM makes up 5.13% of PFM's portfolio and 4.64% of VIG's. As a result, the similar ETFs have similar price performance and dividend yields, although it is not really appropriate to talk about yields for anything other than comparing one ETF's past distributions to another's. This is another thing ETFs dedicated to dividend paying stocks have in common: they do not pay a stable dividend. The distribution amount changes from payment to payment. We can compare yields by looking at what the ETFs have paid in the last 12 months and seeing what fraction that is of their current market price, but it tells us nothing about what we can expect in the future. See box 10 for a snapshot of the dividend payments of a few similar dividend stock ETFs.

ETFs' Dividends Per Share Last 10 Quarters

VIG	PFM	SDY	DVY
$0.29	$0.09	$0.43	$0.46
$0.28	$0.09	$0.42	$0.47
$0.27	$0.06	$0.38	$0.47
$0.31	$0.13	$0.50	$0.44
$0.27	$0.08	$0.44	$0.42
$0.25	$0.05	$0.42	$0.43
$0.23	$0.03	$0.44	$0.42
$0.24	$0.11	$0.42	$0.43
$0.23	$0.06	$0.43	$0.40
$0.28	$0.12	$0.44	$0.40

Box 10

It would be reasonable for one to expect an ETF tracking a dividend stock index to have a sizable yield. For the most part this isn't so. At the time of writing, for example, PFM has a distribution yield of 2.47%. VIG's is 2.12%. These are not that much higher than the S&P 500's (an index that tracks both dividend and non-dividend paying stocks) 1.96% and the Russell 3000's (an index that tracks the 3,000 largest companies) 1.72%, and are in fact lower than the DJIA's 2.65%. Even the dividend stock ETFs with the designation "high yield," like the Power-Shares High Yield Dividend ETF (PEY), do not have a very high yield. While PEY's 3.68% (at the time of writing) is certainly a higher yield than that of the aforementioned ETFs, it's nothing to brag about (or maybe it is—I'm writing at a time when the interest you get in a "high yield" savings account is zero and you are lucky if the bank isn't charging you money).

A final thing in common that all these ETFs have, and why, if your portfolio is large enough, you should stay away from them, is the rate of their portfolio turnover. The turnover ratio is the percent of a fund's holdings that are replaced in a given year. The lower the ratio, the less holdings are replaced. The higher the ratio, the more holdings are replaced. Many of the dividend ETFs have relatively high turnover ratios. PEY's, for example is 44% at the time of writing. That means that from last year to this year 44% of PEY's holdings have been replaced. As stocks are bought and sold, a portfolio's gains and loses are more pronounced. Stocks that are sold at a loss leave less money to buy replacements—which means less dividend income coming in from replacements. Holdings that are sold for a gain leave more funds for replacements. Sometimes this helps and sometimes this hurts. Generally speaking, the higher the turnover rate, the higher the volatility and costs. Note that PEY's turnover is in the high range for dividend stock ETFs, and is lower than that of most mutual funds. Still, it is far higher than that of a portfolio (like mine, say) where most years nothing is replaced.

Whether a dividend stock ETF (and which one) is right for you depends on your objectives. If you are looking for current income, stable income, or steadily growing income, dividend stock ETFs are probably not for you. Their dividend payments are inconsistent because of changes in their holdings and inflows and outflows, which change the number of the ETF's shares outstanding. If, however, you are looking to easily and relatively cheaply build a diversified, relatively less volatile portfolio, along with a dividend, these ETFs might be just the thing you're looking for.

As I mentioned when discussing the MLP ETF AMLP, if you are looking for higher current income, predictable and hopefully ever-rising distributions, buying a fund's top holdings may be the better way to go. For example, at the time of writing, while VIG's unsteady dividend stream has produced a yield over the last 12 months of 2.12%, its top ten holdings, all high quality blue chip stocks, yield around 3.5%. If you're thinking something like, "hey, I can get more than that with PEY," consider the following. Holding the individual stocks not only saves you on the ETF's fees, it also gives you a stable dividend stream that will most likely rise in the future. You will have 0% portfolio turnover, thus lowering your volatility and costs. In ten years your dividend yield will almost certainly be higher. The same cannot be said for all dividend ETFs. (Note that the lower the ETF's portfolio turnover, the less costs it has, and the better it should perform, all other things being equal.)

For example, suppose you bought shares of VIG at inception at $50.01 apiece in the spring of 2006. During the first 12 months you would collect $0.71 a share in dividends, for a yield of 1.4%. During the last 12 months (ending at the end of October 2011, VIG has paid out $1.15 in distributions. That's a yield of 2.3% on your original purchase. In this comparison, the dividend has risen 64%. The ETF has crept up about 8% over this period as well. So this is an example of an ETF portfolio's dividend growth.

Now consider an example of a dividend reduction. Suppose you bought the higher portfolio turnover ETF PEY for $14.88 a share (this was its opening price at VIG's inception) on May 2nd, 2006, because it had a higher yield than VIG. During the following 12 months PEY paid out around $0.63 a share and therefore yielded 4.23% ($0.63 a share in distributions on a $14.88 a share opening price). During the last 12 months, PEY paid out about $0.35 a share. If you bought shares of the ETF at $14.88, your yield of 4.23% the first year (May 2006 through May 2007) would have dropped to 2.35% (12 months before the end of October 2011). (You would also have unrealized capital losses because the ETF's price has dropped too, but that's beside the point.) PEY's higher portfolio turnover and lower quality stocks explains the difference. (And here's a lesson against stretching for yield—a lower yielding ETF composed of high quality stocks now yields about the same as an initially higher yielding ETF does.)

Let's see how owning VIG's original top ten holdings over the same period compares. They were McDonald's (MCD), IBM (IBM), Chevron (CVX), Coca-Cola (KO), Johnson & Johnson (JNJ), Wal-Mart (WMT), Exxon Mobil (XOM), Procter & Gamble (PG), Pepsico (PEP), and United Technologies (UTX).

Of the ten stocks, Chevron increased its dividends the least (44%). Exxon followed with a 46.875% increase. Coca-Cola was next with a 48% increase. Johnson & Johnson hiked its dividend by 52%. Then came Procter & Gamble with a 60.69% increase, topped by Pepsi with a 65.83% dividend raise. United Technologies beat Pepsi with a 75.94% dividend hike. The remaining stocks more than doubled their dividends during the five year time frame. (You would also be sitting on unrealized capital gains. None of the ten stocks were lower at the end of the period.) Your initial yield was higher than VIG's (around 2.2% for the top ten holdings versus 1.4% for VIG), and it increased at around the same rate (about 59%). You would also have saved money by not paying VIG's expense ratio and by having no portfolio turnover.

ETFs Can Be Useful

Nevertheless, ETFs can be very useful. For one thing, not everyone has enough money to invest in many individual holdings. At some point brokerage commissions make it prohibitive. An ETF provides you with a certain amount of diversification in one purchase. For another thing, ETFs can hold stocks that you might not be able to buy. Suppose you want to invest in dividend paying stocks on foreign exchanges. At the time of writing, not many brokers allow you to buy stocks on foreign exchanges. And those that do usually charge exorbitant currency conversion and commission fees. ETFs provide a way around this. The iShares Dow Jones International Select Dividend Index ETF (IDV), for instance, has top ten holdings that trade in Italy, Great Britain, Australia, the Netherlands, and France—companies that you may not be able to buy individually at reasonable cost.

ETFs can also help you invest in an asset class you want exposure to but do not fully understand or do not have time to fully understand. As already mentioned, there are ETFs that focus on preferred shares. Rather than spending hours reading through prospectuses, you can get a relatively diversified holding of preferred shares simply by buying one of the ETFs that track a preferred share index. The same goes for bond ETFs.

ETNs

Exchange Traded Notes (ETNs) are similar to and are often confused with ETFs. Oftentimes ETNs are mistakenly called ETFs. This is because they also trade like stocks and are designed to follow an index. Because of certain tax and other advantages, ETNs are usually much better at tracking their index than ETFs. Additionally, their structure usually lessens the tax headaches investors in some of the more esoteric indexes have to deal with.

The crucial difference between ETFs and ETNs is that ETNs aren't funds. They are notes—unsecured debt instruments (be sure not to confuse these with ETDS, which were discussed in the chapter on preferred shares). An ETN is debt that trades on an exchange and tracks an index. When you buy an ETN what you are doing, in effect, is lending its issuer money for the promise of a return that will track a given index. This has two consequences. First, you cannot keep an ETN forever. They all have maturity dates—usually a few decades in the future. Second, and this is the most important difference for me, because they are debt, they can be subject to default. That is, if the bank that issues the ETN goes bust, the ETN might too, even if its underlying index makes gains. So not only does an ETN have all the risks of the index it tracks, it also has issuer risk. That is, when you buy an ETN, not only are you taking on the risks of the index's holdings, you are also taking on the risks of the bank that issued the ETN.

Here's a real life example. Lehman Brothers, the fourth largest investment broker in the world at the time, issued three ETNs in February 2008. Two were designed to track commodity indexes and one was supposed to track a private equity index. Those investors who were interested in having exposure to those indexes bought the ETNs. One blogger, in discussing the Lehman ETN issuance wrote,

> A major caveat remains, however. Investors should realize that as unsecured notes, their value is underwritten by Lehman Bros. If anything happens to Lehman—which has hardly been immune from the ongoing mortgage meltdown—then their ETN investors could be left out in the cold.
>
> Still, the likelihood of Lehman Brothers going bankrupt is small—the company retains an A-plus rating on its debt from Standard & Poor's and an A-1 ranking from Moody's ratings service. (Murray Coleman, "Lehman Bros. Enters the ETN Market with 'Opta' Commodities, Private Equity," SeekingAlpha, February 20, 2008.)

The second paragraph turned out to be an understatement. Standard & Poor's and Moody's did as poor a job in rating Lehman debt as they did in rating subprime mortgages. In September of 2008, Lehman filed for chapter 11 in what became one of the largest bankruptcies in history. Barclays (BCS) bought some of its assets for pennies on the dollar, but refused to take on any of Lehman's debt obligations. This included Lehman's ETNs. Trading of these ETNs was halted—so investors who bought them couldn't sell—and they were delisted.

It bears repeating, ETNs introduce an extra risk that has nothing to do with the ETN's portfolio: the ETN issuer's creditworthiness. If you distrust banks, ETNs are not for you.

<u>Funds of Funds</u>

Numerous "fund of fund" ETF and ETN products have been introduced in the last several years. These exchange traded products hold other exchange traded products. The two most common funds of funds are both based on asset allocation strategies. So called "target date" funds hold stock, bond, and other ETFs or ETNs in proportions based on when the buyer of the target date fund is supposed to retire. For example, a 2040 target date fund might hold 70% stock ETFs and 30% bond ETFs while a 2011 target date fund's holdings might consist solely of bond ETFs. As the target date draws nearer, the fund owns less stocks and more bonds.

Asset allocation funds, the other type, are similarly constructed, but their portfolio weightings stay the same over time. These funds' holdings are based on investor risk categories. So, for example, "aggressive" allocation funds consist almost entirely of stock ETFs, "conservative" allocation funds consist mostly of bond ETFs, and other risk categories ("balanced," "moderate," etc) are somewhere in between.

These ETFs provide instant diversification. Instead of buying several ETFs to construct a portfolio, you need only buy one. You don't have to worry about rebalancing (more on this in the chapter on diversification), as it is done for you.

The thing to watch out for with these funds is their fee. Not only are you paying the fees of all the funds in the holdings, you are also paying a fee for the fund itself. It might be cheaper, in the long run, just to buy the individual ETFs (or their individual holdings) instead.

Chapter 21 - Closed End Funds (CEFs)

Closed End Funds are investment vehicles, that, unlike mutual funds, ETFs, and other open end funds, do not issue additional shares—hence the "closed end" in their name. They are almost always actively managed, meaning that managers attempt to maximize performance by implementing a strategy instead of replicating an index. Most CEFs use leverage to multiply their returns. That is, in addition to using the proceeds of selling their shares, they invest with borrowed funds. Leverage can amplify returns, but it can also magnify losses. In addition, leverage increases a portfolio's volatility.

As far as costs go, ETFs and ETNs are almost always preferable to CEFs. Most ETFs and ETNs have expense ratios under 1%. Most CEFs, in contrast, have expense ratios over 1%. Some of these funds have expense ratios greater than 4%. What this means is that they have to perform that much better than their benchmark index just to keep up with a comparable ETF or ETN. For example, suppose a CEF focuses on large cap stock investing and charges an annual expense ratio of 4%. Its benchmark will most likely be the S&P 500. Suppose an ETF that tracks the S&P 500 has an expense ratio of 0.11%. This means, first, that all other things being equal, the ETF will underperform the S&P 500 by about 0.11%. Second, this means that the competing CEF will have to beat the S&P 500 by 3.89% just to stay even with the ETF.

There are many CEFs that focus on dividend paying stocks and other income producing assets. Most of them are terrible. Not only do they underperform their benchmarks (i.e., you'd be better off in an index fund), the dividends they pay out are often the bad kind of return of capital (more on this below). That is, these funds just give you your own money back as their share prices decline. If you want this sort of income, just park your cash in the bank and write yourself a check every quarter. At least you won't be taxed for this activity (don't get any ideas, congress!). So if you are in the market for a closed end fund, do not be taken in by a high yield. Be sure to look under the hood to see where those dividends are really coming from.

If you are buying a CEF for its dividends (income is the chief draw of CEFs, considering that their average yield is always a few hundred basis points higher than most other investments available through the stock market—at the time of writing the average CEF yield is around 6.8% while bank interest is 0, blue chip dividend yields are mostly under 4%, and bond yields are even lower), be sure to read the prospectus to understand management's strategy and the risks that come with it. Look at the manager's record to see how he fared in good and bad markets. If the manager has a history of outperforming his benchmark, the CEF might be a good investment (though the manager might just have been lucky and sooner or later his performance will revert to the mean). Also look at the fund's expense ratio. Determine if the CEF's performance justifies it. Finally, the best time to buy the CEF is when it trades at a substantial discount to its net asset value. The worst time to buy it is when it trades at a substantial premium.

The net asset value (NAV) of a CEF is listed on its website. Some funds update it daily, while others do so weekly or on some other schedule. The NAV is the total worth of the fund's holdings, usually expressed on a per share basis (if the fund's holdings total $2 million and it has one million shares, its NAV will be $2 per share, for example). ETFs and ETNs share prices usually track their NAV very closely. When you buy a mutual fund, you always buy it at NAV. Closed end funds, on the other hand, trade all over the place. Sometimes they trade at NAV. Sometimes investors are very interested in their shares and the CEF trades above its NAV. At other times the opposite happens, and the CEF's share price is below NAV. This can last a few hours, days, weeks, months, and even years. Discounts and premiums can be substantial, sometimes exceeding 80%.

When the CEF trades at a substantial premium (that is, substantially above its NAV), its share price can fall even while its underlying assets are going up in value. Investors are often infuriated that their CEF is falling while the market is going up. And when a CEF trades at a substantial discount, its share price can go up even when its holdings are falling in value. That is why it pays to buy a CEF at a discount. As a dividend investor, not only do you get a higher yield than you would at NAV, you also have a cushion against a decline in NAV.

When evaluating a CEF, it is often better to look at its relative discount or premium to NAV than its absolute discount or premium. In other words, a CEF trading at a 20% discount to NAV isn't necessarily a better deal than a similar CEF trading at a 10% discount to NAV or even a similar CEF trading at a 10% premium. Look at these on a relative basis. It may very well be that the CEF trading at a 20% discount has always traded at a 20% discount while the CEF that is trading at a 10% premium usually trades at a 20% premium. In this case, the CEF trading at a 10% premium to NAV may in fact be the better deal: it is trading at a discount to its usual premium while the CEF that's trading at a

20% discount to NAV is not trading at a discount to its usual discount.

For example, suppose CEFA usually trades at a 20% premium to NAV and CEFB usually trades at a 20% discount to NAV. Suppose also that both CEFs have similar investment strategies and yields. If CEFB currently trades at a 10% discount to NAV while CEFA trades at a 10% premium to NAV, CEFA may be the better deal because it is trading at a discount to its usual premium. CEFB, in contrast, may be the worse deal because it is trading at a premium to its usual discount. Over time CEFB might go back to trading at a 20% discount to NAV while CEFA might go back to trading at a 20% premium to NAV.

A Closer Look at CEF Distributions

Some closed end funds, because of their structure, pay taxes on the income they distribute. Others do not. The income is passed through to their shareholders. Check the CEF's prospectus or website to see which kind it is. CEF dividends come in five flavors, depending on their source: regular income, qualified dividends, short and long term capital gains, and return of capital. These are all treated differently for tax purposes. If you own CEFs in a tax deferred account, all other things being equal, you should not care what your CEF distributions are characterized as. Note that a single CEF distribution can be wholly of one type or any combination of types. For example, suppose CEFA pays a quarterly dividend of $0.30. Of this dividend, $0.02 might be regular income, $0.10 might be qualified dividend income, $0.05 might be short term capital gains, and $0.13 might be return of capital. CEFB, on the other hand, might make a monthly distribution of $0.14, all of which is ordinary income.

It pays to know from where your CEF income comes. Regular income comes from ordinary dividends, bonds, and preferred shares. Qualified dividend income comes from common stocks, depository receipts, and any other investment vehicle that pays qualified dividends. Some CEF distributions are treated as capital gains. This is income the CEF earns when it sells something for a profit. Whether it is short or long term depends on the fund's holding period of that asset (it has nothing to do with how long you've held the fund).

Return of capital is probably one of the most confusing aspects of CEF investing. As you recall from the chapter on MLPs, distributions that are classified as return of capital lower your cost basis. If this is in a taxable account, you do not pay taxes on this income until you sell the security that pays you the income or your cost basis falls to zero. This is one of the advantages of MLPs, and it can be an advantage of CEFs. But that depends on what kind of return of capital income it is.

Return of capital from a CEF can be classified as good, bad, or neither. Return of capital is neither good nor bad when the CEF pays this income by passing along the distributions it has collected from MLPs. That is to say, if a CEF invests in MLPs, all or a portion of the CEF's dividends will be classified as return of capital. This is neither good nor bad.

Good return of capital usually comes from unrealized capital gains. Suppose the CEF collects option premiums (more on this in the chapter on options). The gains from these are not realized until the option position expires or is closed. But the CEF can distribute the premium to its

151

shareholders. When it does, this income is classified as return of capital.

The bad kind of return of capital occurs when the CEF makes distributions out of its assets. As mentioned, you are essentially getting your own money back. It is bad because in a taxable account if you ever sell the CEF you'll have to pay taxes on getting your money back. That's like taking money from one pocket, putting it in another, and then writing the government a check for the privilege. Closed end funds with so-called "managed distributions" are most likely to distribute the bad kind of return of capital. Managed distributions are, basically, a constant dividend rate. Every month or quarter the CEF with managed distributions pays the same amount. If the income it has collected from its investments is not enough to cover the dividend, it dips into its assets. For example, suppose CEFC has a managed distribution policy and pays $0.10 a month in dividends. Let's say this month it has collected enough in ordinary income to pay its shareholders $0.08. CEFC reaches into its assets to fill the gap. In this distribution, $0.08 will be treated as ordinary income and $0.02 will be treated as return of capital. The worst CEFs' dividends are almost entirely return of capital. Their net asset values will eventually go down to zero and the funds will be closed. To find out where a CEF's return of capital is coming from, consult their quarterly and annual reports and their SEC filings. Morningstar usually has this information as well.

<u>Funds of Funds (CEFs)</u>

Obtaining market beating returns by investing in actively managed funds is very difficult. To be worth it, as mentioned, the fund has to beat its benchmark by more than the fees it charges its investors. Most funds are not

152

worth your money. You might be tempted, therefore, to have an expert do your fund picking for you.

There are mutual funds, closed end funds, and ETFs that claim to do just that. These are usually actively managed. Some are restricted to holding funds only from their parent company (e.g., a Janus fund of funds only holds Janus mutual funds) while others can buy whatever funds they wish.

As with any actively managed fund, a fund of funds is only as good as its manager. If you are tempted to buy a fund of funds because you are having trouble deciding which particular CEF to buy, a fund of funds will not lessen your trouble. This is because the problem of picking a good manager remains. There are many funds of funds. You have to decide which one to pick.

Furthermore, the problems of fees and portfolio turnover are compounded with funds of funds. There are two layers of fees in these investment vehicles. As mentioned, the first is the fee that the fund of funds charges you. The second is all the fees that the funds in its portfolio charge. This latter fee is often not listed anywhere—be aware that the expense ratio on a fund of funds may be much higher than is listed on the fund's website. You should look for something called the acquired expense ratio or acquired fees. This will tell you what the underlying holdings charge. You can add what the fund of funds charges on top of it. A fund of fund's performance thus must be even greater than the average CEF's if it is worth investing in. Since most active managers underperform the market, it is almost certainly better to invest in an index fund instead of a fund of funds.

The problem of portfolio turnover is also compounded because not only does the fund of funds flip its holdings, so do the funds that it owns. To find the true portfolio turnover rate is very difficult and would involve examining all of the funds that the fund of funds owns. Also keep in mind that the problem of leverage is compounded if the fund of funds uses leverage to invest in other funds that also use leverage.

At the time of writing I am aware of one ETF that holds a portfolio of CEFs: the PowerShares CEF Income Composite (PCEF). It charges a 0.5% fee on top of the fees generated by the CEFs that it holds. At the time of writing this is an additional 1.12%. PCEF follows an index designed to track the universe of CEFs that invest in income producing assets (bonds, preferred shares, dividend stocks) or engage in option writing, about 123 CEFs. The ETF's portfolio is adjusted quarterly and it has a turnover rate of 29%. To determine the actual turnover rate, as mentioned, you would have to look at PCEF's individual holdings. The biggest draw of PCEF is its monthly dividend and high yield (at the time of writing over 8%).

The benefit of PCEF and other funds of funds is that it provides instant diversification. Performance information is scant, but by the time of writing PCEF is underperforming the market.

Business Development Companies (BDCs)

Business development companies (BDCs) trade on the exchanges like any other stock. They are similar to closed end funds. The difference is that they invest in private, usually small businesses by providing them with loans and or by buying their stock (note that some CEFs also invest in private companies). Congress created BDCs in the 1980s to encourage investment in private business. One of the requirements to be treated as a BDC includes distributing at least 90% of the company's taxable income to shareholders. As a result, BDCs have fairly high yields. Many BDCs pay a monthly dividend. Their distributions are taxed as ordinary income. Different BDCs, like CEFs, have different strategies and can specialize in different industries. For example, one BDC might specialize in providing loans to small telecommunications companies while another may invest in small banks, private equity, or architecture firms.

The advantages of investing in BDCs include having exposure to private companies and participating in small business growth. BDCs provide one of the few, maybe the only, ways of investing in Main Street through Wall Street. As with closed end funds, the risk associated with investing in BDCs are of two different kinds. The first is portfolio risk and includes economic contractions, small businesses going under, and the particular strategy the BDC uses being out of favor. The second is management risk. The BDC's management might just not be very good. They can make terrible investment decisions. As a result, two BDCs with similar strategies can have very different performance. An additional risk is rising interest rates. If interest rates rise, the BDC's share price might fall because investors can get higher yields in safer instruments (e.g., government bonds).

By and large BDCs did not fare very well during the financial crisis. Their share prices swooned with the rest of the market, but unlike other funds, by late 2011 their shares were still down. Some have also lowered their distributions.

A good place to find a list of BDCs is QuantumOn-line.com. There are also a few ETFs and ETNs that hold BDCs, and there will probably be more on the way. One available at the time of writing is the PowerShares Global Listed Private Equity Portfolio ETF (PSP).

Final Considerations

Never buy a CEF on its IPO (initial public offering)— when it first starts trading. Studies have found that after five months of trading, closed end funds averaged a return of -12.6%. (Kathleen Weiss Hanley, Charles M.C. Lee, Paul J. Seguin, "The Marketing of Closed-End Fund IPOs: Evidence from Transactions Data," *Journal of Financial Intermediation*, Vol. 5 (2), pp. 127-59. April 1996.) Indeed, if you look at the chart of any number of CEFs, you will find that most of them decline in price. If you examine their net asset value performance, you will see that it too declines in most cases.

If you are comparing a chart of a CEF with an index, say the S&P 500, or some other, more appropriate benchmark, don't forget to include the dividends. Although a price chart might show significant price underperformance by the CEF, if you compare the total returns (price plus dividends), it might not be as bad as it looks.

In sum, CEFs are an investment vehicle for the savvier investor. It takes some skill to find a fund that will perform better than the market over the long term. If you decide to invest in CEFs because they spew mounds of cash, pay special attention to where this cash comes from and what fees you are paying to get it. Moreover, pay attention to how the CEF is trading with respect to its NAV, both on an absolute and relative basis. Consider funds of funds but be mindful of their limitations and imposition of extra fees and portfolio volatility.

There are a number of excellent websites that may help you with closed end fund research. These include CE-

FConnect.com, CEFA.com (Closed End Fund Association), and QuantumOnline.com.

Chapter 22 - Bond Funds

There are many mutual funds, ETFs, ETNs, and CEFs that focus on bonds. They come in all sorts of flavors, from region (North America, Asia, etc), to type (sovereign debt, corporate bonds, investment grade, junk, municipal, asset backed), to duration (short, medium, long, ultra long), and strategies from passive index to active, to leveraged, and combinations of these. Most of these funds pay a monthly "dividend." CEFs are more likely to pay the same amount from month to month. ETFs and mutual funds are more likely to pay varying amounts with each distribution. Most distributions from these funds are treated as ordinary income for tax purposes, though some of the payments can be (especially at the end of the year) short and long term capital gains. CEFs are most likely to have distributions that count as return of capital.

All of the risks and advantages that I've outlined about funds above hold true for bond funds. There are, however, a few more disadvantages that are unique to bond funds.

When you hold the bonds individually, you collect interest payments until the bond matures. When the bond matures, you get your principal back (so long as you bought the bond at or below par, the bond's face value). Every bond has listed on it what the debtor will pay at maturity. Depending on the price of the bond when you buy it, you usually get a small capital gain. Bonds trade like any other security. They rise and fall daily. Over the course of many years, bond prices can change dramatically. If you hold to maturity, this doesn't matter for you. So long as the bond issuer does not default, when it matures you will get whatever price it says on the bond.

Bond funds, however, typically do not hold their bonds until maturity. For instance, an intermediate duration bond fund usually holds bonds that will mature between five and seven years from now. Once a bond's maturity is in four years, say, the bond fund sells it on the open market and uses the proceeds to buy another bond whose maturity is farther out. This can result in capital losses for the fund (I mentioned this when discussing the portfolio turnover problem with ETFs). Moreover, ETF and mutual bond fund prices are linked to their net asset values (like all open end funds). This changes daily. So it is very possible that the net asset value will decline after you buy shares of the fund. With individual bonds, on the other hand, you will get the bond's face value at maturity (which means you will have a capital gain if you buy the bond below par or face value and a capital loss if you buy the bond above par).

If you do not have enough money to buy a number of individual bonds, one solution to get around the problem of portfolio turnover is to buy a laddered fund. A bond ladder (you can also do this with certificates of deposit) is a bond portfolio consisting of bonds of different maturity dates. Every bond in the portfolio is held until it matures. The proceeds at maturity are used to buy a new bond at the furthest maturity. For example, suppose you have $20,000 to invest in bonds. Instead of putting all the money into one bond, you put $2,000 each into a one year bond, a two year bond, a three year bond, and so on, with your last $2,000 going into a ten year bond. You hold all these bonds until they mature. When each bond matures (this will be the one year bond), take the proceeds and use them to buy another 10 year bond. Every year the one year bond will mature, and every year you will buy a 10 year bond—but you will always have a bond for every year (the ten year bond becomes a nine year bond becomes an eight year bond, and so on, until it matures).

The disadvantage of a bond ladder is that you would be better off buying one type of bond and holding it to maturity if, between your purchase of it and maturity, interest rates fall. The advantage of a bond ladder is that it is less interest rate sensitive than an individual bond. Since in a ladder you are constantly replacing a short term bond with a long term one, if interest rates rise you do not have to wait long before your portfolio pays you a higher rate. With an individual bond, on the other hand, you are stuck with a fixed interest rate.

A laddered bond fund has these advantages over regular bond funds. In addition, a laddered bond fund does not have the high portfolio turnover rate problem. Here's an example. The PowerShares 1-30 Laddered Treasury Portfolio (PLW) holds bonds that will mature in each of the next 30 years. Its annual portfolio turnover is just 1%. Compare this to its category average turnover rate of 51.2% (that's for passive ETFs). PLW's performance is hard to compare to other bond ETFs because they all stick to owning bonds of certain maturities (e.g., five to seven year bonds, ten to twenty year bonds, etc). But consider this: from inception to the time of writing, PLW's index outperformed the Barclays Capital US Treasury Index and the Barclays Capital US Aggregate Index (the most popular ETF tracking this index, and probably the most popular bond ETF in general, is the iShares Barclays Aggregate Bond ETF [AGG], which has a whopping turnover rate of 406%) by 12.58% and 13.51%, respectively. Note, however, that since bonds trade daily, their prices change. A bond fund's NAV is thus af-

160

fected. When you buy the laddered bond fund, therefore, it is not the same as buying it at inception or holding your own ladder in individual bonds. For instance, PLW's weightings are skewed toward the long term bonds because these have gone up in price since PLW bought them.

If you are interested in laddering corporate bonds through ETFs, you might consider the Guggenheim Bullet Shares ETFs (note that there are two varieties: investment grade and high yield, also known as junk; be sure not to confuse these). Like PLW, each of these ETFs holds most of its bonds to maturity (ideally, the Bullet Shares will have no portfolio turnover at all until the bonds they hold mature or default). Unlike PLW, the Bullet Shares ETFs hold corporate bonds, and each ETF holds bonds that mature in a specific year. For example, all of BSCC's holdings mature in 2012, all of BSCD's holdings mature in 2013, and so on. Once the holdings start to mature, the fund transitions to cash and cash equivalents (e.g., short term US Treasuries). By the end of the year in which all of the fund's holdings mature, all of the cash, net of the fund's expenses, is given to shareholders of the fund (just as what happens when an individual bond matures). In effect, each Bullet Shares ETF is like an individual bond (the difference being that it is diversified among many companies and there is an expense ratio [comparable to other bond ETFs]). You can use several of these ETFs to building a corporate bond ladder—but with a lot less money than would be required were you to own all of their holdings individually. At the time of writing, the Bullet Shares investment grade ETFs go up to the year 2017 (BSCH). (If you are interested in buying such funds, note that they are not very clear about exactly what investors will get per share once the fund closes. It is understandable, as some of their bond holdings, while unlikely, may default while others may be called before maturity (which can result in a capital gain or loss, depending on where they were trading at purchase, and will result in lower distribution payments). Be aware that you may lose principal when buying these funds, as the cash that they return to you when they close can be less than you put in.

Another important risk that bonds and bond funds are very vulnerable to is inflation. As inflation rises, bond prices tend to fall (because investors want a higher yield or coupon, as it is called). Even if you get your entire principal back at maturity, this money will have less buying power than it did when you first bought the bond. Moreover, as bond interest payments are usually stable—like those of preferred stocks and unlike those common stock dividends —they cannot keep pace with inflation (inflation protected bonds, and presumably the funds that hold them, are an exception).

High Yield Corporate Bond Funds

There is a difference between investment grade and high yield (aka "junk") bonds. The latter are viewed by many experts as more like stocks than bonds. This is because they are riskier than investment grade debt (the ratings agencies determine this—whatever that is worth, but so does the market, by demanding higher yields). It is also because their returns are similar to those of stocks. From July 1983 through August 2011, stocks have returned around 10% per year while high yield corporate bonds have returned 9.33%, but with less risk. Viewed from a risk perspective, high yield corporates have returned 0.55% per unit of risk while stocks have returned 0.35% per unit of risk (Source: Zephyr StyleADVISOR). When diversifying your portfolio among different asset classes, therefore, consider adding high yield bonds to your holdings and treating them as stocks. There are a number of high yield bond ETFs, including the SPDR Barclays Capital High Yield ETF (JNK) and the iShares iBoxx HY Corp Bond Fund (HYG). Both pay monthly dividends and the trailing twelve month distribution rate is usually over 7%.

If you are thinking about buying shares of an actively traded bond or preferred share fund, don't just look at mutual funds. Closed end funds might be better for you, so long as the fees are about the same and the closed end fund doesn't use leverage. There are three reasons for this.

First, the dividends will be more stable with CEFs. This is because their shares trade on the secondary market. That is to say, the number of their shares outstanding is stable. Open end funds (mutual funds and ETFs), on the other hand, create new shares as new investors come in and cancel shares as investors leave. This makes the distributions per share unstable. Open end funds rarely pay out the same dividend per share in every payment period because sometimes there are more shares outstanding, sometimes less.

For simplicity's sake, let's say an open end fund invests in bonds and collects $1 million per month in interest, which it distributes to its shareholders monthly. Suppose that the first month it has one million shares outstanding. The first month's distribution is therefore $1 per share. So if you own 100 shares, you'll get $100.

Suppose that investors buy more of the fund's shares during the second month and the fund hasn't put their money to work yet (this takes a while). Let's say the fund has issued an extra 200,000 shares. It collects $1 million next month, but now must distribute this amount to 1.2 million shares. This comes out to a distribution of $0.8333 per share. If you own 100 shares, you will get around $83.33.

Suppose during the third month investors get skittish about bonds and there is an outflow of 400,000 shares. These are canceled and the fund has 800,000 shares outstanding. It collects $1 million. Distributed over 800,000 shares, this comes out to $1.25 per share. If you own 100 shares, you will get $125.

In this simplistic example, the mutual fund's distributions ranged from $0.8333 to $1.25 per share. A closed end fund that collects $1 million per month and issued one million shares, on the other hand, would pay $1 per share per month. If stable income is important to you, a closed end bond fund might be better than an actively managed bond mutual fund. (Note that in our example the mutual fund actually paid out more in dividends than the closed end fund—this may or may not be the case in real life. The point was to show how open end fund distributions can be more variable than closed end fund distributions. Note also that because open end funds trade at net asset value, total returns are not at all affected by the per share distributions. This is because the fund's share price drops by the dividend amount on ex-dividend day.)

Second, open end funds are affected by inflows and outflows in another way. When investors put money in, the fund manager must invest this new money. When investors take money out, if the fund doesn't have enough cash, it must sell something. This can negatively impact returns, especially because investors tend to sell when prices are down (forcing fund managers to liquidate positions that have unrealized capital losses) and buy when prices are up (forcing fund managers to initiate positions when prices are high). Since closed end funds do not have to issue new shares for new investors or cancel shares for old investors, they do not suffer this problem. This may explain why over the long term closed end funds that focus on municipal bonds have outperformed municipal bond mutual funds.

Third, you may be able to get a larger income with a closed end fund than an open end fund. Mutual funds trade at net asset value. Closed end funds, on the other hand, rarely trade at NAV. If you buy a closed end bond fund at a discount to NAV, you will have a higher income than if you bought a mutual fund that had the exact same number of shares and invested in the exact same thing. For example, suppose again that the mutual fund has one million shares outstanding and collects $1 million dollars in interest per month from its investments. As mentioned, shareholders will receive a distribution of $1 per share. A closed end fund that also has one million shares outstanding, invests in the same bonds, and collects $1 million, will also pay $1 per share. Both funds have the same net asset value. If, however, the CEF is trading at a discount, say 10%, its yield will be higher.

Let's say NAV is $100 per share. You can buy the mutual fund, therefore, for $100 per share. The closed end fund, on the other hand, trades at $90 per share (10% discount). Compare a $10,000 investment in each fund. Putting $10,000 into the mutual fund will get you 100 shares, and you will receive $100 per month in income (pretending for the sake of simplicity that there are no inflows and outflows) or $1,200 per year. Putting $10,000 into the closed end fund, in contrast, will get you 111 shares. You will receive $111 per month, or $1,332 per year. That's more than an extra month's worth of income even though you're investing in essentially the same thing.

Mutual Funds

There is no chapter on mutual funds because they are just like ETFs and CEFs. They can hold all of the same assets, follow the same indexes, and so on.

There are some differences. Mutual funds are purchased and sold at the end of the trading day at net asset value. Some mutual funds have purchase and sales fees (loads), and a variety of other fees. Mutual funds, like ETFs and all other open end funds, issue new shares when money is brought in and cancel the shares when money is taken out. Closed end funds, in contrast and as mentioned, only issue shares once (that's why they're closed), and when you buy their shares you do so in the secondary market. Mutual funds can track an index like ETFs and ETNs, and they can be actively managed, like ETFs, ETNs, and CEFs. That's about it.

Part Five - Dividend Reinvestment Plans and Bypassing Your Broker

Investors sometimes wonder whether they should reinvest their stock, unit, or fund distributions. By reinvesting you get more shares or units in the company or fund. In this part I go through some of the advantages and drawbacks of doing so.

Chapter 23 - Pros and Cons of Dividend Reinvestment

There are two ways of reinvesting the distributions you receive from your stock, partnership, bond, and fund holdings. If it is available through whatever medium you hold your investment (through broker, mutual fund company, direct ownership, etc), automatic dividend reinvestment programs use the distributions you receive to purchase more shares of the security that made the distribution. For example, if stock XYZ pays you a $200 dividend, that $200 is used to buy more shares of XYZ.

All other dividend reinvestment schemes are manual. With these, the dividends pile up in your account and you can use the cash in whichever way you want, including buying more shares of the security that paid you the distribution or investing the money in some other asset.

Advantages

1. If the stock goes down, you are automatically lowering your dollar cost per share because you are buying more shares at a lower price. If the stock later goes up, you will break even more quickly, receiving higher returns if it continues its assent than you would if you did not reinvest your dividends. If the stock goes up, you are buying less shares. This is also good, as your average dollar cost does not go up as much. You are buying more when the stock is cheaper and less when it's more expensive. As you are not adding any extra money out of pocket, that is, as all new shares are coming from your dividends, this is a good thing.

2. My favorite reason for reinvesting dividends is that it compounds dividend payouts. Reinvesting gets you more shares, so your future dividends, as long as the company does not cut the payout, are larger.

For example, say you buy one share of a company for $100, and let's say the company pays out a quarterly dividend of $1 a share, giving out $4 a share per year in total. For the sake of ease, let's say this stock remains flat, trading at $100 a share for a year.

For the first quarterly dividend, you get $1 and reinvest it. (This example assumes you are buying the stock either directly from a company that allows fractional shares, or through a broker that has automatic free dividend reinvestment in a tax deferred account). As the stock remains at $100 a share, after reinvesting the $1, you now have 1.01 shares. That is, with that dollar, you've just bought 1/100 of a share.

For the second quarterly dividend, you get $1.01. That's because you received a dollar per share and have 1.01 shares. Once again, assuming the stock remains at $100 a share, if you reinvest the dividend, you get an additional .0101 shares. You now have a total of 1.0201 shares.

When the third quarterly dividend comes around, you get $1.0201. Reinvesting this, again assuming the stock stays at $100, you get another .0102 shares, bringing your total to 1.0303 shares.

Your fourth quarterly dividend will be $1.0303. If the stock stays at $100, reinvesting this amount will get you an additional .0103 shares, bringing your total to 1.0406 shares.

So, after starting off with one share, you have 1.0406 at the end of the year without putting in any extra money. Had you not reinvested the dividends, you would have gained $4. Having reinvested the dividends, the total payouts received from the company amounted to $4.0604. That's a 1.5% greater return by doing nothing. Looking at it another way, not reinvesting the dividends would give you a

4% yield on the stock. Reinvesting them would give you a 4.06% yield. These sums are tiny, sure, but imagine this process with many shares and over a greater period of time.

As I've repeated, the example assumes that the stock remains flat. Had the share price fallen and you reinvested your dividends, your payout would be greater still. Had the share price risen, your payout would be smaller than in the example, but still larger than if you didn't reinvest the dividends.

As long as the company does not reduce its dividend, reinvesting dividends compounds your dividend returns. When you retire and decide to start collecting your dividends, you'll find that your original yield has skyrocketed.

Box 11 provides a comparison with a real life example. In 2008 I received 94.3 shares of Philip Morris International (PM) as a spinoff from Altria (MO). I had my dividends automatically reinvested. By the time of writing, a little over three years later, because of reinvestment I've received over 8% more in dividend payments than I would have if I didn't reinvest ($847.38 with dividend reinvestment versus $779.84 without dividend reinvestment). As long as PM continues to may the dividend at the current rate or higher, this spread will widen. From the time I received the shares to the time of writing, PM has raised its dividends by around 67%. But because I reinvested my dividends and therefore bought more shares (I currently own 110.07, up from 94.3), my most recent dividend payment is almost double the first one (from $43.39 a quarter in 2008 to $84.31 a quarter in late 2011).

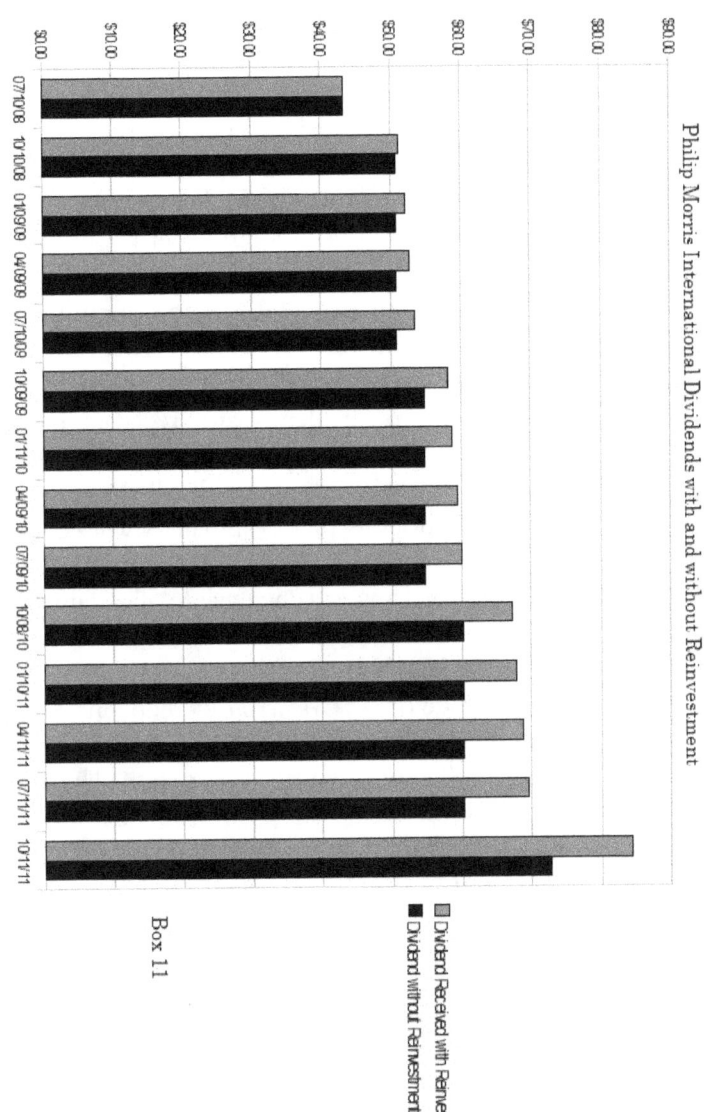

Philip Morris International Dividends with and without Reinvestment

Box 11

171

Compare also my effective dividend yield with reinvestment with what my effective yield would be without reinvestment. I received the PM shares at $51.06 apiece when PM paid a quarterly dividend of $0.46 per share. My yield at that time was 3.6% annualized. Since then, PM has raised its dividend to $0.77 a share. On my original cost basis of $51.06 per share, this comes out to a little over 6% annualized. In other words, if you had invested in PM when Altria spun it off and held it to late 2011 (the time of writing), your dividend yield on the stock would be 6%. This is without dividend reinvestment.

Since I reinvested my dividends and received more shares, my dividend yield is 7%. And as long as the company does not reduce its dividend, my yield will continue to rise every quarter. (My hope is that eventually I will collect more per year in dividends than I originally invested in the stock. That is, I hope that my effective yield will eventually top 100%.) Compare these yields to 4.3%, the yield someone would get in late 2011.

3. According to one of *The Motley Fool's* many infomercials on the subject, from January 1926 to December 2006, "41% of the S&P 500's total return" came from dividend reinvestment. As another example, also from *The Motley Fool*, if you invested $2000 in Pepsico (PEP) in 1980 and reinvested the dividends, you'd have over $150,000 by late 2011. Doing the same with Philip Morris (now Altria) (MO), you'd have over $300,000.

<u>Disadvantages of Dividend Reinvestment</u>

As there is no free lunch, here is the darker side of dividend reinvestment.

1. Reinvesting dividends in a company that goes out of business or whose stock tanks because its dividend is cut or

eliminated can hurt. Imagine reinvesting in Kodak (EK) or General Motors (GM) (now better known as Government Motors). If you hadn't reinvested, your loses would be lower, because you'd have gotten some of your money back through dividends. If this happens in a taxable account, not only do you lose your money, you lose extra by having to pay taxes on the dividends as you collect them (if you own the shares in a taxable account).

2. Reinvesting dividends can create a nightmare at tax time when you decide to sell your shares. This is because you will have many purchases, all with a different cost basis. Depending on how long and how often you've been doing the reinvesting, it can be a lot of work to figure out your gains and losses at tax time. This doesn't apply to tax deferred accounts such as IRAs.

3. Reinvesting dividends in an all stock portfolio may make it too concentrated. You might want to think about using the dividends toward the purchase of some other asset class, such as bonds or commodities.

4. Similarly, reinvesting dividends may deprive you of cash you could use in a better way. That is, there are opportunity costs, and you may get a better return by using the dividend in some other way. Perhaps when deciding to reinvest dividends, you should think about whether you can do something better with that money instead. If you cannot, you should reinvest.

Reinvesting Dividends In Mutual Funds

Note that mutual funds are required by law to distribute most of their income and capital gains, which are usually taxed at different rates. They usually do so at the end of the year. The good and bad here are pretty much the same as above. There is, however, something to consider.

173

Stock prices fluctuate throughout the trading day. Mutual funds, on the other hand, are priced at the end of the trading day. This is determined by the market value of the mutual fund's net assets, divided by the number of outstanding shares, which is the net asset value (NAV), as previously mentioned.

People use many different ways of evaluating stocks, including share price divided by earnings (PE), sales divided by earnings, etc. When a stock goes ex-div, its price drops by the corresponding dividend. The P/E falls, as do most other measures of the stock's value, and the yield rises, making it look cheaper to investors. You may recall, also, my argument earlier in the book that stock dividends can force the share price to rise. This does not happen with a mutual fund. Recall that the cash distributed as a dividend lowers the fund's NAV.

In other words, as a stock's price depends on the buying and selling of it, the dividend payout does not affect the stock's price as much as it does a mutual fund's. While a mutual fund's NAV depends somewhat on the amount of cash it has, most of its price movement comes from the market value of its other assets—stocks, bonds, etc. What this basically means is that reinvesting a mutual fund's dividends gets you to the same position you would have been in if there were no dividend. You get more shares, but they are worth less than before. The same can be said with a stock, as in my reinvesting example above, but since a stock's price does not depend on net asset value, after dividend reinvestment your total position could be worth more than it was before the dividend. Of course, it could be worth less as well (as when the share price drops after reinvestment). Is this good or bad? It's something to consider.

Additional Considerations

Some companies and closed end funds offer investors a choice between cash and stock dividends. If you're going to reinvest anyway, stock dividends are probably better. These are often given at a discount to the market price. For example, the share price might be $100, but your stock dividend gets you shares at $98. That's a pretty good deal.

If you are thinking about investing and reinvesting into a closed end fund, be sure to examine their dividend reinvestment policy. Some funds allow you to buy shares at net asset value or market price, whichever is cheaper. Others choose one or the other.

Although brokers are the most common way to buy funds, stocks, and publicly traded partnership units, in many cases you can purchase shares either directly from the company or through a transfer agent. When you buy stock directly from a company, the company acts as its own transfer agent. When you buy shares through a transfer agent, the shares are purchased from the company, on the open market, or both.

A **transfer agent** is a financial institution that keeps records of investors, transactions, and account balances for a corporation. They issue and cancel the company's share certificates, and are involved in other, similar activities. Most companies use transfer agents in their direct investment programs because it is costly and time consuming to do it themselves. Many of the participants (shareholders) in the direct investment programs own so few shares that it can cost more to maintain their accounts than the shares are worth.

Transfer agents are better able to handle lots of small accounts because it is their business expertise (whereas the corporation might be engaged in food processing, mining, refining, manufacturing, etc) and because they can use the same infrastructure to serve many corporate clients. That is, they can turn this record keeping into a profitable business even when what they charge their corporate clients is less than what the corporation would have spent if it were its own transfer agent.

Advantages

There are a number of advantages to directly investing in a company instead of going through a broker. First, it can be much cheaper. Transfer agents charge a number of fees (enrollment fee, purchase fee, sale fee, reinvestment fee), but many companies pay some of them for you when you buy their shares. While it depends on the policies of the company you invest in, if you plan to buy its shares periodically, you will usually save money by enrolling in a direct investment program.

For example, suppose you want to enroll in Pepsico's (PEP) direct investment program. Bank of New York Mellon is PEP's transfer agent. It costs $10 to enroll and you must invest at least $250 for your initial investment (some companies have no investment minimum, others want you to invest at least $1,000 your first time, and pretty much all the other corporations are somewhere in between, clustered at the low end of the range). There are no charges for subsequent investments (which for PEP must be $50 or over) or dividend reinvestments because Pepsico pays these on your behalf. If you decide to sell your Pepsi shares, there is a $5 fee and a charge of $0.10 per share sold ($10 for every 100 shares). You can invest a maximum of $10,000 per month.

Compare this to a broker. Let's say the broker charges you $7 per trade. Suppose you want to invest $50 per month into PEP. With the direct investment program, you'll end up paying $10 and investing at least $250. After your initial investment you won't be charged any other fees until you sell. So, investing $50 per month for a year won't cost you anything more than the $10 you already paid. With the broker, on the other hand, if you invest $50 per month you'll be paying a transaction fee of $7 twelve times a year, or $84. That's a month and two thirds worth of investment money.

(Note that there are brokers out there that, for a set fee or if you keep your account balance above a certain threshold, allow you some number of free trades per month. These may be comparable to or cheaper than direct investment plans, depending on the company's policies and how many investments per month you make. Note also that not all direct purchase and dividend reinvestment plans are alike. Some can be more expensive than investing through a broker. For example, Kraft's transfer agent charges a 4% fee, up to $2, for each dividend reinvestment, in addition to a $3 fee for optional cash investments, $0.80 for automatic withdrawals, and $0.03 per share purchased. Coca-Cola's transfer agent charges $3 per cash purchase, $2 for automatic investments, $0.03 per share purchase fee, and a 5% dividend reinvestment fee up to $2. In contrast, most brokers do not charge a per share fee, and their dividend reinvestment plans are usually free.)

(Note also that you may incur tax liability for any of the transfer agent's fees that the company you invest in pays on your behalf. In other words, if the transfer agent charges a trading fee and the company you are investing in pays the transfer agent on your behalf, that fee will be listed on your 1099 form as a dividend payment from the company to you. So, for example, let's say you decide to buy Pepsi stock through the company's transfer agent BNY Mellon. You open an account and make an initial purchase of $250. You incur a $10 service fee for the initial transaction. The remaining $240 is used to buy shares of stock. BNY Mellon charges a trading fee of $0.10 per share. Let's say at the time of your purchase PEP stock trades at $64.87. You acquire 3.6997 shares. The transfer agent therefore charges you a $0.37 trading fee. Pepsi bears this cost. The company pays the $0.37 on your behalf. At the beginning of the next year, when you receive your 1099 form from BNY Mellon, you will notice that it says you have collected an extra $0.37 in dividends than you actually received. The trading fee that Pepsi paid on your behalf counts as a dividend paid to you. So, if you pay a 15% tax on dividends, you'll owe the government $0.06 more than you would have if the fee hadn't been paid on your behalf. If you think this is stupid, write your congressman and tell them to stop taxing you.)

Second, dividend reinvestment plans can be more flexible and more rewarding with transfer agents than with brokers. Most brokers do not charge you anything for automatically reinvesting your dividends. But if you want to reinvest only a portion of your dividends, you cannot use the automatic reinvestment program. That is, you must manually reinvest your dividends. For example, suppose a company pays you $1,000 a quarter in dividends and you only wish to reinvest half of this amount ($500). Dividend reinvestment plans (DRIP) at most brokers are an all or nothing affair. You either reinvest the $1,000 at no charge, or you do not enroll in the program and instead have the money deposited to cash. Afterward, you keep $500 and invest the other $500. But this comes with a broker fee because you're making a trade.

With a transfer agent, on the other hand, partial dividend reinvestments are allowed. You are able to choose what percentage of your dividend you want to keep and what percentage you want to reinvest.

Reinvesting dividends with transfer agents can also be more rewarding. I don't mean rewarding in the sense that "helping underprivileged kids is rewarding." Rather, I mean it pays you money. Some companies, to encourage dividend

179

reinvestment, offer a discount when you reinvest. The typical discount is usually between 4 and 6%. So suppose on dividend reinvestment day the company's shares trade at $100. If the company offers a 4% reinvestment discount, you reinvest in those shares at $96 per share instead of $100 per share. You therefore get around 4% more shares with your dividend proceeds than you would have otherwise. (Note that some broker DRIPs also have discounts.)

Third, you can buy fractional shares with a direct investment plan. With most brokers, however, you can only buy full shares. For example, let's say stock XYZ trades at $40 per share and you want to invest $250. With a direct investment plan you'll buy 6.25 shares ($250 divided by $40). With most brokers, however, you will only be able to buy 6 shares. You'll have $10 left sitting in your account. In other words, you will have invested $240 with the broker. The direct investment would yield you more dividends as a result. (Note that some brokers, Sharebuilder for example, allow you to make fractional share purchases—but you probably have to pay a trade commission each time or a monthly fee.)

Fourth, and this is for those people who are wary of financial institutions and are afraid that their account data might become "lost" and their shares stolen: you can order physical share certificates from the transfer agent, usually at little to no cost. You can store these in a safe like in the old days before computerized book entries.

Disadvantages

As with practically everything in life, there are disadvantages. With a broker you can specify at what price you want to buy or sell a stock. You cannot do this with a direct investment plan. Instead, the shares are purchased for you at market price sometime during the day (or the average price of a batch order—based on all of the orders for the stock that the transfer agent processed). And when you choose to sell the shares, the direct investment plan sells the shares at market price. As a result, direct investment plans are terrible platforms for trading.

Another disadvantage is that you cannot write covered calls on your stocks with direct investment plans. (Covered calls will be explained in a later chapter). Also, if you sell your shares with a broker you can use the proceeds to buy another stock immediately (if you do not have a margin account, you have to wait three days to sell this second purchase). With a transfer agent, however, if the other company you want to invest in does not have a plan with that transfer agent, you have to take your proceeds and give it to another transfer agent or to a broker. This can be very frustrating and time consuming. There are actually two disadvantages here. One is that direct investment plans aren't for trading (although this can be considered an advantage). The other is that a transfer agent only does business with certain companies. This means that if you want to buy Pepsi stock and Coca-Cola stock, for example, you will have to register with two different transfer agents. With a broker, on the other hand, you can buy any stock you want as long as it trades on your country's exchanges (and some brokers allow you to invest in foreign traded stocks).

Moreover, if your investment is time sensitive, transfer agents aren't for you. It can take longer than a week for shares to be purchased into your account once you initiate an order. This is partly because the money for the purchase must first be transferred from your bank.

A fourth disadvantage is that direct investment plans do not have margin. With a typical broker, on the other hand, if you meet the balance threshold, you can get a margin account. This allows you to borrow money to buy more shares (I shall remain silent on the merits of this—my point is just that you can't do this with a direct investment plan) and short sell shares. Finally, a related disadvantage is that if you want to hedge your stock portfolio (with options or other instruments) you must have a brokerage account. This means that if you want to do these things (margin, options, hedging) you need to use a broker anyway, so it might not be worth it to enroll in a direct investment plan.

In sum, direct investment plans are great for those investors that are in it for the long haul. They are not very good, on the other hand, for people who do a lot of trading.

Now that we've looked at some of the advantages and disadvantages of using transfer agents instead of brokers to buy stock, the following is a list of the main transfer agents and some of the companies with which they do business.

American Stock Transfer & Trust Company

<http://www.amstock.com/>

At the time of writing, American Stock Transfer & Trust Company had 304 stocks available. Some of the more famous ones include Under Armour (UA), Rite Aid (RAD), and Yum! Brands (YUM). (If you haven't heard of the last one, it owns Pizza Hut, KFC, and Taco Bell, and used to be part of Pepsico.)

BNY Mellon Shareowner Service
<http://www.bnymellon.com/shareowner/equityaccess/>
At the time of writing 561 companies and funds were available. These included American Express (AXP), Costco (COST), Pepsico (PEP), MasterCard (MA), and many others.

Computershare
<http://www-us.computershare.com/>
At the time of writing, 421 stocks were available. Among the companies you probably heard of there were AT&T (T), Wal-Mart (WMT), ExxonMobil (XOM), and Coca-Cola (KO).

Continental Stock Transfer & Trust Company
<http://www.continentalstock.com/>
At the time of writing, Continental had one stock available, Armour Residential REIT, Inc. (ARR).

JP Morgan
<https://www.adr.com/Home>
At the time of writing, there were 108 depository receipts (DRs) available. DRs are financial instruments issued by a bank to represent foreign corporations' publicly traded stock. Basically, they are equal to shares of foreign companies' stock but trade on local exchanges (e.g., Baidu [BIDU] is a Chinese company. Its common stock trades in China. Its depository receipts trade in the United States on the NASDAQ). Among the available DRs there were Canon (CAJ), Honda Motor Co. (HMC), and Sony Corp (SNE).

Wells Fargo Shareowners Services

<https://www.shareowneronline.com>

At the time of writing, there were 120 stocks available for purchase. These included 3M (MMM), Hewlett-Packard (HP), and Kraft (KFT).

Walt Disney (DIS) and Procter & Gamble (PG) are two major corporations that run their own shareholder investment plans. Until several years ago many other big companies ran their own investment plans. They either discontinued them or are now using a transfer agent for the reasons outlined earlier (costs, efficiency, and so on). With the above transfer agents and Disney and Procter & Gamble, pretty much all of the large dividend paying corporations whose shares and depository receipts trade on US exchanges are available for direct investment. If you are in it for the long haul and would like to make periodic additional investments, signing up with these transfer agents will most likely enable you to bypass brokers altogether. So if you're such an investor and are tired of paying commissions, you should give direct investment plans a shot. Be sure to compare the fees of buying a stock through a transfer agent with buying the same stock through a broker, and be aware that like broker fees, transfer agent fees can increase at any time.

Finance channels on television and radio stations occasionally air commercials for books that promise to give you information about how to invest in companies without a broker. Essentially, they tell you everything in this chapter. Their bulk is devoted to lists of stocks, brief descriptions of them, and which transfer agent they use. Don't waste your time or money on these directories. Just go to the investor relations website of the company you would like to invest in and check to see if they have a direct purchase plan. If they do, they will have a link to the transfer agent that sells their stock.

If for some reason the links to the transfer agents listed above do not work, you can easily find them by searching for their names in a search engine like Google.com. But again, the best way to find the right transfer agent is by visiting the investor relations website of the company in which you'd like to invest. It may be tempting to look at one transfer agent's list of available stocks and just to choose from these. Do not invest in companies on the basis of availability. Invest based on what is right for your portfolio.

Chapter 25 - Buying Funds without a Broker

As mentioned, some transfer agents sell fund shares. Another place to buy funds, especially mutual funds, is directly from the company. Writing, calling, or visiting their website are some of the ways to find out more about them (but be aware that their materials are promotional material). Investment publications and financial newspapers (*Wall Street Journal*, *Barron's*, and so on) usually have more neutral information about the current state of the fund industry, which funds are worth considering, and which are best to avoid.

Morningstar is one of the best places to do fund research. It has heaps of information about funds, from their portfolios, to their turnover rate, taxation, fees, how long the manager has been there, etc. Morningstar also ranks funds by star, one being worst and five being best. These rankings are based on past performance. Most people rely on the star ratings and put their money into the higher ranked funds. Studies have shown, however, that one and two star funds usually outperform these four and five star funds in the next three years. Of course, some five star funds will continue to do well and some one star funds will continue to do poorly. But when people sell their one star funds and buy five star funds what they are doing is selling low and buying high. Ignore the Morningstar ratings. So how do you choose a fund? Easy. Pick the one that tracks the indexes your portfolio is to be composed of with the lowest fees and turnover. That's it!

Much of the information Morningstar offers is free, but if you want detailed write-ups of specific funds you will have to pay a subscription. There are a couple of ways to get around the subscription fees (or rather, to avoid paying twice, because in most cases you are already paying for them in one way or another) for research services and investment publications. Your broker's research section may give you access to research reports from Morningstar and others (S&P, Ned Davis, Zach's, etc). If you (or someone in your family) is a university student, it's likely that you can access financial news and research through the university library's website. Finally, your local public library may also give you access.

Advantages of buying funds directly include being able to mail in orders (this is for those people who do not use computers), bypassing broker fees, not having to search for brokers that sell the fund (if the fund isn't available through your broker), and lessening counter party risk (when you buy and hold a security through a broker, not only does your risk include the security itself, it also includes the risk that the broker will go out of business and/or lose your account information).

The disadvantages of buying funds without a broker include having to keep track of extra accounts (each fund company will necessitate a new account), which means you'll receive more statements and will have more work at tax time. If you want to switch funds this may also involve more accounts and hassles. Having more accounts means that more firms will have your personal and financial information, increasing the likelihood that this information will fall into the wrong hands. It might also be the case that buying a fund through a broker, because of the broker's agreement with the fund company, will be cheaper than buying the fund directly. Moreover, some funds may only be purchased through a broker.

Part Six - Strategies

Chapter 26 - Using Options to Get Extra Income and Reduce Portfolio Risk

Some of the strategies outlined below will not be available in tax deferred accounts, where you can get the most out of dividend paying stocks. It all depends on the broker. Some brokers do not allow any options trading in IRAs, others allow only covered call writing, a few others allow call buying, cash secured put selling, and even spread buying. (If you do not know what these terms refer to, they will be explained below.)

Because one option typically controls 100 shares of a stock or ETF, smaller portfolios will not be able to use options in the way outlined below.

As most people are unfamiliar with options, I will begin with a summary of the terminology, explain briefly how options work, and then outline the ways in which they can be used to make extra income and/or reduce portfolio risk.

An option is a contract for the right to buy or sell something (house, car, painting, shares of stock, etc) for a certain price within a certain period of time.

Covered Call Example 1: suppose you have a car that I'm thinking about buying. I'm not sure if I want to buy it yet, but while I think about it, I don't want anyone else to buy it from you. Let's say you're willing to sell the car to me for $10,000. I propose the following deal with you: I may or may not buy the car from you for $10,000 between now and May 20th of this year. In return for you waiting for me to decide, I'll give you $100 right now. If I end up buying the car before May 20th, I'll give you $10,000 for it. If I decide against buying the car between now and May 20th, you keep the $100 and the car. If we agree to these terms and I give you the $100, we've just entered into an option contract. (More precisely, we've entered into a call option contract.)

There are two types of options: calls and puts. Both of these types of options can be bought and sold like anything else that is bought and sold. In the example above, for instance, if we agreed to the deal, I bought a call option from you, and you sold it to me. I can then go ahead and sell someone else this contract, which is the right to buy your car for $10,000.

Although options are bought and sold, to avoid confusion we say "write" or "wrote" instead of "sell" or "sold" when talking about initial options positions. So, in the example above, you wrote a call option and I bought it. To illustrate the difference between "write" and "sell," consider that I may later sell the call that I bought from you to someone else. Note the distinction. If I sell the call, I am selling someone the right to buy the car from the writer, which is you, not me. So, if I say that I sold a call, this can mean one of two things: that I sold a call I had previously purchased, or that I started a new contract. Using "write" for the latter eliminates the potential confusion.

Calls

A **call option** is a contract where the buyer, in exchange for a **premium**, has the right to buy the **underlying asset** from the writer for the **strike price** between the time the contract is formed and the **expiration date**. The call buyer does not have to buy the underlying asset—he has the *right* to buy it but not the obligation to do so, and therefore may choose not to do so. The **premium** is the amount that the option writer is paid and the option buyer pays. No matter what happens, the option writer keeps the premium that he is paid. In our example, whether I buy the car from you or not, you get to keep the $100. The **strike price** in a call option is the amount to be paid to the call option writer by the call buyer for the **underlying asset**, if the call buyer chooses to exercise the contract (if he does, he *calls* the underlying asset from you in exchange for the strike price) before it expires. The underlying asset, or simply **the underlying**, is whatever asset the contract is for (shares of stock, a house, a car, etc). Finally, the expiration date is the day on which the contract expires. Options are worthless after they expire.

In our example above: the premium is $100, the strike price is $10,000, the underlying is the car, and the expiration date is May 20th of this year.

Here is another example.

Covered Call Example 2: Suppose you are in the market to buy a house and find one that you like. The seller is asking for $200,000. The housing market is volatile at the moment. You want to wait a few months before doing anything because the house might drop in price. On the other hand, you're afraid that prices might turn up and in a few months someone might offer more for the house. You're also afraid someone might buy the house before you for the current asking price of $200,000. So you propose the following deal to the homeowner: you will pay him $5,000 now for the right to buy his house from him for $200,000 between now and four months from now.

If you and the homeowner agree to the deal, no matter what happens, the homeowner keeps the $5,000 premium. You, on the other hand, have four months to decide what to do—as the call buyer you have the right, but not the obligation, to buy the house from the owner for $200,000 within the next four months.

Call Scenario 1: By expiration date, house prices have dropped, as you have feared. Let's say the home is now valued at $175,000. If you had bought it at $200,000, you'd be losing $25,000. Since you bought the call option instead, however, you're only out $5,000. You can simply walk away. Or, you can buy the house now for $175,000. If you choose to buy the house, your total purchase price will be $180,000 (what you pay to the owner for the house plus the call premium you have already paid him). Either way, it has worked out for you: you've saved $20,000.

The homeowner, the call writer, is probably not happy that his house went down in price, but he's also better off (of course he'd have been much better off if you had agreed to buy the house four months ago for $200,000). That is because you've already given him $5,000. This has lessened his losses. Suppose you walk away and the homeowner can't find another buyer. Although his house is now valued at $175,000, down from $200,000, he's lost $20,000 instead of $25,000. He gets to keep his house and the $5,000. In a sense, he hasn't lost anything, given that he still has his house. He's also gained $5,000—he has made income off of his asset.

Call Scenario 2: By expiration date, house prices have gone up. Let's say the home is now valued at $275,000. Congratulations, you've made a $70,000 profit, provided that you exercise your call option by buying the house from the owner for $200,000 or sell the contract to someone else before it expires. (If you sell the contract to someone else, they may be willing to pay more for it than $75,000 if they think the home's price will continue to rise.) We derive a $70,000 profit because the house is now worth $75,000 more than the strike price and you have paid a $5,000 premium for the contract.

The homeowner would have been better off if he didn't enter into the contract with you, because he'd now be able to sell you or someone else the house for $275,000—$75,000 more than four months ago. Nevertheless, he's better off now than he would have been had he simply sold you the house for $200,000 four months ago. This is because you've paid him a $5,000 premium. That is, if you exercise your call, you'll have bought the house from him for a total of $205,000. This is better for the homeowner than $200,000.

Call Scenario 3: By expiration date, house prices have stayed flat. The market price for the home is still $200,000. As the call buyer, you can buy the house or walk away. While you haven't gained monetarily, you were given time to see how things played out and you made sure that no one else would swoop in and buy the house out from under you. But you are out $5,000.

The homeowner made an extra $5,000 off of his house. Whether you or someone else buys it, the total purchase price will be $205,000. And if no one buys it, the homeowner has made $5,000 in income. If you walk away, the contract will expire worthless. The homeowner might then write another call contract with another buyer, and collect another $5,000 premium.

Puts

A **put option** is a contract where the buyer, in exchange for a premium, has the right, but not the obligation, to sell the underlying to the writer for the strike price between the time the contract is formed and the expiration date. Here's an example.

Put Example 1: You have a car that is currently worth $10,000. You're thinking about selling it, but you're not sure. You fear, however, that the market price for the car will drop in the meantime. You propose the following deal with me: at any time between now and May 20th of this year you will have the right to sell me your car for $10,000. In exchange, you will give me $100. If we agree and you give me the $100 premium, we have formed a put contract. At any time between now and May 20th, you can put (sell) the car to me for $10,000. You do not have to do so. You simply have the right to do it. Whatever you decide, I get to keep the $100 premium. In this example you are the put buyer and I am the put writer.

Note how in our put option example, derived from Covered Call Example 1, many of the elements are the same: the underlying, expiration date, and the premium (this will not necessarily be the same in real life). The major difference is which party has a right, and what that right is. To review, **a call option buyer has the right**, but not the obligation, **to buy** the underlying at a certain price within a certain time. **A put option buyer**, on the other hand, **has the right to sell** the underlying at a certain price within a certain time. A call buyer may call (buy) the underlying asset. A put buyer may put (sell) the underlying asset. The buyers control the disposition of the underlying. The writers collect premiums.

Here's another example. **Put Example 2**: You are in the market for a home. You find a house you like and the owner is willing to part with it for $200,000. He's not sure that he's willing to sell yet, however. He thinks maybe housing prices have hit a bottom and there will be a rise in the near future. But he's also worried that prices can fall further. You really like the house and are willing to take the loss if its value drops. So you offer the owner the following deal: he gives you $5,000 now. In exchange, he can sell you the house at any time between today and two months from now for $200,000. If you agree and he gives you the $5,000 premium, you have entered into a put contract. You wrote the put and he bought it. He has the right, but not the obligation, to sell you the house at any time between now and when the contract expires.

Put Scenario 1: The housing market continues falling. Let's say the home is now valued at $175,000. Before the option contract expires, the owner puts the home to you for $200,000. He's better off because he just saved himself $20,000 ($200,000 sale price minus the $5,000 put premium minus the home's $175,000 current value). He will have saved more if home prices continue to plummet. You're also better off, in a sense. You wanted the house for $200,000, but ended up paying $195,000 for it ($200,000 strike price minus the $5,000 premium you were given). Instead of losing $25,000, you're losing $20,000. It is not good that you are losing money, but you ended up buying something for less than you originally intended.

Put Scenario 2: The housing market did hit bottom. Other buyers have approached the homeowner and the most recent bid is $275,000. The homeowner is better off because he can now sell for $70,000 more than you offered (the $200,000 strike price minus the $5,000 premium he has given you). You are also better off, in a sense. You've pocketed $5,000 just for being a ready, willing, and able buyer. Nothing stops you from placing a bid for the house now, it'll just cost you more. You can also write another put, if the owner is interested.

Put Scenario 3: By expiration date, house prices have stayed flat. The market price for the home is still $200,000. The homeowner might decide to sell to you or someone else, or he might keep the house. He's out $5,000, but he considers it a small price to pay for being able to sleep at night for the past couple of months because he knew that no matter what, he would be able to sell the house for $200,000 or more. If he decides to keep the house, he might buy another put from you or someone else. You are also better off. If the homeowner exercises his put, you end up buying the house for $195,000 instead of the $200,000 asking price (because you were given a $5,000 premium). If the homeowner decides to keep the house or sell it to someone else, the put expires worthless and you've made a profit of $5,000.

Some More Terminology You Will Encounter with Stock Options

Most of the major stocks and ETFs have puts and calls at various strike prices and expiration dates trading daily on the Chicago Board Options Exchange. Each option contract is typically for 100 shares of the underlying stock or ETF. So when an option sells for $4, for instance, you have to shell out $400 for it. If you buy 25 calls that are each selling for $0.75, you will spend $1,875 ($0.75 x 100 x 25).

When you **sell to open** (write) an option position, you are going **short** that option. In your brokerage account you will have a negative symbol in front of the quantity. For example, if you write three calls on stock XYZ, you will have a -3 displayed in the quantity column for the calls in your brokerage account. If you **buy to open** three calls you will be going **long**, on the other hand, and you will have 3 displayed in the quantity column for the calls you bought.

Whenever money goes into your account, whether from closing a long position (selling stock or options) or opening a short position (short selling stock or selling to open options), that money is called a **credit**. When you buy a stock or option or close a short position, the money going out of your account is called a **debit**. Suppose you write calls for a credit of $500 and you buy a few other calls on the same underlying asset for a debit of $300. Your **net credit** will be $200 ($500 minus $300). If, on the other hand, you take the other side of this trade and buy a few calls for $500 and write a few other calls for $300, your **net debit** will be $200.

Option positions are sometimes called **legs**. When you buy an option, you are going long. As such, this option position can be referred to as a **long leg**. When you write an option, you are going short. This position is thus called a **short leg**.

All brokers have two choices on their trading screen when you are buying or selling stocks or options: "**market order**" and "**limit order**." If you select "market order," this tells the broker that you want to buy or sell the equity or option at whatever price the market is trading when your order is executed. Use this choice when you want to buy or sell something immediately. It works fine for stocks and options that are heavily traded, but you should not use the "market" choice with a thinly traded security. This is because you can get ripped off. If you are buying, you are more likely to be overcharged. If you are selling, you are likely to sell for less than you could have otherwise.

If you select "limit order," you must enter a price for which you want to buy, if you are buying, or sell, if you are selling. If you are buying, the limit order tells the broker that you want to buy at the price you entered or lower. If you are selling, the limit order tells the broker that you want to sell at the price you entered or higher. If you place a market order for a stock trading at $30, you will receive that stock for $30. If you place a limit buy order of $25 for a stock that is trading at $30, nothing will happen until the stock falls to $25 or below. If you place a limit sell order for $35 and the stock is currently trading at $30, nothing will happen until the stock goes up to $35 or above.

You will have noticed that in my call examples above I use the term "**covered call**." A **covered call** is a short call position where the call writer owns the underlying asset. For example, if you write a call on stock XYZ and you own 100 shares of XYZ, you are writing a covered call. But if you write a call on XYZ and do not own 100 shares of XYZ, you have written a **naked** call. If your stock is called away and you wrote a covered call, money is deposited (how much depending on the strike price) into your account and your stock is taken away. If the call holder exercises the call and you wrote a naked call, money is deposited into your account, but you have no stock to give the call buyer. You therefore go short the stock, or, depending on your broker, your broker buys the stock for you at the current market price (taking money out of your account) and hands it over to the call buyer.

There are also a few put positions. A **covered put** position is initiated when you are short a stock (100 shares for every put you write) and you write a put. The put is **naked** when you write it and you do not have a short position in the stock. As you will recall, when you write a put you give the owner of the put the right to sell you the underlying asset at the strike price. If you have enough funds in your account to buy the underlying should it be put to you, this is called a **cash secured put**.

There are four different terms that refer to what you are doing when you initiate or close an option position. When you initiate a short leg by writing a call or put, for example, you **sell to open**. When you close a short option position, you **buy to close**. You receive a credit when you sell to open and a debit when you buy to close. For example, suppose you want to write 12 puts for $3 each. You sell to open the puts and select a limit price of $3. If your order is executed, you receive a credit of $3,600 (12 x 3 x 100). Suppose some time later the puts fall in price and now trade at $1.25. You decide to close the position. You buy to close the 12 puts and select a limit price of $1.25. You incur a debit of $1,500. Since you bought back the puts at a lower price than you wrote them, the two transactions yield a net credit of $2,100. That is your profit on the trade.

When you initiate a long leg by buying a call or put, you **buy to open**. When you close a long option position, you **sell to close**. You incur a debit when you buy to open and receive a credit when you sell to close. For example, suppose you want to buy 12 puts for $3 each. You buy to open the puts and select a limit price of $3. If your order is executed, you incur a debit of $3,600. Suppose some time later the puts fall in price and now trade at $1.25. Fearing more losses, you decide to close the position. You sell to close the 12 puts and select a limit price of $1.25. You receive a credit of $1,500. Since you bought the puts at a higher price than you sold them, the two transactions yield a net debit of $2,100. That is your loss on the trade.

When you sell to open an option and buy to open the same type of option (both legs are calls or both legs are puts) of a different strike price and/or expiration this is called a **spread**. If you receive a net credit, you are **selling the spread**. If you incur a net debit, you are **buying the spread**. (There are other terms related to this, like bull, bear, vertical, and diagonal spreads, but they are not relevant to the strategies outlined below.)

There are a few more terms that options traders often use. When an option's strike price is very close to the price of the underlying (e.g., the $25 strike for a stock currently trading between $24.50 and $25.50) we say that the option is **at the money**.

When a call's strike price is below the current price of the underlying, we say that the call is **in the money**. If the call's strike price is very far below the current price of the underlying, we say that the call is **deep in the money**. Calls are most likely to be exercised before expiration when they are in the money or deep in the money, especially before the ex-dividend date.

When a call's strike price is above the current price of the underlying, we say that it is **out of the money**, and when the call's strike is far above the underlying's current price we say that the call is **far out of the money**.

When a put's strike price is below the current price of the underlying, we say that the put is **out of the money**. If the put's strike is far below the underlying's current price, we say that the put is **far out of the money**. If the put's strike is above the current price of the underlying, we say that the put is **in the money**. And if the put's strike is far above the current price of the underlying, we say that the put is **deep in the money**. Puts are most likely to be exercised before expiration if they are in the money or deep in the money, especially on or soon after an ex-dividend date.

The farther out of the money an option is, the less it sells for. It has no intrinsic worth. It only has time value. The deeper in the money an option is, the more intrinsic worth it has and the more it sells for. Typically, at the money options have the most time premium. See box 12 where AFLACK (AFL) trades at $45.29 per share in November.

Listed in box 12 are 14 different call contracts for AFL that expire on February 18, 2012. Column 1 is the strike price for each contract. For example, where it says "40," that means that that is a contract for the right to purchase 100 shares of AFL stock at $40 per share.

Column 2 lists all of the call contracts' ticker symbols. Let's take a look at the first one to see the format: AFL120218C40. The letters "AFL" refer to the underlying stock (AFL is the stock's ticker symbol). The numbers following the stock ticker indicate when the option will expire. They are arranged by 2-digit year, 2-digit month, and 2-digit day. Here we have 12 for the year, meaning 2012. We have 02 for the month, meaning February. And we have 18 for the day, meaning the 18th day in February. If you look down the list in box 12, you will notice that all of the options are identical in this regard. This is because they all have the same underlying stock (AFLACK) and all expire on the same day: February 18, 2012. If all of the options expired on March 17, 2012, all of their tickers would begin with AFL120317.

AFL Feb Calls with Premium

1 Strike	2 Symbol	3 Last Trade	4 Bid	5 Ask	6 Premium to 45.29	
40	AFL120218C40	7.6	7.3	7.5	2.01	
41	AFL120218C41	6.9	6.55	6.8	2.26	
42	AFL120218C42	5.05	6	6.1	2.71	
43	AFL120218C43	5.4	5.35	5.45	3.06	
44	AFL120218C44	4.95	4.7	4.85	3.41	
45	**AFL120218C45**	**4**	**4.15**	**4.25**	**3.86**	In the money / **At the money**
46	AFL120218C46	3.66	3.6	3.75	3.6	
47	AFL120218C47	3.1	3.15	3.25	3.15	
48	AFL120218C48	2.78	2.71	2.79	2.71	
49	AFL120218C49	2.39	2.31	2.39	2.31	
50	AFL120218C50	1.98	1.93	2.02	1.93	
52.5	AFL120218C52.5	1.17	1.2	1.28	1.17	
55	AFL120218C55	0.75	0.7	0.77	0.75	Out of the
60	AFL120218C60	0.23	0.2	0.24	0.23	money

Box 12

202

Following the numbers indicating the date is the letter C. This indicates that the option is a call. If the option were a put, there would be a P instead of a C. That is to say, AFL120218C is a call that expires on February 18, 2012 and AFL120218P is a put that expires on February 18, 2012.

Following the C is a number. That number is the strike price. So, for example, AFL120218C41 is a call to purchase 100 shares of AFL for $41 per share, and the call expires on February 18, 2012.

Column 3 represents the last price for which each contract was traded. Column 4 is the bid, and column 5 is the ask. The bid is what buyers are offering for the option. The ask is what sellers (both people who are long the option and want to sell it—sell to close—and those who want to write a new contract—sell to open) want for the contract.

Column 6 is not usually present on your broker's or financial website's screen. It is something I included to show that at the money options, in our example the 45 strike price (because AFL is trading at $45.29 per share) have the most time value.

An option's trading price has two basic components: intrinsic value and time value. For calls, the intrinsic value is derived by subtracting the strike price of the call from the price at which the underlying stock is trading. For puts, the intrinsic value is derived by subtracting the price at which the stock is trading from the strike price of the put. (For both calls and puts, if the intrinsic value is negative, we say that the intrinsic value is 0). In our example, AFL is trading at $45.29 per share. This means that the $40 strike call has an intrinsic value of $5.29. At the same time, a $41 strike call has an intrinsic value of $4.29.

Note that the $40 strike call isn't trading for $5.29. Sellers want $7.50 and buyers are willing to pay $7.30. This extra amount over the intrinsic value is the time value of the option. Time values are determined by options traders. The options market tries to guess the price of the underlying stock at expiration and also factors in any dividends that the stock might pay. An option's time value thus depends on a number of things: the underlying stock's volatility, the overall stock market's volatility, uncertainty about the future price of the underlying, dividends, interest rates, and how much time there is left until the option expires. All other things being equal, the same strike option further into the future will have the same intrinsic value, if any, and a greater time value. For example, the March $40 strike AFL call has the same intrinsic value as the February $40 strike AFL call, but because the contract lasts a month longer, its time value will be greater. While AFL120218C40 trades for $7.50, AFL120317C40 might trade for $7.90, and the November $40 strike call (AFL111119C40) might trade for $5.35.

In the money options have both intrinsic and time value. Out of the money options have only time value. At the money options usually have the most time value, and that is what column 6 in box 12 is trying to show.

Investors and speculators buy and sell options for a number of different purposes, including capital gains, income, and hedging. Option prices are set by the market but are related to their underlying stocks (for example, a call option at the $50 strike will trade for at least $4 if the underlying trades at $54). Generally speaking, calls rise when the underlying rises and fall when the underlying falls. Puts rise when the underlying falls and fall when the underlying rises. But note that this is not always the case. There are many scenarios in which calls fall when the underlying rises and puts fall when the underlying falls.

Options are much more nuanced, complicated, and interesting than I have outlined above. And you can do much more with them than what I've said and am about to say. Nevertheless, what I have discussed is enough for our purposes here. If you are interested in learning more, a great book on the subject is *Option Volatility and Pricing* by Sheldon Natenberg.

Using Covered Calls to Generate Extra Income from Your Stocks

Covered Call Example 3: Let's say you own 100 shares of insurer AFLACK (AFL). You bought it at $40 a share, and on November 4, 2011 it trades at $45.29. AFL pays an annual dividend of $1.32 a share in quarterly installments (that's a 3.3% yield on your purchase price). Hoping to collect some more income from the stock, you look at where the calls that expire on February 18, 2012 are trading (see box 13). All things being equal, you would like to keep the stock. That is, you'd rather not have the stock called away. You want the contract to expire worthless.

AFL Feb Calls

Strike	Symbol	Last Trade	Bid	Ask	Volume	Open Interest*
40	AFL120218C40	7.6	7.3	7.5	15	670
41	AFL120218C41	6.9	6.55	6.8	15	126
42	AFL120218C42	5.05	6	6.1	17	941
43	AFL120218C43	5.4	5.35	5.45	4	2482
44	AFL120218C44	4.95	4.7	4.85	50	800
45	AFL120218C45	4	4.15	4.25	30	418
46	AFL120218C46	3.66	3.6	3.75	5	277
47	AFL120218C47	3.1	3.15	3.25	3	797
48	AFL120218C48	2.78	2.71	2.79	32	544
49	AFL120218C49	2.39	2.31	2.39	28	649
50	AFL120218C50	1.98	1.93	2.02	5	808
52.5	AFL120218C52.5	1.17	1.2	1.28	5	231
55	AFL120218C55	0.75	0.7	0.77	7	430
60	AFL120218C60	0.23	0.2	0.24	55	302

Box 13

*Open interest = the total number of options contracts not closed or delivered

206

You examine the charts and think that AFL will probably not break $50 per share in the next three months. So, you figure that the $50 strike February call will expire worthless. The bid on the 50 strike Feb call is $1.93 per contract. The ask is $2.02. Let's say you decide to write the covered call. You place a sell to open order for one $50 strike call with a limit of $1.97.

Suppose this order is executed. $1.97 (minus commissions, but we'll exclude these for simplicity's sake) per share is deposited into your account. Since each option contract for this stock represents 100 shares, you have just written a call for $197. No matter what happens, that money is yours to keep. You've just generated $197 in extra income—this is in addition to the dividends you already get. That is 4.925% of your purchase price.

Scenario 1: You were wrong. AFL continues its rally. It bursts through $50 a share and by February 17, 2012 it trades for $55. You have a couple of choices. If you really want to keep the stock, you can buy back the call. As it is the $50 strike and the stock trades for $55, the call is worth at least $5. Let's say it's trading for $6. You will spend $600 buying the call back. Since you previously took in $197, you will have lost $403 on the call. (But note that AFL was $45.29 when you sold the call. At the current stock price of $55 a share, you are making almost $1,000 on the appreciation.) After you buy to close the call, you can write another one, say for May or June. The premium, depending on which strike price you select, may lower your losses on the February call or may even cover it completely and leave some extra cash. If you buy back your call and write another one further out, this is called **rolling**.

Another choice you have in this scenario is to do nothing. The stock will be called from you and $50 per share ($5,000) will be placed in your account. Although you would have been better off, from a capital gains perspective, if you hadn't written the call (or written it later for a bigger premium), it's still not that bad an outcome. You end up selling the stock at $50 per share. Since you bought at $40, you've made $1,000 in capital gains. On top of that, you've made the call premium of $197, bringing your total gain to $1,197.

What is bad about this scenario is that you have a stock taken away from you that you planned to keep. If you want it back, you'll have to get it for the current $55 a share, thus paying an extra $500, or you'll have to wait for it to drop in price. This can happen, but it might also be the case that AFL will never go lower again. These are some of the risks of writing covered calls: you limit your potential capital gains, and if a stock is called away from you, you might never get it back for a decent price.

Scenario 2: You were right. AFL met resistance at $50. Unfortunately, there was a downgrade by some big fancy investment bank and AFL shares have crashed. As the option expiration approaches, the stock trades for $35 a share.

The $50 strike call will expire worthless and you will get to keep your stock. You are better off having written the call than just holding the stock because the $197 premium you took in has reduced your losses. One way to look at it is that the call premium reduced your cost basis in the stock by $1.97 a share. Instead of having a cost basis of $40 per share, your new cost basis is 38.03. You're still losing money ($3.03 per share) but it's less than if you didn't write the call (you'd be losing $5 per share had you not written the call).

Another way to look at it is that you collected an extra $197 in income (that's more than the annual dividend). The stock would have dropped anyway, so writing the call proved to be the right thing to do. Everything went pretty much according to plan. You collected some money and got to keep your stock. After the call expires you might consider writing another one for a future month, or just holding the stock.

Scenario 3: You were right. AFL met resistance at $50. It has since bounced around between $45 and $50 a share and, as the February expiration approaches, currently trades between $45 and $50 a share. The closer to $50 that the stock trades, the more the call will trade for—because there is a possibility that it will close above $50. If you are worried about this and wish to keep the stock, simply buy to close the call. It might be a lot cheaper (depending on how far from the strike price it is) than when you wrote it three months ago. Typically, the out of the money call will lose most of its value long before expiration date, in which case you can buy to close earlier (and possibly write it again if the stock price rises).

You're better off for writing the call for the same reasons as in *Scenario 2*. The difference here is that you do not have any capital losses. If the call expires worthless or you close the position, you are free to write another one. Let's say the $50 strike in May 2012 now trades at $2 and you decide to write it. That's another 5% income on your original purchase price of $40 per share.

If AFL continues paying dividends, over the year you will have received $1.32 per share. You will also get to keep the $1.97 per share from the February call and the $2 per share for the May call. That's a total income of $5.29 a share, making for a yield of around 13.23%. If something similar to *Scenario 3* plays out in May, you can write another call for August, and in August for November, and in November for February (2013) again. If you can write a call on AFL every three months for around $2, you'll make $8 per share per year in income in addition to the $1.32 per share you receive in dividends. On your initial purchase of AFL at $40 per share, the $9.32 annual income would give you a yield of 23.3%.

The longer you can keep this up, the more income you will earn. Some investors manage to do this sort of thing for years, earning more in income than they spent on buying the stock (note that even without covered calls, in a long enough time a good dividend paying stock will pay you more in income than you originally paid for its shares).

Most people, however, will not. The likelier outcomes are *Scenario 1* and *Scenario 2*. The trouble with *Scenario 2*, especially if the stock keeps dropping, or if the stock is below your initial purchase price in general, is that calls at strike prices above your initial purchase price will sell for less and less. Depending on how low the stock goes, strike prices above your initial purchase price might pay no premium at all. That is, they might have no bid (which means no one is willing to buy the call from you).

If this happens, if you want to continue writing covered calls you will either have to write the calls further out into the future (say six months, a year, or two years, if these are available) or write calls for lower strike prices to get the same premium. With the former, you will be tying yourself down to the stock for a longer period of time and for a much lower annualized return. A number of things might happen between when you write the call and expiration, including something like *Scenario 1*. It might give you lots more grief than you bargained for. With the latter, you risk having the stock called away from you for lower than you paid for it, thereby locking in capital losses.

Covered Call Example 4: suppose you bought AFL for $40 per share. It currently trades at $30 per share. The $40 strike calls for all expiration dates pay very little. Not content with the $0.50 bid for the $40 call that expires in two years, you decide to write the $33 strike call three months out for $1.50. The stock may continue falling, or it may stay flat and below $33. If it does, writing a covered call turns out to be a good idea. But suppose the stock bottoms just as you write the call and goes on a tear up to $50 a share. You either have to close the call at a loss or have the stock taken away at $33. Either way you lose money.

In sum, covered calls offer a way to increase your equity income, but the trade off is that your gains are capped and your potential losses are mitigated only slightly.

One extremely important thing that I have not made explicit is that when you write a call, the underlying stock can be called away at any time before the call expires. This is much more likely when the call is in the money (whether because you wrote an in the money call or because the underlying's price increased above your strike price). As far as dividend paying stocks are concerned, they are often called away right before ex-dividend date if the call is in the money. This is because the call holder wants to capture the dividend. Keep this in mind when writing calls.

Reinvesting Covered Call Premiums

If you have no need for current income and are already reinvesting your dividends, you may want to consider reinvesting your covered call premiums. As we have seen, when you write covered calls, cash is deposited into your account. You can use this cash to buy extra shares of the stock you wrote the covered calls on, a different stock in your portfolio, a new stock, or add it toward the purchase of an ETF or bond. Your option premium might not be enough to justify a transaction, depending on your broker's fees. You may have to wait, allowing all your call premiums to add up before reinvesting them. You'll save money in the long run (more on this in Chapter 30).

Once you do reinvest your call premiums, the advantages and disadvantages are the same as with reinvesting dividends. Your reinvestment gets you more shares which pay you their own dividends (and for every extra 100 shares you buy, you get to write another call). Another advantage is that when you reinvest dividends and/or covered call premiums, if your stock is called away, you still have some shares left over that will participate in the rally.

To sum up, we have so far dealt with writing covered calls. The strategy has the potential to increase your income from equities whether you keep the cash or reinvest it, but it also comes with certain risks. These risks include having to pay extra to keep your stock and missing out on potential capital gains.

Covered Call Funds

A number of "buy/write" closed end funds have sprung up with the advent of the CBOE S&P 500 Buy-Write Index (BXM). At the time of writing, there are about two dozen CEFs, one ETF, and a couple of mutual funds whose strategies focus on covered call writing. This may be an attractive option, pardon the pun, for those investors who find covered call writing appealing but do not have the time, a large enough portfolio, or confidence to engage in it. Most of these funds sell calls on a portfolio of stocks, but a few sell calls on a portfolio of bonds.

You can find these funds on the web at sites such as CEFConnect.com and the Closed End Fund Association <cefa.com>. If you are looking to buy these funds, make sure that you understand their strategy before making your purchase. (Note that while distributions classified as return of capital are generally bad, they are not necessarily so with buy/write funds. This is because call premiums paid as dividends can be classified as return of capital.) Although at first glance the CEFs might all look the same, there are some important differences apart from the usual differences like yield, discount, and fees. Before buying, determine how the covered call strategy is implemented. Which indexes do the funds follow? Some own only S&P 500 stocks, others NASDAQ, and others some other index or a combination of indexes. Some funds sell calls on index options. These are cash settled—stock is not called away. Other funds write calls on their individual stock holdings. The time to expiration and the type of call (at the money, in the money) can differ with each fund. Moreover, what the fund does if by expiration the calls it sold are in the money can also differ. Some funds let their stocks get called away. Others buy back the calls and sell new ones further out into the future. All of this affects returns.

Speaking of returns, most buy/write funds' NAVs and share prices are lower every year. Comparing their price performance on a chart versus an index will almost always show the index outperforming by a wide margin. Be sure to take account of the fund's distributions and the index's dividends over the same period to see the entire picture. Also related to returns, some strategies, at least theoretically, seem to make long term underperformance inevitable. For example, if the fund is strictly rules based and writes calls on all its holdings every month no matter what, it is destined to terrible performance. Those of its stocks that perform well will be called away. The fund will end up buying them back at a higher price. Those of its stocks that do poorly, on the other hand, will remain in the portfolio. In other words, the fund will sell its winners (and buy them back for a higher price) and will keep its losers. It will end up writing calls on the losers that will be at lower strike prices than their original purchase. When these stocks bounce back, they will be called away at a loss. When the fund buys them back, many will be bought at a higher price than they were sold. Over a long enough period, such a fund's NAV will go to zero.

<u>Puts</u>

As with covered calls, small investment accounts cannot take full advantage of the strategies outlined below.

<u>Using Puts to Generate Income from Your Stocks and ETFs Before You Buy Them (or, Buying Stocks for a Discount)</u>

Suppose you want to buy 100 shares of a stock or an ETF. You can buy them outright for the price they are trading. If you want to pay less for the stock, you can wait to see if it drops. Perhaps it will, but it might not. Another way to purchase the stock for less, or earn income if you're unable to buy it because its share price goes higher, is through a cash secured put. As you will recall, a cash secured put is writing one put for every hundred shares you want to buy and having enough cash in your account to fund this purchase should the stock be sold to you.

Put Example 3: You want to buy 100 shares of AFL, which currently trades at $45.29. Although you think this is a good price, rather than paying $45.29 you decide to write a cash secured put. You decide to look three months out. See box 14. Let's say you want to write the $45 strike put. You enter a sell to open order with a limit of $4.35. If the order is executed, $435 is deposited into your account. For the next three months, the put buyer will be able to put the stock to you for $45 a share. If he does, $4,500 will be withdrawn from your account and 100 shares of AFL will be deposited. You therefore make sure to leave $4,500 in your account just in case this happens.

Scenario 1: AFL trades at $50 a share at expiration. The put you wrote expires worthless. You don't get the stock, but you've made $435 in income from it. If you want, you can write another put.

AFL Feb Puts

Strike	Symbol	Last Trade	Bid	Ask	Volume	Open Interest
30	AFL120218P30	0.75	0.74	0.79	21	382
31	AFL120218P31	1.05	0.85	0.9	17	215
32	AFL120218P32	1.18	0.97	1.03	110	156
33	AFL120218P33	1.12	1.1	1.16	3	490
34	AFL120218P34	1.49	1.25	1.3	18	583
35	AFL120218P35	1.44	1.42	1.47	26	626
36	AFL120218P36	1.65	1.6	1.65	18	558
37	AFL120218P37	2.23	1.8	1.86	3	72
38	AFL120218P38	2.09	2.02	2.09	18	516
39	AFL120218P39	2.33	2.27	2.34	1	278
40	AFL120218P40	2.4	2.55	2.61	10	386
41	AFL120218P41	3.25	2.84	2.92	28	407
42	AFL120218P42	3.25	3.15	3.3	40	2708
43	AFL120218P43	4.15	3.5	3.65	13	222
44	AFL120218P44	4.05	3.95	4.05	252	1061
45	AFL120218P45	4.25	4.35	4.5	530	673
46	AFL120218P46	5.97	4.85	4.95	5	86
47	AFL120218P47	4.05	5.35	5.5	5	162
48	AFL120218P48	7.15	5.9	6.05	2	444
50	AFL120218P50	5.8	7.1	7.35	10	40
52.5	AFL120218P52.5	7.56	8.8	9.3	49	58
55	AFL120218P55	9.5	10.75	11.55	5	45

Box 14

216

Scenario 2: AFL trades around $45 per share at expiration. If the stock closes above $45, the put expires worthless, and as in Scenario 1 you've made $435 in income off of it and can write another put if you wish. If the stock closes below $45, it will be sold to you for $45 a share. Since you already collected $435, the stock, from one perspective costs you $4,065 ($4,500 minus $435) or $40.65 per share. In other words, you wanted to buy it for $45.29 a share but ended up buying it at almost a 10% discount. Since you paid only $40.65 a share and AFL pays an annual dividend of $1.32 per share, your dividend yield on the stock is 3.25%. Had you simply bought the stock for $45.29 a share three months ago, your dividend yield would be 2.91%.

Another way to look at it is that you bought the stock for $45 a share and earned $4.35 a share in income (9.67%).

Either way, now that you own the stock, you will receive dividends. You can earn extra income by writing a covered call.

If you decide against owning the stock and you're afraid that it will be put to you, you can buy to close your put. The put will be trading for less than you wrote it, how much less depending on the exact price of the stock, how much time is left to expiration, its volatility, and other factors. Whatever it costs to close the position will take away from the premium you collected in writing the put.

Scenario 3: AFL trades at $30 per share at expiration. The stock will be put to you and $4,500 will be taken from your account unless you buy to close the put. Anyway you look at it, you have unrealized capital losses. But note that writing the put was a better decision than simply buying the stock for $45.29 a share. That is because your losses were mitigated by the $435 premium you collected. You now own the stock. As in *Scenario 2* you can sell a covered call on it (but keep in mind the risk that it can be called away from you for less than your purchase price if the stock rises), and you will receive dividends as long as the company pays them.

Scenario 4: AFL is put to you before expiration date. There is always the possibility that a stock will be put to you if you have written a put on it. This is less likely to happen if the stock trades above the strike price (and if for some strange reason it does happen, you are better off). People usually exercise their puts when the underlying is trading below the strike price. If the underlying pays dividends, it is less likely that a stock will be put to you before ex-dividend day if there is one between when you write the put and when the put expires. A put is most likely to be exercised when the underlying is trading below the strike price and ex-dividend day has passed. Should a stock be put to you before expiration date, the situation is the same as in *Scenario 3*, the difference being that the date is earlier.

As discussed in the section on calls, you can (re)invest your put premiums into more shares of the stock. You can also mitigate potential losses (but lower your put income in the process) by adding a long put leg when you write puts. For example, suppose that in addition to writing the $45 strike put for $4.35 you buy the $40 strike put for $2.61. This will reduce your income to $174 ($435 minus $261) but it would come in very handy in *Scenario 3*. There, your long leg (the $40 strike) will be worth at least $10 a share. Given that you spent $2.61 for it, you would save $7.39 a share ($739) in capital losses. The risks of adding a long leg to a cash secured put include: you reduce your income and the strategy is most useful in the event that the underlying drops in price significantly. If the stock does not drop significantly and finishes above the long put strike, you will probably have been better off not buying the long leg (especially if you want to own the stock no matter how long it goes). Indeed, you'd save on broker costs simply by writing a lower strike put. Note, however, that if you are writing puts (or naked calls) for income with no intention of owning the underlying stock, buying a long leg is a worthwhile hedge (especially with uncovered calls, where potential losses are unlimited).

Combining Covered Calls with Cash Secured Puts

Now that we have seen how one can generate income by writing covered calls and cash secured puts, you may be wondering whether there is a way to combine them. There is, but you need to have enough cash to buy 200 shares of the underlying stock. As such, the following strategy involves an even bigger portfolio (in terms of money invested) than either covered calls or cash secured puts alone.

Here's a popular way to go about it. Sometimes called the "three legged position" because it involves a short call leg, a short put leg, and a long stock leg, the strategy is otherwise known as either "covered short straddle writing" or "covered short strangle writing." The names depend on what the strike prices of the calls and puts are. If you write the put and call with the same strike price and expiration date, it is a short straddle. And if you write a put whose strike is different from the call's but has the same expiration date, it is called a short strangle. Both of these strategies are "covered" when you also buy, or already have, 100 shares of the underlying stock for every call.

Suppose you want to buy 200 shares of AFL, which trades at $45.29 a share. To implement this strategy, you buy 100 shares of the stock for its asking price (or place a limit order and wait for it to drop) and you write a covered call on it. In a separate transaction, or simultaneously if your broker gives you this capability, you write a cash secured put for the other 100 shares you want to buy. Let's combine our previous examples.

<u>Covered Call-Cash Secured Put Combination Example 1</u>: You buy 100 shares of AFL at $45.29 and sell to open a $50 strike call three months out for $1.97 a share. At the same time, you sell to open a cash secured $45 strike put, also three months out, for $4.35 a share. When the broker executes your orders, you end up with 100 shares of AFL, -1 $50 strike call, and -1 $45 strike put, both expiring in three months. $4,529 is deducted from your account for the purchase of the shares, while $632 from the option premiums is deposited. You therefore have a net debit of $3,897. Remember to keep an extra $4,500 in your account so that you can pay for the other 100 shares of AFL if they are put to you.

Scenario 1: AFL trades at $55 a share at expiration.

Unless you fork over at least $500 (which, as discussed previously, will be mitigated by the $197 call premium and in this example by the additional $435 premium you received from writing the put) your stock will be called away and $5,000 will be deposited into your account.

The put, on the other hand, expires worthless. You don't get the other 100 shares of AFL, but you've made $435.

Your total profit in this scenario if you choose not to keep the stock is $471 in capital gains ($5,000 minus

$4,529), $632 from option premiums, and any dividends that the stock paid during the time you held it. That's a profit of $1,103 plus any dividends received. Since you earned the $632 as income, we can say that you earned about 7% in income (more if you received dividends) from the stock ($632 in income on a risk basis of $9029, $4,529 plus $4,500).

Scenario 2: AFL trades between $45 and $50 a share at expiration. Your call will expire worthless, but if at expiration the stock trades near $50 and you want to keep the stock, you can buy to close the call. This will cost you less than the premium you took in, how much less depending on where the stock is trading and other factors previously mentioned. For simplicity's sake, let's say the call expires worthless. You have pocketed the $197 premium from writing the call.

As in Scenario 1, the put you wrote should expire worthless too. If so, you've made $435 from it. Depending on how close to $45 AFL trades, if you don't want to buy 100 more shares of the stock and want to make sure that you don't, you should buy to close the put. It will be trading for less than the $4.35 a share you wrote it for three months earlier. The difference between $435 and what it costs you to close the position will be your profit on this leg of the trade.

When both options expire worthless, you will be left with 100 shares of stock. The $632 in option premiums that you collected can be seen in one of two ways. You can look at it as having reduced the cost basis of your stock by $6.32 a share. In other words, you can look at it as if you bought AFL for $38.97 a share instead of $45.29 ($45.29 minus $6.32).

From an income perspective, you can look at the result as though you earned $632 in income from your AFL holdings. As mentioned previously, that's around 7% of how much you risked. Given that you still have 100 shares of the stock, you might choose to sell the shares, or write another covered call, write another cash secured put (for the extra 100 shares you wanted) or write both a covered call and a cash secured put. If you're able to do this four times a year and get about the same income on average, you will have made around 28% in income off the stock plus dividends. Do this successfully for eight quarters, and your option and dividend income will have more than paid for the 100 shares of AFL that you continue to own.

Scenario 3: AFL trades below $45 a share a expiration. Let's say it's $30. The call you wrote therefore expires worthless. The $197 call premium you collected mitigates your unrealized capital losses.

Since AFL is below the $45 strike price, the stock is put to you. One hundred additional shares of AFL are deposited into your account and $4,500 is withdrawn. The $435 put premium you collected also mitigates your unrealized capital losses.

After expiration date, you end up with 200 shares of AFL. You bought the first 100 shares for $45.29 and the second 100 shares for $45. Your total capital outlay is therefore $9,029 ($4,529 plus $4,500). There are, as usual, two ways to look at it. The first is that the option premiums you collected reduced your cost basis by $632. Looking at it this way, your cost basis is $8,397 ($9,029 minus $632) or $41.985 per share ($8,397 divided by 200). Even though you have unrealized capital losses, given that the stock is trading at $30, you are better off than you would have been had you simply bought the 200 shares for $45.29 each three months earlier.

Another way to look at it is that you spent $9,029 on 200 shares and generated $632 in income, almost 7%. You also might have received a quarterly dividend during the three month period, which would increase your yield.

Now that you have 200 shares of AFL you can sell one or two calls on it (but be mindful of the risks previously mentioned). If you want to buy another 100 shares, you can write another put.

Scenario 4: AFL trades between $40.65 and $45 per share at expiration. Your call expires worthless. You get to keep the $197 premium.

Unless you buy to close the put (which might be trading for less than you wrote it, depending on where the stock is trading) the put will be exercised by its holder and you will receive another 100 shares at $45 apiece. This scenario is similar to *Scenario 3* except that if you take the put premium into account, you do not lose anything on the second 100 shares. This is because the put premium you collected covers the entire loss. One way to look at it is that when you wrote the $45 strike put for $4.35, if the stock were put to you, you would end up buying it for $40.65 a share ($45 minus $4.35). Therefore, you are only worse off on the put leg if the stock trades below $40.65 a share. Anything above that is a gain on these 100 shares.

This three legged strategy of buying 100 shares, writing a call, and writing a put has many variations. You can select different strike prices from the ones in the example above. Moreover, you do not have to write the call or put right away. You can buy the 100 shares, for instance, wait for the stock to gain, and then write the call. You can also wait for the stock to fall before writing the put. The strategy works best in a bull market, but it reduces losses (as compared to buying 200 shares of the stock at the current market price) when things go wrong.

<u>Writing Cash Secured Puts Instead</u>

While it has its advocates, the covered straddle/ strangle strategy also has its detractors. You may be better off writing two cash secured puts instead of buying stock, writing a call, and writing a put, for example. First, instead of paying three separate commissions (for stock, call, and put), you only pay one (just for the puts). Second, you only have to deal with the bid and ask spreads of the puts, instead of three separate securities. In other words, your order is more likely to be filled, and for a better price.

When comparing the two strategies, consider when the stock goes ex-dividend, how much the dividend will be, and what your cost basis will be if by expiration the stock drops below the puts' strike price. (Also keep in mind that options don't pay dividends but their prices account for them—in fact, options often predict what the declared dividend will be.)

Here's an example. Let's say in early November AFL trades at $45.29 and you are looking at writing February options. You can (1) buy AFL for $45.29 a share, write a call, and write a put. Or, you can (2) write two puts.

In choice (1), your cost basis if the put is assigned will be the following: $45.29 a share for the first 100 shares, $x a share for the second 100 shares where x is the put strike, minus the call premium per share, minus the put premium per share, minus any dividends received.

So, let's say you decide to write the $47 call for $3.15 and the 40 put for $2.55. Your cost basis is $7,929 if the stock drops below $40 and you buy the second 100 shares at expiration ($4,529 plus $4,000 minus $315 minus $255 minus $30 [estimated dividend per share]). That's $39.645 per share which is certainly a lot better than buying 200 shares at $45.29 each. So, if AFL goes down to zero, you will lose $7,929 with the covered strangle as compared to $9,058 if you simply bought the shares.

Now let's look at your maximum gain, which would occur if AFL closed above $47 a share on expiration day. The max you'll gain on the 100 shares is $47 (call strike) minus $45.29 (purchase price), or $1.71 per share. To this we add the estimated dividend of $0.30, along with the call premium of $3.15, and the put premium of $2.55. The maximum gain is therefore $7.71 a share or $771. Remember that in the real world these gains will be lower because of broker commissions and tax.

In choice (2), your cost basis for the shares if the put is assigned will be the following: $x per share where x is the put strike price minus the put premium. Let's say you sell two $44 strike puts for $4 each. If the puts are assigned, your cost basis for each 100 shares will be: $44 minus $4, for a total of $40 per share or $8,000. Compare this with buying 200 shares at $45.29. Writing the two puts also gives you a higher cost basis than the covered strangle, whose cost basis is $39.645 a share or $7,929.

Now let's look at your maximum gain, which would occur as long as AFL closes above $44 per share on expiration. The max you'll gain is the put premium, which is $4 per share for 200 shares, or $800. This is slightly more than the $771 potential gain for the covered strangle, but you've risked more money (lose at most $8,000 with the put strategy and lose at most $7,929 with the three legged

225

strategy). The potential gain on the covered strangle results in an 8.5% return on the money put up for the trade. The potential gain on the cash secured puts results in a 9.1% return on the money put up for the trade. Note that to reach max profit with the three legged strategy, AFL has to close above $47. To reach max profit with the put strategy, AFL has to close above $44. The latter is likelier than the former, and is something else to consider.

Returns and risk vary depending on the strike prices of the options you write and where the stock is trading at the time. That is to say, while the strategies can yield similar results, it is hard to make a perfect apples versus apples comparison, as we could have picked different strike prices for both strategies. If choosing between the two strategies, ask yourself which gives you a better return for the same amount of risk.

A Penny Saved is a Penny Earned (Buying Puts for Protection)

While in the above I discussed writing puts for income or for getting shares cheaper than the market price, puts can also be used as insurance or price protection. When you buy one put for every 100 shares of a stock you own, the most money you can lose during the life of the contract is the put premium plus the difference between the put strike price and the price at which you bought the shares.

Put as Insurance Example 1: Suppose you buy 100 shares of stock XYZ at $40 a share and buy a put, three months out, at the $38 strike for $1.50. You spend $4,000 on the stock plus $150 on the puts. Between now and when the put expires, you can always sell the 100 shares for $38 a share by exercising your put. If, between now and when the put expires XYZ's share price drops, the most you can lose is the $150 you paid for the put plus $200 ($4,000 for the shares minus the $3,800 you can sell the shares for), or a total of $350. This loss is lessened if XYZ pays any dividends during the period.

Investors often buy puts when they think a downturn is coming but they want to hold on to their shares. It helps them sleep better at night knowing that no matter what happens, there is a limit to their potential losses. They want to continue owning the shares to collect the dividends and participate in any capital gains, but they want to be protected from potential price drops. Oftentimes, investors will finance the purchase of their puts by writing calls. Depending on which strike prices they choose, the stock's volatility, and so on, a covered call may lessen the cost of a put to pennies, and sometimes the transaction even results in a net credit. When one sells a covered call and buys a put on the same security, the trade is called a **collar**. This is because, if you recall, a covered call limits your potential gains (at the written call's strike price) and the bought put limits your potential losses (at the put's strike price). So the stock is "collared" between the two strike prices. You keep it if by expiration the stock remains between the two strikes, and you sell it if it goes above the call strike or below the put strike. Your gains or losses depend on where you originally bought the stock, what dividends you collected, where the stock trades at expiration, and what strike options you used.

<u>Collar Example 1</u>: Suppose you bought 100 shares of AFL at $40 a share. The stock now trades at $45 a share. You want to hold the stock, but are afraid that it will drop in price. You can sell a covered call, which, if AFL does fall, will lessen your losses somewhat (as we have seen). You can also buy a put, but you are reluctant, as buying a put means shelling out cash. You're in it to collect cash, not give it away. So you decide to open a collar position. There are many combinations of puts and calls to choose from, let's say you decide to write the $46 strike call, three months out, for $3.60 and buy the $43 strike put, for the same expiration, also for $3.60. Excluding broker fees, you initiate the transaction for a net credit/debit of $0.

Scenario 1: At expiration, AFL trades above $46 a share. Your put will expire worthless. If it still has some time value and your net credit from closing the position will be greater than your broker's commission fees, you should sell to close the put. If you want to keep the stock, you should buy to close the call. How much this costs will depend on where AFL is trading, time left to expiration, and other factors. If you do not close the call position, AFL will be called away from you for $46 a share. Your total gain on the stock will be $600 ($4,600 you sold it for minus $4,000 purchase price) plus any dividends you receive, plus whatever you salvage from the put, if you sell it.

Scenario 2: At expiration, AFL trades between $43 and $46 a share. Both your call and put will expire worthless. How much they trade for before expiration will depend on where the stock trades, and so on. If the put still has some value left, you should close it, provided that the net credit will be greater than your broker fees. You get to keep the stock. Your gain is the dividends you received during the period plus what you are able to salvage by closing the put, if you close it. Your unrealized capital losses will depend on where AFL trades. If it's still $45 a share, you're in the same position you were three months ago.

Scenario 3: At expiration, AFL trades below $43 a share. Your call will expire worthless. If you want to keep the stock, either sell to close your put or inform your broker that you do not want to exercise it. If you decide to keep your stock and sell your put, your unrealized capital losses from three months ago, when AFL was $45 a share, will be lessened by the credit you receive from selling the put. For example, if AFL now trades at $40 a share, your put will trade for at least $3 at expiration.

If you decide to sell AFL, you will exercise your put (this will happen automatically at most brokers if the stock closes below the put strike at expiration) and sell the stock to the put writer for $43 a share. You will have lost $200 (mitigated by any dividends you received during the period) from the $45 a share price three months ago. Your total gain will then be $300 plus dividends, as in this example you bought the stock for $4,000 and sold it for $4,300. In sum, collars limit potential losses at the expense of capping potential gains.

Using Puts to Limit Your Potential Losses While Leaving Gains Open

Another strategy is to take your losses up front by buying puts on a stock at the same time you buy the shares. If you simultaneously buy shares of a stock and a put for every 100 shares, this transaction is called a **married put**. You might wonder why anyone would do this. Here's one reason. One of the biggest problems that individual investors have is that they sell their losing stocks too late and their winning stocks too early. Most people do not have the discipline to sell their losing stocks, and end up doing so when it is either too late or just before a stock rebounds. Basically, most individual investors buy high and sell low, despite their initial plans to the contrary.

While I think it's great to own dividend paying stocks and not to pay attention too much to the stock price as long as the company does not cut its dividend, many people freak out. They have trouble sleeping at night. Their stock is down 30% from their purchase price and they can't take any more pain. So they sell. What usually happens next is that the stock falls some more and the investors thank the heavens that they sold when they did. But then, in most cases with good companies, other investors are attracted to the great dividend yield, and the stock rallies. It is soon higher than our worried investors' purchase price. Had they held on, they would be sitting on capital gains and would have collected dividends during the period. Now they wonder whether they should get back in at the higher price. Married puts are used to avoid such situations.

Married Put Example 1: Suppose dividend paying stock XYZ has dropped in price sharply. The reasons could be a product recall, class action law suit, an earnings drop (that may or may not be temporary), etc. Let's say, for this example, that XYZ makes cigarettes and a very important court ruling is due soon. If the court rules against the company, it will have to pay out a massive judgment and future sales will be in jeopardy. It may never be profitable again. It may even go out of business. Whether it does or not, if the court rules against the company, its dividend will almost certainly be cut or eliminated. Currently, the stock pays an annual dividend of $2 a share and trades at $20, down from $40 a share a few months ago. The stock's historic average dividend yield is 5%. Currently, it sports a dividend yield of 10% ($2 divided by $20 and expressed as a percentage).

If the court rules in favor of the company, the dividend will remain the same or rise. XYZ is either a screaming buy or a yield trap. Investors have sold the stock off in fear. Analysts at fancy investment banks, and pundits on television are saying that the stock can fall as low as $10 a share, if the company survives, should the ruling be against it. Now you are thinking of buying it. What are you to do?

Let's say you want to limit your potential losses to 7% of your investment. You can buy stock and set for yourself a plan: "if it declines 7%, I'm selling." If you are able to do this, good for you. Most people are not. Another strategy, and I think the better one, is to buy a married put, several months out, that limits your losses to the same percentage. The disadvantage of the married put, as compared to the loss limit plan, is the situation where XYZ rebounds immediately after you buy it. In every other way, the married put strategy is better, because it gives the stock time to bounce around. XYZ can keep dropping after you buy it. If you're using the mental stop loss method, for example, you might sell the stock only to see it rebound.

The way many investors approach this strategy is to buy a put for every 100 shares of the stock, several months out—say six months, at a strike price above where the stock currently trades. That is, they buy in the money puts. This is because, if you recall, the greatest option premium is at the money. Out of the money and in the money options almost always have less time value.

So, suppose you buy 100 shares of XYZ at $20 a share ($2,000) and at the same time you buy a $23 strike put, six months out, for $4.50 a share ($450). Your total debit for this married put is $2,450. The most you can lose in the next six months if the stock goes down is $150, or around 6.5%. The most you can gain is unlimited. Here's how we get $150: you shell out $2,450 for 100 XYZ shares and one put. During the next six months, you can sell your XYZ shares for $23 a share, or $2,300. $2,450 minus $2,300 is $150, and $150 is around 6.5% of $2,300. The $150 loss will be lessened by any dividends XYZ pays out during the six months. Now you can sit and watch, knowing that no matter what the stock does, the most you can lose is 6.5%.

Scenario 1: The court rules in favor of XYZ. The stock rises sharply as dividend investors swoop in to capture the great dividend yield. By options expiration, XYZ has almost recovered its share price, trading at $35. It has continued paying out dividends, and may raise them in the future.

Your put will expire worthless. Nevertheless, you will be sitting on $1,500 of capital gains, lessened by the $450 put premium you paid. That is, if you decide to sell the stock now, you will have a capital gain of $1,050. Added to your gain will be any dividends you received.

Of course, you can also keep the stock and continue to receive dividends. In this case, your cost basis for the stock will be $2,450 ($2,000 spent on shares plus $450 spent on the put). If the dividend rate stays at $2 a share, your effective dividend yield is 8.16% ($2 dividend divided by $24.50 per share cost basis and expressed as a percentage). Nice!

Scenario 1a: But you can make even more money (or at least lessen your cost basis) in this scenario. For example, when the court rules in favor of the company, you can sell your put. Your credit from the transaction will depend on how much the put trades for, and this will depend on where the stock is. You might sell the put for more than you bought it, or you might not. But whatever credit you receive will be subtracted from your cost basis of $2,450, thereby lowering it. For instance, if you sell the put for $3 a share

($300), your cost basis will drop to $2,150 ($2,450 share and put total purchase price minus $300 for selling the put).

If it seems like the court will rule in the company's favor and the stock starts to rise, but you aren't certain enough to sell the put and leave your shares uninsured, another thing you can do is roll your put up. For example, suppose that XYZ moves up to $23 a share a few weeks to a couple of months after you buy it. You think it's going to rebound further, but aren't sure. What you can do is sell your $23 strike put and use the proceeds, plus a little extra, to buy, say, a $26 strike put for the same expiration. This transaction is worthwhile as long as your total debit for it is less than the difference between the strike prices. Here, the difference between the strike prices is $3 per share, or $300. If you can roll your $23 strike put up to a $26 strike put (sell to close the $23 strike and buy to open the $26 strike) for a net debit less than $300, you should. This is because once you own the $26 strike call, you can sell the stock for $26 a share at any time between now and expiration.

This is possible because, as already mentioned, at the money options have more premium than in the money options. For example, when XYZ is at $23 a share, the $23 put will still have a lot of time value left. It might trade for, depending on how far away expiration is, $1.80 per share. The $26 strike put might trade, at the same time, at $4.20 a share. If you sell the $23 strike put for $1.80 and buy the $26 strike put for $4.20, your net debit will be $2.40 a share, or $240. If you do this, your cost basis, which was $2,450 will go up by an additional $240, for a total of $2,690. But, since you now have the right to sell the shares for $26 apiece (if you exercise your put), the most you can lose now is $90 ($2,690 minus $2,600). If XYZ continues paying $2 per year in dividends, over the six month period you should collect $1 per share ($100) in dividends. Excluding taxes, that means you will be ahead by $0.10 a share, or $10. In other words, if you roll your put up as described, and XYZ pays you two quarterly dividends, (excluding taxes) you can no longer lose any money. The least you can gain is $10 and your potential gains are unlimited.

Suppose XYZ continues to rebound and now trades for $26 a share. Your $26 strike put still has time value. Let's say it trades for $1.70 a share. Let's say the $29 strike put trades for $4.25 a share. You can roll your $26 strike put to the $29 strike for a net debit of $2.55 ($255) ($4.25 minus $1.70). The $255 debit is added to your cost basis. Your total cost basis is now $2,945 ($2,690 plus $255). Since you now have the right to sell the shares at $29 each ($2,900), the most you can lose is $45 ($2,945 cost basis minus $2,900), which is 1.5% of your investment (that's down from 6.5%, if you recall). If you receive $1 per share ($100) in dividends during the period, excluding taxes, you cannot lose any money. That is because you gain, at a minimum, $55 (we've now gone from a loss of, *at most* 6.5% to a gain of *at least* 1.87%).

At this point you can wait for the stock to go up some more and roll your put again, or you can sell a covered call. (Remember that covered calls limit your potential capital gains.) Do you see how the rolling of puts on a dividend paying stock can be considered an income strategy even though you incur a net debit with each transaction? Options are powerful tools.

Note that while *Scenario 1a* is possible (I have done it a few times), it only works in certain market conditions (the stock has to rise within the life of your puts, and so on).

Also note the married put strategy's advantages over the mental stop loss strategy. In our example, with the married put you have six months to see what happens and your losses are fixed. With the mental stop, you might be forced to sell too early (the stock can continue falling only to rebound after you sell). Moreover, you might not have enough discipline to enforce your mental stop. A positive analyst note or something a pundit says might keep you in the stock after it goes lower than your mental stop price. You might, therefore, lose more money than you planned if the stock keeps falling.

Scenario 2: The court rules against the company. It can no longer sell its products because of the court ruling. The dividend is cut, and the share price tanks to $10. The put is worth at least $13. You can exercise it at any time before expiration. If you do, you'll sell the stock to the put writer for $23 a share, losing, as discussed, $150. Alternatively, you can sell your put. If the stock continues its decline, the most you can lose is an additional $1,000. If the stock gains, on the other hand, your $150 loss will be mitigated by the rise. You might even make a profit.

Scenario 3: The court rules against the company and it goes out of business. Its cash reserves are used to pay the court judgment. The rest of the company's assets are put up for auction. The proceeds will be used to pay the bond holders. If there is anything left, the remainder will be used to pay XYZ's preferred shareholders. If there's a remainder, it'll go to holders of the common stock, like you. Let's say that while XYZ is in bankruptcy court the stock, now on the Pink Sheets, trades for $0.12 a share.

Your put will be worth at least $22.88. You can exercise it and sell your shares to the put writer for $23 a share at any time before the put expires. You will lose $150 in total, as discussed above. You can also sell your put for the going rate if you think that after all the company's senior creditors are paid off you and the other common stockholders will receive more than $0.12 a share. If you do this and are wrong, at most you'll lose an additional $12. If you are right, your $150 loss will be mitigated by whatever you get back per share.

The best time to buy a dividend paying stock is when everyone hates it. The yield is higher than it would otherwise be and there is potential for capital gains. Most people are too scared to do this and miss out on great gains. Married puts are the antidote for fear and potential losses. Consider them when there's a market crash, everyone is panicking, and it seems like it's the end of the world.

Chapter 27 - Dividend Capture Strategies and Why They Usually Don't Work for Individual Investors

Now that we have looked at options in some detail, I can discuss the various "dividend capture" strategies out there. The short version is that dividend capture strategies usually don't work for individual investors because of transaction costs. If you want to know the longer version, read on. (The following, with some alterations, previously appeared on my blog and on *Seeking Alpha*.)

A popular strategy among those people who trade actively is dividend capture. There are several different ways to implement it, and I would like to go through some of the more prevalent ones.

Recall that the last time to buy a stock and be eligible to receive its dividend is the day before ex-dividend day. That is, if ex-dividend day is December 15, one must buy the stock on December 14 (or the last trading day before December 15) at the latest. If you sell your stock on ex-dividend day, you are eligible for the dividend as long as you bought it, or exercised a call to buy it, the day before.

At the heart of every dividend capture strategy is the fact that on ex-dividend day, all other things being equal, a dividend paying stock opens lower than its previous close by the amount of the dividend. For example, a stock that closed at $50 a share on the day before ex-dividend and which pays a $0.50 dividend, should open, all things being equal, at $49.50 the next day. Given trading and other factors, in reality the stock may open substantially higher or lower than the previous close. The trader who wants to capture the dividend wants to buy the stock for $x and sell it for $x or higher. The dividend and the amount over $x is his profit, less commission costs and taxes.

Dividend Capture Strategy (1)

The most common dividend capture strategy, and the worst, at least in bear markets, is the following. The trader buys a stock shortly before ex-dividend day. As the stock trades on and after ex-dividend, its price will of course fluctuate. The trader who bought the stock for the dividend in this first strategy will want to proceed in one of two ways after holding the stock overnight. The trader will either (a) sell the stock immediately after it reaches or exceeds the price at which he bought it, or (b) he will wait at least 61 days and then try to sell it for the price he paid or higher. In both cases, the trader uses the sale proceeds to move on to the next dividend paying stock. He will receive the dividend payment on the pay date, which for most stocks is usually a few weeks after ex-dividend day. The person who does (a) potentially has access to his money much faster, thus being able to put it back to work more quickly. In some cases, the dividend paying stock can be sold on ex-dividend day for a profit. However, the dividend this person receives is taxed as ordinary income. The person implementing (b) will optimally sell for a profit right after holding the stock for 61 days. This person can receive up to six dividend payments on the same sum of money per year and be taxed at the qualified dividend rate. If strategy (a) can be implemented successfully on a regular basis, it is likely better than (b) in terms of after tax profits.

Critics of the strategy often say the dividend capture is a myth. I am inclined to agree, especially with regard to (a). What the trader is really doing is trying to get a capital gain. It is the stock's move up after ex-dividend that results in the profit. This is the same as buying any stock, not necessarily dividend paying, at any time and waiting for it to go up some specified amount before selling it. (I did argue in Part One that dividends force a stock's price to go up, but this happens over a long period of time.) Strategy (b) has more right to be called a dividend capture strategy, but it too relies on capital gains in order to be successful.

With both strategies there is no guaranty that the stock will go back up to the price the trader paid for it. There is also no guaranty of how long it will take for the stock to go back up. Sometimes it never does.

<u>Dividend Capture Strategy (2)</u>

Another dividend capture strategy involves buying a stock before ex-dividend day while simultaneously selling a deep in the money call. The trick is to find a call whose delta (a measure comparing the changes in price of the option contract to the changes in price of the underlying—the closer to 1 this ratio is, the more likely the option contract is to move along with the stock. For example, if the underlying stock moves up $2 per share, an option on that stock whose delta is 1 will also move up $2 per share) is as close to 1 as possible and whose premium at least compensates you for all your transaction costs should the stock be called before ex-dividend day (exercise notices are accepted until 4:30 P.M. Central Time). The trader then sells the stock and buys back the call on or immediately after ex-dividend day. The gain in this transaction is taxed at ordinary income rates (even if you hold the stock for 61 days or longer).

Why the highest delta? The higher the delta on the call, the more likely it is that one can exit the position for the same price that one entered into it, regardless of the stock's price movement (provided it doesn't fall too sharply, in which case the call might be more expensive compared to the stock's price if it becomes in or out of the money).

Here's an example. Stock XYZ trades at $30 a share before ex-dividend day. It is supposed to pay a $0.40 per share dividend, and the pay date is a month from now. At the same time, a $5 strike call is trading for $25.20. (This is rare, but it does happen). The trader proceeds to enter a multi-leg order, usually called a "buy write" on the order screen of his brokerage account (strategy (2) is not worth doing without a muli-leg order; that is, if you have to make two separate transactions, you might lose money if the prices change too quickly). This order has two legs, one to buy the stock and one to write the call. In leg one, the trader buys 100 shares of XYZ. In leg two he sells to open 1 XYZ $5 strike call. Where he specifies the price, the trader enters a net debit of $4.8. If the order is filled, the trader will receive 100 shares of XYZ into his account and he will be short 1 call, while $480 (plus commissions) leaves his account.

The next day, ex-dividend day, if the trader's shares haven't been called, he will enter into another transaction. He will proceed to the same screen on his brokerage account, except now he will sell 100 shares of XYZ in leg one and buy to close 1 call in leg two. Where he specifies the price, he will enter a net credit of at least $4.8. If his order is filled at $4.8, he will receive $480 in his account (less commissions), he will no longer have the XYZ shares, and he won't be short the XYZ call. A month later, he will receive XYZ's dividend of $40. This, minus commissions and taxes, is his profit from the entire enterprise. If he is able to reverse his position for a higher net credit than his debit, this will add to his profit.

Note that the stock's price action does not matter unless it goes down substantially. If XYZ went up by $5 a share to $35 during the two days, the call would also go up by $5 to at least $30. If the stock went down by $6 to $24 a share, as another example, the call would go down by $6 to around $19.

The trader does not lose money unless the stock goes below his net debit. In the example above this would be XYZ going below $4.80 per share. Also, since only the net debit leaves the trader's account, the dividend can be greatly leveraged. Notice that in the example above the trader used $480 to receive a $40 dividend, less commissions. A trader using strategy (1) above would have to put $3,000 at risk (if XYZ is trading at $30 per share) to get the $40 dividend. The trader in strategy (2) can buy 600 shares for less than $3,000, and the dividend he would receive would be $240, less commissions. Now that's leverage, and very low downside risk.

It is important to mention again that calls are most likely to be exercised the day before ex-dividend day. This is why it is necessary to find a call that offers a time premium, so that if the shares are assigned early the premium compensates the trader for his transaction costs and may even leave some profit. To be worthwhile, the net debit of the transaction must be below the call's strike by at least the amount of all the broker fees the trader will incur for initiating and closing the position.

I believe (2) can more appropriately be called a dividend capture than strategy (1), as the strategy seeks to minimize all potential capital gains and losses. The main source of profit is the dividend payment. The problem with this strategy is that it can't be implemented with any consistency. It is rare that a deep in the money call will offer a premium high enough to compensate you for all the transaction costs. And it is even rarer that the deep in the money call won't be exercised shortly before ex-dividend day.

Dividend Capture Strategy (3)

Along the same lines as strategy (2), but with no leverage at all and with the use of a lot more money but almost no risk, the trader buys the dividend paying stock the day before ex-dividend day while at the same time buying an in the money put. The deeper in the money the put is, the more likely the trader will receive an advantageous price for it. Just as in (2), the trader's aim is to enter and exit the transaction for the same price. That is, the net debit for entering the transaction should equal the net credit for exiting it. The dividend received, minus transaction costs and taxes, is the profit.

Here's an example. Stock XYZ trades at $30 a share. The $50 strike put trades at $20. Before ex-dividend day, the trader enters a multi-leg transaction on his brokerage screen, typically called a "protective put." In leg one he buys 100 shares of XYZ. In leg two he buys to open 1 XYZ $50 strike put. Where he specifies the price, he enters 50. If his order is filled, $5,000 will leave his account (plus commissions) and he will receive 100 shares of XYZ and 1 XYZ 50 strike put. On ex-dividend day or after, the trader will either attempt to close out his position by doing the same multi-leg order in reverse--sell 100 shares and sell to close 1 put—for a net credit of 50 or more, or he will exercise the put, whichever is cheaper in terms of commissions, unless the net credit is sufficiently over his original debit to give a profit, in which case he will do the multi-leg order.

For example, if the trader can sell the shares and put for a credit of 51, he will earn an extra $1 per share of profit (less commissions). In the worst case, the trader will exercise his put. That is, in the worst case, he will receive the $5,000 back into his account, no matter what the stock does. On the pay date, he will receive the dividend, which will be his profit, less commissions and taxes.

Note that here there are no adverse stock moves. Suppose XYZ goes to $0. The trader can exercise his put and get his $5,000 back. Or suppose the stock goes above $50 a share. The trader can still get his $5,000 back, but if the stock rises enough, he can get more. For example, suppose XYZ goes to $50 per share. The trader will now be making $20 per share on the stock. If the put is worth more than $0, which it should be since it's at the money, the trader will receive more than $5,000 in closing out his position by selling the stock and put. As another example, suppose XYZ goes up to $100 per share. The trader will make $70 per share on the stock, but the put will probably be worthless. Still, he'll make $5,000 by selling the stock. That is, he'll receive $10,000 for selling XYZ, resulting in a $5,000 profit.

As this dividend capture strategy is a no lose situation (except if the stock doesn't pay the dividend, in which case the most one can lose is commission costs and put premium, if any), in the money put sellers have long factored in the dividend. It is rare when one can find a stock trading at $30 with a $50 strike put trading at $20. This happens occasionally, but more likely than not the put will have some time value.

Thus, strategy (3) is only worthwhile if the dividend payment will cover all commission costs and taxes and the difference between the strike price, the stock price, and what the put is trading for. That is, suppose XYZ pays a $0.40 dividend and trades at $30 before ex-dividend day while the $50 strike put trades at $20.10. The transaction will cost the trader $50.10 per share plus commissions. Let's say total commissions, for entering and exiting the position, equal $0.10 per share. That means that the entire transaction will cost the trader $50.20 per share, or, if this is for 100 shares, $5,020. Implementing strategy (3) in this case would still be worthwhile, because the dividend is $0.40 per share. Here, the trader's profit would be $0.20 per share, or $20. This does not factor in taxes, which would be based on the entire $0.40 dividend and which would be charged at the ordinary income rate regardless of when the position is exited.

If there is still a profit after taxes and commissions, and the investor has a lot of money to work with, he can potentially make a consistent and practically risk free return on the same sum of money every day. That is, the transaction is entered into on Monday before XYZ goes ex-dividend on Tuesday. The position is closed on Tuesday, and the proceeds are immediately invested into ABC, which is going ex-div on Wednesday. The ABC position is closed on Wednesday and the investor immediately invests the proceeds into ZYX, which goes ex-dividend on Thursday. And so on. It is hard work, but it may be very worthwhile, for there is practically no risk.

Note that in strategy (3), it is OK if the net debit exceeds the strike price, as long as the dividend more than covers the difference and all the costs. Unlike in strategy (2), there is no risk for the investor of losing his shares. This is because as the option holder he controls whether and when the option is exercised, so long as the option's expiration date is after ex-dividend day.

Just like strategy (2), the profit for strategy (3) comes from the dividend minus transaction costs. It is therefore more appropriately called a dividend capture strategy than (1). For tax reasons, strategies (2) and (3) are best implemented in a tax sheltered account. Most broker IRA accounts allow covered calls. Protective puts should also be allowed, but each broker has its own policies. (Note that because retirement accounts don't allow margin, you would be unable to buy and sell with the same money daily. For example, say you have a total of $10,000 in your account. You use the sum to buy stock. Now you have $10,000 worth of shares. You can sell these shares and use the proceeds to buy another stock. If you sell this second stock before settlement (three business days after you buy it), this will count as a round trip or "free-riding." Your broker will warn you, if it even lets you make the sale before settlement. If you make another round trip, your broker will most likely freeze your account. Were you to do this in a taxable account, you would be warned after the first round trip. After the second, you'd be classified a day trader and would be required to open a margin account.)

While the strategy is almost risk-less, like (2) it is hard to implement consistently. Commission costs and taxes will likely make it impossible for individual investors to profit from it.

Variations on the Above Three Strategies
Dividend Capture Strategy (4)

One variation on strategy (1) is take advantage of the difference between a deep in the money call's price plus the strike and the price at which the stock is trading. Typically, assuming there are no commission expenses, it is cheaper to buy a deep in the money call and exercise it than it is to buy the stock. For example, Verizon (VZ) is trading at $30.62 as I'm writing, while the January 2010 5 strike call has a bid of

25.45 and an ask of 26. If I can buy the call for under 25.62, it is more worthwhile for me to do so and immediately exercise the call than it would be to buy the stock, if we assume there are no commissions. Suppose I am able to buy the call for 25.50. When I exercise it, an additional $5 per share exits my account, and I end up buying the stock for $30.50 per share, $0.12 lower. Doing this before ex-dividend day offers a little protection over strategy (1). The person implementing this strategy, just as in (1), hopes the stock will go up by at least the amount of the dividend on or soon after ex-dividend day. The profit will be the few cents earned on the call along with the dividend payment to be received, minus transaction costs and taxes.

Dividend Capture Strategy (5)

Another variation on strategy (1) is to combine (4) with (2). That is, it involves buying deep in the money calls and exercising them at the same time as selling other or same strike in the money calls and hoping these are not exercised. While the optimal time to exercise a call option early is the day before ex-dividend day, some number of calls are not exercised. This may be because the call holder forgets, doesn't have enough money to do so, or doesn't think it's worthwhile.

Just as in (4), institutional investors frequently engage in this activity. Commissions usually make this strategy cost prohibitive for individual investors.

Dividend Capture Strategies (6) and (7)

Do the same thing as strategies (2) and (3), but use margin to get more shares than you could otherwise afford by using cash only. Profit is increased by the extra dividends received, minus the margin borrowing rate and the extra commissions for selling or buying more option contracts.

* * *

You may be tempted to buy a closed end fund that specializes in dividend capture strategies. There might be some that excel, but I haven't found any yet. For the most part they look like scams. They return your own money to you in the form of dividends as their net asset value approaches zero. Be careful!

Part Seven - Building Your Portfolio

Most investors try to beat the market. Most of them fail. If you want to beat most investors, invest in the market. That is, determine your asset allocation (I discuss this in the chapter on diversification), and pick the index funds that track these assets most cheaply. Decide whether you want to reinvest the dividends or not. That's it, you're done. After all, your money should be working for you and not the other way around. Use your spare time to do something you enjoy or to work a second job.

Although it's probably the most prudent thing to do for most people, most of us are not index investors (you wouldn't be reading this book if you were). We try to find individual stocks. We read articles and listen to pundits on TV as they talk about PE ratios and so on. It's not that we're trying to work for our money instead of letting it work for us. We actually enjoy doing research. The websites we frequent the most are finance related. We read the business section of the newspaper and if we're home during the day our TV is probably tuned to a channel with a ticker running across the bottom. The stock market is somewhere between a second job and a hobby for us. The remaining chapters of this book are for us. In them I will try to persuade you that you shouldn't do much research. Let the indexes do the work for you even when you are buying individual securities.

Chapter 28 - Mostly Useless Stock Metrics

For all of the ratios in this and the next chapter, consult more than one source for every stock you evaluate. You will find that different websites and research services will provide you with different numbers for the same ratios. This can be the result of error, different time periods being used, and other factors. When you are in doubt, go straight to the source: the investor relations website of the company you are evaluating. They don't usually provide you with the ratios, but you can figure these out yourself by plugging in the company's numbers.

Among the popular financial research services, my favorites are Yahoo! Finance and Morningstar. They both have similar information, though I think Morningstar's is more thorough. For example, it lists what bonds a corporation has outstanding, what they currently yield, and when they mature. Not only can this help you find investments, it can also tell you how much the corporation needs to service its debt, and help you identify potential trouble spots. Some brokers have very good research sections. Fidelity has the most information among the brokers I've used (this doesn't mean that I recommend them).

Most corporate statistics and valuation ratios are useless because they tell you very little, if anything, about the future. And they tell you even less about how investors will react. Management can change, the company might launch a new product line, the government might raise taxes, compliance and raw materials costs might rise, a product might have a major design flaw, competitors might become stronger, customers' needs and preferences might change, and so on. Therefore, I separate them into "mostly useless" and "less useless" categories. The mostly useless statistics, perhaps unsurprisingly, are the ones the financial media mentions most. The less useless statistics have some worth because they can alert you to potential trouble at a company and when it might be a better time to buy or sell, relatively speaking. But for the most part, I think the statistics are a waste of time and are a crutch for people with little to say. Some of them are outlined in this and the next chapter, but feel free to skip these. The most important ratio is the dividend yield.

The PE Ratio

Many stock market participants favor the PE ratio when trying to figure out a good time to buy a stock. Pundits talk about stocks' PE ratios breathlessly when they're pumping and dumping on the financial news channels. "Its PE is only 12," they say. "It's a buy right here! Buy buy buy!"

Although the PE gives you some information about a stock, I think it's pretty much useless. Standing for "price to earnings," the PE ratio is a stock's share price divided by its earnings per share. We find earnings per share by taking the company's earnings and dividing them by the number of the company's shares outstanding. For example, if a company earns $3 million and has 1 million shares outstanding, its earnings per share will be $3. And if the company's stock trades at $30 per share, its PE will be 10 ($30 divided by $3).

People tend to think, and are encouraged to think by the financial media, that stocks are cheap when PE ratios are low, and expensive when PE ratios are high. Others argue that the PE ratio by itself does not matter. The important thing is growth. If the PE is below the company's earnings growth rate, they say, the stock is cheap. If it's above the growth rate, it is a sign that the stock is expensive. I think the only useful information a PE ratio shows is what portion of the stock price a company's earnings are.

Suppose company XYZ trades at $80 per share and has earned in the last 12 months $4 per share. It has a PE of 20. We also know that earnings account for $1/20^{th}$ the company's share price. (This is called the "earnings yield." One way to think about it is that it shows what the dividend yield would be if the company paid out all its earnings.) That's it. Is it cheap? Is it expensive? Who knows. PE ratios often expand and shrink because of things that have nothing to do with the company. When the future looks bright and there's not a worry in sight, people put more money into the stock market. PE ratios expand. XYZ can still be earning $4 a share, but if buyers of its stock outnumber its sellers, the share price and therefore the PE will go up. Say the stock now trades at $100 a share. Its PE will be 25. Then suppose the future doesn't look as bright. Bad times are coming. Instead of happy news, it's all doom and gloom on the financial channels. Stock market participants become more risk averse and are no longer willing to pay $100 a share. The stock falls and eventually stabilizes at $40. It still earns $4 a share. Its PE is now 10.

Nothing has happened to the company's day to day business. It's the same as it was when it traded at $80 and $100. It is the share buyers' attitudes that have changed. They are no longer willing to pay $20 or $25 for every dollar the company earns. Now they'll pay only 10. If the PE stays at 10, XYZ will have to double its earnings to trade back at $80.

One may argue that this is an example of why PE ratios are useful: PEs of 20 and 25 were too high. XYZ was too expensive when it sported these figures. Now that the PE is 10, the stock may be cheap. Okay, great. But how do you know when a PE is too high? A stock with a PE of 100 can easily have a PE of 200 in a few months. And a stock with a PE of 10 can easily have a PE of 5 in the future (its share price doesn't even have to fall—earnings just have to go up). History has shown that a seemingly high PE can go ever higher, irrespective of the company's earnings growth, and a seemingly low PE can go lower, also irrespective of the company's growth. Share prices also seem detached from the notion that a high PE makes a stock expensive. In 2002, for example, Apple traded with a PE over 270. Was it expensive at the time? Maybe, but its share price is 15 times higher at the time of writing.

To add a little more detail, the PE depends on three things: share price, earnings, and the number of shares outstanding. For example, if the share count decreases while earnings stay the same, earnings per share will rise. If the share price remains the same, the PE will fall. If the number of shares rises while earnings stay the same, earnings per share will fall. If the share price stays the same, the PE will rise. Theoretically, the more shares there are, the less valuable each one is. The less shares there are, the more valuable each one is. If the number of shares stay the same, the PE will change when the share price and earnings change. If the share price stays the same and earnings fall, the PE will rise. If the share price stays the same and earnings rise, the PE will fall. If earnings per share stay the same while the share price falls, the PE will fall. And if earnings per share stay the same while the share price rises, the PE rises.

Phew! As mentioned, people normally assume that a low PE indicates that a stock is undervalued while a high PE indicates that a stock is overvalued. But a PE can be low (and often is!) when a company's earnings are shrinking. For example, this can happen when a company buys back its own stock. Suppose the company earned $12 million last year and earns $6 million this year. Its earnings growth is negative. If the stock price stays the same, the PE will double. But if the company buys back half its shares, the PE ratio will also stay the same. And if the company buys back more than half its shares, the PE ratio will shrink. But this will certainly not mean that the stock is a good value (it might be, if the earnings slip is a slight hiccup, but probably not).

The above is about the PE ratio that we see daily in stock tables and what financial pundits usually talk about when they make their cases for buying and selling. The earnings part of the ratio is usually over the last twelve months. As such it is called the trailing twelve months PE or ttm PE for short. You will notice that most stock quoting services display "ttm" in their PE statistics. (If you see "mrq," this stands for most recent quarter.)

There's also something called the "forward PE." This is the same as the ttm PE ratio, except that instead of taking earnings over the last 12 months as its denominator, the forward ratio uses the projected earnings for the next 12 months. So, suppose that XYZ is once again trading at $80 per share. The average analyst estimate is that in the next year the company will earn $8 per share. That makes XYZ's forward PE 10. Pundits might scream that the stock is cheap, given that it historically trades at a PE of 20. Buy buy buy!

But there's a funny thing about analysts. They tend to be overly optimistic during good times and overly pessimistic during bad times. This usually results in stocks' forward PEs being low just before the market tops out and stocks fall, and being high just before the market puts in a bottom and stocks rebound. What the forward PE tells you is what analysts think. If it's below the trailing 12 month PE, analysts think earnings will grow. And the lower it is, the more optimistic they are. If the forward PE is higher than the trailing 12 month PE, analysts think that earnings will shrink. The higher the forward PE, the more pessimistic analysts are. That's about it. For these reasons I think the PE ratio is mostly useless.

Price to Sales (Revenue) Ratio

The price to sales ratio (or P/S) is calculated by taking the share price and dividing it by sales per share over the past year. Sales, also called revenue, is the amount of money a company brings in. Suppose a company sells 10 million widgets for $3 each. Its revenue is $30 million. If the company has 6 million shares outstanding, its sales per share is $5 ($30 million divided by 6 million).

Now let's say that the company's shares trade at $100. Since its sales are $5 per share, that means the company's price to sales ratio is 20 ($100 divided by $5).

The ratio is used to compare a stock's value to that of other firms, its industry, the broader market, and to its own past. The higher the ratio, the more investors are paying for the company's sales. The lower the ratio, the less they are paying for the company's shares. Typically, the higher the ratio, the more expensive a stock is. The lower the ratio, the cheaper it is.

Many investors favor the price to sales ratio over the PE because it is not as prone to accounting tricks. Earnings can be artificially lower or higher, depending on the accounting method and management's intentions. Revenue, on the other hand, is just the money the company takes in. It's harder to fake that. Moreover, a sharp drop or rise in earnings can be attributed to one time events, like a court award or judgment, an acquisition, and other things that aren't part of the company's normal business. But when sales rise or fall, this is usually due to the company selling more or less of its product.

The price to sales ratio can therefore be a more reliable gauge of a stock's value than the PE.

Price to Book Ratio

The price to book ratio can be a better indicator of whether the company's stock is selling at a discount or premium. It is calculated by dividing the share price by the last quarterly book value per share. The book value per share is the company's book value divided by the number of shares outstanding. So, if the book value is $7 billion and the company has 1.5 billion shares outstanding, the book value per share is $4.67. The book value is derived by subtracting the company's intangible assets (e.g., patents, copyrights, trademarks, goodwill) and liabilities (debts, bills) from its total assets. So, suppose all of a company's assets (copyrights, patents, buildings, computers, desks, chairs, etc) total $10 million. Let's say the company's intangible assets are worth $2 million and that the company has $5 million in debt. Its book value will be $3 million ($10 million in total minus $2 intangible assets minus $5 million in debt).

Note that the book value can be negative (as when the company's debt is greater than its tangible assets, which might be a bad sign; on the other hand, a company's book value can be negative because it owns a very valuable copyright and patent portfolio that dwarfs its tangible assets like buildings and cash). The book value per share is, in simplest terms, what shareholders would receive if the company stopped its business and liquidated all its assets.

Generally speaking, you are getting a great deal on a company's stock if you're buying it at a price to book ratio of 1 or less (1 or less means that you are buying the shares at or below book value). This is like buying a CEF for a discount. Also, generally speaking, if you are buying shares at a price to book above 1, you may be paying too much. As with everything, there are many caveats. For example, a low price to book ratio might mean that there is something terribly wrong with the company.

Decades ago, it was not a rare occurrence if a stock traded at or even below its book value. At the time of writing, however, most healthy stocks trade above 1. Procter & Gamble's (PG) shares, for example, trade at a price to book of 2.7.

Unless the price to book is significantly above or below 1, the ratio does not really tell you much by itself. You should look at the company's earnings growth and return on equity (a measure of how much profit the company generates from the money it received from shareholders). For example, a high price to book ratio combined with a low return on equity can mean that the stock is too expensive. To get a better picture, be sure to compare the company to its competitors. The entire industry might be over or undervalued, but by comparing the companies within it, you can get a sense of which companies are the industry leaders.

Cash per share

Related to the book value measurements that pundits sometimes scream about is the cash per share figure. As its name suggests, cash per share is calculated by taking the company's total cash and dividing it by its shares outstanding. If a company has $5 billion in cash and 2 billion shares outstanding, it has $2.50 in cash per share. Pundits often say that a stock is a screaming buy when cash per share is a significant portion of the share price. They evaluate the share price as follows.

Suppose a stock trades for $60 a share and has $28 in cash per share sitting in its treasury. Pundits and analysts often subtract the cash per share from the share price. In this example, they would take $28 away from $60, saying something like, "the stock is really trading for $32." They will then calculate the PE ratio based on this share price.

Theoretically speaking, it is much better for a company to have lots of cash in its bank account than very little. Practically, however, lots of cash on the company's books can mean a few things. First, it can reveal that the company has not found any worthwhile projects to invest in. If so, growth may slow in the future. Second, it can reveal the company's attitude toward shareholders. Why is it hoarding the money instead of giving it to its owners? The directors may not be very good stewards. Third, as discussed in the first two chapters, when a company has a lot of cash it is more likely to overspend on acquisitions, wasteful projects, and buying its shares back at inflated prices. Inefficiencies are also more likely to go unaddressed. Employees may be sitting around with nothing to do. Expensive employee perks and programs might be started that will later cripple the company. Innovation may stall. Or the economy might simply go downhill.

These things might not happen, but they are more likely to occur when a company is flush with cash rather than when it is trying to save every penny. Lots of cash on the books (especially with little or no debt) means that the company has been very successful in the past. Whether it can continue this success is another matter. For example, in 1995 Chrysler's cash per share net of debt amounted to 30% of its share price. Pundits screamed that you could buy the company for a 30% discount. A decade and a half later the company needed to be bailed out by the government.

It is not unheard of to find a company that has more cash in its bank account than its market capitalization. That is, sometimes companies have more cash net of debt per share than their share price. Awesome buy, no? You're buying it at a discount, aren't you? It depends, but usually the answer is no. When a company trades so low in proportion to its cash, it means investors think it has no future prospects. Most of the time they're right. If they're not, some bigger company swoops in and attempts to make an acquisition. Such a move would usually raise the share price above the cash and other asset value (because shareholders will demand more money to let go of their shares). If the company to be acquired has no growth prospects, therefore, it will not be worth it for the bigger company to buy it at a premium. So, what ends up happening is the stock sits there and decreases in price as the company runs through its cash to fund operations (basically having the executives come in to work to do nothing). It is eventually bought for a much lower price or simply goes out of business. Adaptec

(ADPT), since transformed into Steel Excel Inc (SXCL), is one example. My dad was a shareholder from the company's glory days of the tech bubble in the late 1990s. He would lament practically every time he looked at his statements about why the company hadn't been bought out by someone. "Look at all that cash," he would say. Yeah, but what will they do in the future? After the company became Steel Excel, my dad exclaimed, "they misspelled steal!" So much for having lots of cash and trading below book value. Once again, having a lot of cash in relation to share price is an indication of past success. No one knows the future.

Chapter 29 - Less Useless Stock Metrics
Interest Coverage Ratio

The interest coverage ratio is a firm's earnings before taxes and interest divided by the firm's interest expenses over the same period. Suppose last quarter the company paid $6 million in interest and earned $30 million before interest and taxes. The company's interest coverage ratio is 5 ($30 million in earnings divided by $6 million in interest).

The ratio gives you a quick look at how easy or hard it is for the company to pay interest on its debt. If the ratio is 1, that means the company's earnings are just enough to cover interest payments. If the ratio is below 1, the company's earnings do not cover interest payments. That means it has to borrow or dip into its cash reserves (if it has any) to pay its creditors. Generally, it is a red flag if the interest coverage ratio is below 1.5—if the company pays dividends, they may be cut or suspended. In general, therefore, the higher the interest coverage, the better.

The interest coverage changes over time because it depends on the firm's earnings, the size of its debt, and the interest rate. A rise in earnings or a reduction of debt or interest will increase the ratio. A reduction of earnings or an increase in debt or interest will lower the ratio. Firms with no debt do not have an interest coverage ratio (because you cannot divide by zero).

Look at what the firm's interest coverage is over time. How low does it go during recessions? How high does it go during boom periods? The interest coverage ratio can tell you lots of things about a company, including how well it manages debt, how well management plans ahead, and how different economic conditions and interest rate environments affect the company—is its businesses stable or volatile? Comparing the company's interest coverage over time to its industry will shed further light on these questions. You cannot know the future, but how a company did in the past can be a good indication of what to expect.

Debt to Equity

The debt to equity ratio is the company's liabilities divided by shareholders' equity. (Shareholder's equity is calculated by subtracting a company's total liabilities from its total assets.) So, for example, if a company owes $3 billion and its shareholders' equity is $7 billion, its debt to equity ratio is about 43%.

The higher this figure is, the more indebted a company is. This can be a bad sign, but isn't necessarily so. What is considered high depends on the company's business. Thus, the ratio should be put in context by comparing a company with its peers instead of with other, random companies or the broader market average. When comparing the debt to equity ratios of one or more companies, also make sure that the debt on their books is calculated in the same way. For example, short term debt might not count toward one of the companies' total liabilities while it does for the other —this would tend to skew your comparison's results.

One liability that is often not listed on the balance sheet but has killed many companies is the employee pension fund (also known as a defined benefit pension plan). With these plans employees know what their future benefits will be, and it is up to the company to fund this amount. This is entirely different from the 401k. Pension fund numbers are found in a maze of footnotes in the form 10-K in companies' annual reports. Low interest rates and poor market returns sometimes make it necessary for companies to put extra cash into their employees' pension plan. For ex-

261

ample, in 2009 Lockheed Martin injected $1 billion into its pension fund, taking an earnings hit and suffering a decline in share price. As of 2011, the company's pension fund still faced a shortfall of over $14 billion. Pension funds are one of the greatest long term threats not only to dividend payments but also to company survival. At the time of writing, the following major companies, besides Lockheed, had significant shortfalls (over 25% of their market cap) in their pension funds: Ford (F), Goodyear Tire & Rubber (GT), US Steel (X), Sears (SHLD), Raytheon (RTN), Whirlpool (WHR), and Alcoa (AA).

Earnings Growth

Earnings growth is the measure of a company's change in earnings from one time period to another. For example, if the company earned $10 million last month and earned $12 million this month, its earnings grew by 20%. If, however, the company earned $10 million last month and earned $8 million this month, its month to month earnings fell by 20%.

A company's most recent earnings are compared to its earnings in the past. The current quarter is compared to last quarter, the current quarter is compared to the same quarter last year, the current year is compared to the previous year, or the previous number of years. Generally, earnings are growing if the earnings growth number is positive. And earnings are shrinking if the number is negative. This may seem obvious, but it might not be, depending on what you're looking at. As already mentioned, earnings are subject to accounting tricks and one time gains or expenses. Whenever possible, try to take out the one time events for a better comparison, and always remember that earnings can be restated. Moreover, if you are looking at earnings per share, be sure to check the share count. A decreasing share count will make earnings look higher than they are. That is to say, the company may be making less money this year than last, but because it has bought back shares, earnings per share have increased.

It's usually better to compare the current quarter not to the three months immediately prior to it, but to the same period in a prior year. For example, instead of comparing the earnings from January, February, and March to October, November, and December, compare them to January, February, and March of last year. This smooths out seasonal differences. For example, sales from October, November, and December might be much higher than other quarters because of the holiday shopping season. Also note that some quarters are longer than others. For example, the current quarter might have one or two days less than the same quarter last year.

Sales or Revenue Growth

This ratio is just like earnings growth, but instead of earnings, sales are measured. Again, it is best to evaluate similar time periods (e.g., current quarter to same quarter last year) to smooth out seasonal differences.

When looking at a company's sales growth, remember that there are two ways to increase this ratio. The most obvious is to sell more widgets. The perhaps less obvious way is to sell the same number of widgets (or even lower) as before, but for a higher price. For example, suppose last year the company sold 10 million widgets for $3 apiece. Its sales were $30 million. This year, it sells 12 million widgets for $3 each. Its sales are $36 million. Sales grow, year over year, by 20%.

Now suppose that this year the company sells 10 million widgets for $3.60 apiece. Its sales are also $36 million, and therefore grow by 20%.

As a last example, suppose that this year the company sells 8 million widgets for $4.50 each. Its sales are $36 million and therefore grow by 20%.

It depends, of course, but I would say that these three scenarios are arranged from best to worst. Even though the company brings in the same amount of money, it has no unit sales growth in the second example and a unit sales decline in the third. As long as prices stay about the same, it is generally better that the company sells more widgets than less.

So, the sales growth figure does not give you the entire picture. If growth is negative, you know there is a problem. But there may also be a problem even when sales growth is positive. Be sure to examine unit sales (the number of individual items that the company sold) if this figure is available.

For those companies that have physical retail locations (restaurants, stores, etc), in addition to sales growth, you should also look at "same store sales growth." This is because such companies can grow sales in two ways: revenues can increase in the stores they already have, and they can open up new stores. As long as revenues stay the same at all the old stores, new stores will make revenues grow (as long as they generate at least one new sale). Therefore, the more important number is same store sales growth. If this is declining, the company has a problem. Don't look at sales figures from a one or two year period. This is just noise. Sales figures over a longer period, on the other hand, can make a trend.

Return on Equity

Return on equity (ROE) is a measure of a company's profitability. It shows how much profit a company generated with the money shareholders invested. The ratio is the company's net earnings (after preferred share dividends are paid out) divided by shareholder's equity. Shareholder's equity is derived by taking the company's total assets and subtracting its total liabilities.

So, for example, if the company's net income is $20 million and its shareholder's equity is $100 million, the company's return on equity is 20% ($20 million is 20% of $100 million). As this figure may change from period to period, it should be compared with periods in the past. A steadily rising figure may indicate that the company is improving its efficiency. A shrinking number might indicate that the company is becoming less efficient, or is not using its investors' money in the most productive way.

Return on Assets

Return on Assets (ROA) is similar to return on equity, except that it does not subtract the company's liabilities. The ratio is calculated by dividing net income by total assets. So, if net income is $20 million and total assets are $150 million, the company's return on assets is 13.33% ($20 million divided by $150 million and expressed as a percentage).

Thus, return on assets indicates how efficient the company is in using its total assets. For this reason, this ratio is also known as return on investment. This is because a company can earn money on its liabilities as well as its assets (e.g., if it borrows money and generates a higher return than it pays in interest, which is the goal of borrowing).

265

The return on assets tells you how well the firm converts its funds (borrowed and not) into income.

As with return on equity, the higher the return on assets, the better. The goal of management, after all, is to make as much money from each dollar invested as possible while limiting risk to an acceptable level. That is, it's far easier to make $5 million if you invest $100 million than it is to make $5 million when you invest $20 million. The manager that makes $5 million on a $20 million investment will have a return on assets of 25%. The manager that makes $5 million on $100 million, however, will have a return on assets of only 5%. The manager with the higher return on assets is probably doing a better job.

A company's return on assets depend on the business in which it is engaged. Supermarket chains tend to have a different ROA from utilities, utilities tend to have a different ROA from REITs, and so on. It is therefore important to compare a company's return on assets to its competitors' and peers' rather than to that of companies not in its industry.

Dividend Payout Ratio

The dividend payout ratio is the annual dividend per share divided by the company's earnings per share. Suppose the annual dividend is $3 per share and over the course of the year the company earned $12 per share. The firm's dividend payout ratio is 0.25, or 25% ($3 divided by $12).

Generally speaking, the lower the payout ratio, the more easily the company can pay its dividend, and the more likely it is that the dividend will increase in the future. Any ratio below 1 means that the company makes more money than it pays out in dividends. A ratio above one means that the company makes less money than it pays out in dividends. Typically, a ratio above 0.8 or 80% is a warning sign (but it does depend on the industry) and a ratio above 1 cannot be sustained. A ratio above 1 or 100% means that the company is borrowing or dipping into cash to pay the dividend. Stay away from common stocks that have ratios near or above 1. Their dividends will most likely be cut or eliminated.

Note that there are exceptions. As discussed earlier, REITs must pay out at least 90% of their taxable earnings through dividends. Moreover, companies that have lots of infrastructure, equipment, and other tangible assets that can be depreciated will often have payout ratios greater than one. Companies that fall into this category include MLPs, REITs, telecoms, and utilities. For these firms the payout ratio displayed on the popular financial websites and in magazines may be misleading because of depreciation and other accounting items (the PE too—if you ever read an article where PEs or payout ratios are used to compare MLPs with each other or other stocks, be aware that the writer does not understand what he's writing about).

To calculate the dividend payout ratio of such companies, you should look at the payout ratio from free cash flow instead. That is, instead of dividing the dividend per share by earnings per share, divide the dividend per share by free cash flow per share. (Free cash flow, which is usually listed in the company's statistics, is the cash that the company produces from its operations minus the money the company uses to upgrade, maintain, or acquire its physical assets.) For example, a dividend payout ratio based on earnings might be well over 100%, but it can be 60% on a free cash flow basis. This would indicate that the dividend is probably safe.

Look at the company's dividend payout ratio in relation to the dividend rate over time. If the dividends are growing, is it because the company is earning more (i.e., the ratio stays about the same) or is it because the company is just paying out more of its profits (the ratio increases)? The latter kind of dividend growth is unsustainable. Also, watch out for one time items. Earnings can jump or plummet because of law suit judgments, asset sales or acquisitions, and so on. Even in the normal course of business earnings are bumpy. They are not "sticky" like dividends. Looking at the ratio over time will smooth out these fluctuations and provide you with a better picture of the company's ability to pay dividends.

Finally, compare the company with its industry. Is its payout ratio lower or higher? Is management stingy with its dividend policy? Is management not prudent enough? But it bears repeating that no one knows the future. Companies with low payout ratios may suffer a decline and suspend their dividends. Companies with high payout ratios may continue paying and raising their dividends forever.

<u>Dividend Growth Rate</u>

The dividend growth rate is the rate at which the company's dividend payout grows over time. It is usually expressed as a percentage, and can be measured over any period you want. A positive number means that the dividend has been raised, a negative number means that the dividend has been reduced, and zero means that there have been no change in the dividend. A history of dividend growth is a good indication that the company will continue raising its dividend. It usually means that the company has a solid, profitable business. Some companies have been raising their dividends every year for decades.

Not all companies that raise their dividends every year do so at the same rate. Financial websites, as well as the investor relations sites of the companies usually have a history of dividend payments. To determine the rate of dividend growth, simply take the most current annual dividend and subtract a prior year's dividend from it. Then, divide your result by the prior year's dividend.

For example, suppose that this year a stock pays $2 per share in dividends and that last year it paid $1.75. We take the difference, which is $0.25, and divide it by $1.75. The result is 0.1429. Expressed as a percentage, that's 14.29%. In other words, the dividend grew by 14.29% from last year to this year.

The dividend growth rate is used in a popular method of valuing stocks called the Dividend Discount Model. Investors use the model to figure out what a stock is worth by taking the predicted dividends and discounting them to present value. It is based around the idea that a dollar today is worth more than a dollar a year, two years, a decade, a century, etc from now. That is because a dollar today has more buying power than a dollar in the future (if we factor in inflation). A dollar today is also worth more than a dollar in the future because a dollar today can be earning interest. Hence, we use a discount rate to estimate how much the dollar today will be worth in the future.

For example, suppose you'll be given $100 a year from now. Let's say you can safely earn 10% interest on the money you have now. If we use this 10% discount rate, the $100 a year from today is worth $90.91 to you today ($100 divided by [1 plus 0.10]). That's because if you had $90.91 and received 10% interest on it ($9.09), you would have $100 in total in a year's time. So, receiving $100 in a year's time, if you can safely invest your money today at 10%, is the same as receiving $90.91 today.

In the dividend discount model, we discount the dividends we expect to receive in the future to their value today. According to the formula, the value of a stock is equal to the dividends we expect per share divided by the difference between the discount rate and the dividend growth rate. If the price of the stock is below what you calculate by using the formula, that means the stock is under-valued. If the stock trades above your calculated future price, the stock is overvalued, and if it's the around the same price as your calculation, the stock is fairly priced. Then again, it could be that your estimates, either for the dividends you expect to receive, the discount rate, the dividend growth rate, or some combination of these are wrong.

If you would like to use the dividend discount model, there are a number of handy calculators available online. The best I've been able to find are at Moneychimp <http://www.moneychimp.com>.

One of the trickiest things about discount models is figuring out the expected dividend. While past dividend growth gives you some idea of how the dividend will grow in the future, the figure can be unreliable for a number of reasons. First, the dividend may grow more in the future because past growth has been hampered by a sluggish economy or inefficiencies in the company. Second, the dividend may grow at a slower rate in the future because the company is now larger and can't maintain its growth rate, there may be a recession or depression, and so on. The typical way investors get around this problem is by consulting the company's average return on equity and using this figure as a factor in their dividend growth projections.

Another tricky thing about discount models is choosing the discount rate. That is, the rate at which money can be safely invested. Do you pick a number out of thin air? Do you look at the rate of bank certificates of deposit or savings accounts? Most investors choose the 10 year Treasury yield, which currently yields below the rate of inflation.

Remember that no one knows the future. The past can be a guide, but that's all it is. Things can change suddenly and drastically for the better or worse. A stock that the model shows to be undervalued is suddenly overvalued (without a change in its share price or business prospects) because interest rates have changed, for example. It is therefore important to recalculate and reevaluate your portfolio as you receive new information.

If you are interested in obtaining lists of companies that have raised their dividends in the preceding years, there are two popular indexes (both of which have outperformed the broader market). The S&P High Dividend Aristocrats Index consists of companies in the S&P 1500 that have raised their dividends every year for at least 25 years in a row (a few companies, like Procter & Gamble, have raised their dividends every year for over 50 years). As of writing, the index includes 60 companies. If you're interested in owning them all or cherry picking a few for further research, the SPDR S&P Dividend ETF (SDY) is a good place to look.

Another index is the Mergent Dividend Achievers Select Index. It includes companies that have raised their dividends every year for at least 10 years in a row. At the time of writing, the index includes 127 companies. If you want

to buy the entire thing or cherry pick, check out the Vanguard Dividend Appreciation ETF (VIG) or the Power-
Shares Dividend Achievers ETF (PFM). Another place to
find lists of dividend raisers is at The Dynamic Dividend
<http://dynamicdividend.com/dividend-dynamos/>.

Dividend Yield

Although dividends tend to support a company's stock
price, investor optimism and pessimism can have an effect
on a stock's dividend yield. A stock's price can shoot up
during an optimistic period, making its yield go lower. A
stock's price can go down during a pessimistic period, making the yield go higher.

In terms of potential capital gains, the dividend yield
can be a good indicator of whether a stock's price is under
or overvalued. It can also provide a warning sign that there
is something wrong with the business and that the dividend
is not sustainable (if it is extremely high). Looking at the
stock's historical dividend yield can quickly tell you if the
stock has always been a high yielder or if investors think
that there is something amiss. If the stock's dividend yield
is not within its historic norms, investigate further as to
why. Is it experiencing trouble? Are the company's competitors also sporting dividend yields that are higher than normal? Has the stock market in general gone down?

If the dividend yield is higher than normal and you can
find nothing wrong with the company (this includes up-
coming changes in laws), the stock is undervalued and is
therefore a good buy. (You have probably seen financial
news articles about "the dogs of the Dow" every January.
The strategy is to buy the top 10 (or 5, or 4) yielding stocks
in the Dow Jones Industrial Average at the start of the year.
At the end of the year, dump these and buy the stocks that

yield the most at the time. It might be the same ones, but a few or most might be different. The idea is that the highest yielding Dow stocks are undervalued, and are therefore good buys. Although it has many detractors, according to DogsoftheDow.com the strategy has given investors a 17.7% average annual return since 1973, compared to 11.9% for the Dow Jones Industrial Average over the same time period.)

If you find something wrong with the company—the reason why its stock has fallen—determine whether this is a temporary setback or a fundamental problem. Will the company's future earnings sustain future dividends? Or will the dividend be cut? This is usually hard to figure out and is more akin to speculation than investing. Buying such a company's stock should be done with extreme caution. You may want to consider incremental buying (dividing the amount you want to invest into several portions and buying the shares over a period of time instead of all at once) and/or married puts.

Different Kinds of Yields

Dividend yields displayed by stock quoting services can often be misleading. There are a few things to watch out for. As mentioned in Part One, the yield that most stock quoting services list is based on the total of the distributions the stock or fund has made in the previous 12 months. This is called the trailing 12 month yield, often written as "ttm yield."

Sometimes, however, the yield displayed is based on the most recent distribution. It's usually called "most recent quarter" (mrq) or "most recent distribution" (mrd). For example, suppose a stock in the last quarter paid a dividend of $0.30. A stock quoting service might display a dividend rate of $1.20 per year and use this number to calculate the yield. The $1.20 is derived by annualizing the $0.30. That is, the $0.30 is multiplied by four because there are four quarters in a year. As another example, suppose an ETF pays a monthly distribution of $0.20. The most recent distribution is annualized (that is, it's multiplied by 12 because there are 12 months in the year) to calculate the yield. Since this figure annualizes the most recent distribution, it can be very misleading. For example, the stock or fund might not pay any more dividends after this, it might pay dividends of different amounts in the future, both greater and smaller, and so on.

There is also what is called the SEC yield. This is most useful when looking at funds. The SEC yield is based on the most recent 30 day period and is supposed to show the net dividends and interest earned by the fund. Since this figure is mandatory for all bond funds, it can be helpful if you want to compare two funds. It is not very helpful for much else, however, because most bond funds, as mentioned, don't hold their bonds until maturity. This is to say, if you buy a fund and its SEC yield is 6%, this does not mean that you can expect to receive 6% in distributions over the next year. You might get more, and you might get less. Looking at the fund's historical distributions will give you a better indication of what to expect.

Finally, there is a seven day SEC yield, which is mostly used by money market funds. This is what the fund's yield would be if it paid income for the entire year as it did in the last seven days. It is similar to the 30 day yield, and is most useful in comparing similar funds. It is otherwise not very useful.

Make sure, therefore, that when you compare yields between a stock and its past, between stocks, between stocks and funds, and between funds and funds that you are comparing figures that have been calculated in the same way. Be sure to also never take anyone's word for it. Check the figures yourself. Publications often list yields that are incorrect, or derived by some unconventional method. A stock yielding 2% might be displayed as yielding 8%, for example. It helps tremendously to understand how a yield was calculated so that instead of comparing apples to oranges you're comparing apples to apples and oranges to oranges.

The Real Importance of Yield

The yield on a stock with a stable dividend (i.e., one that is never lower than a previous year's) is probably the best valuation measure there is. It's not just an indicator of under-, over-, or fair value. It tells you the annual return you can expect from a given stock. The same goes for bonds and other income generating assets.

Chapter 30 - Save on Costs Whenever Possible

Don't buy and sell securities frequently. It increases your portfolio volatility and the only one who'll make money will be your broker (there's a corny joke that brokers are called brokers because they make you broke). Furthermore, if you're purchasing a fund (mutual fund, ETF, ETN, or CEF), pay close attention not only to the expense ratio, but also to the fund's portfolio turnover rate, how closely it tracks its index (or by how much it outperforms) compared to similar funds, and how it is taxed. Sometimes it is better to pay a higher expense ratio if you save on taxes or have better performance. That is, a fund that has low fees but that saddles you with taxes and underperforming its benchmark may be worse than a fund that charges a higher fee but is tax efficient and outperforms its benchmark (but remember the past does not guarantee the future).

As I've mentioned earlier, try limiting your commission per trade to one percent or less. This means that if your broker charges you $6 per trade, for example, each of your trades should be at least $600 ($606 in total with the commissions). The greater the portion of your investment that a trade commission is, the more the security you're buying has to go up for you to break even.

Here's an extreme case. Suppose your broker charges $6 per trade and you decide to buy a stock that trades for $6 a share. Suppose you only have $12 to invest. If you buy the stock, you'll be able to get one share. You'll pay $6 for it, and you'll fork over another $6 (100% of the trade) to your broker. The stock has to double from here if you are to break even. And don't forget that it'll cost you another $6 in broker's fees to sell. That means if you are to break even the stock has to go up from $6 to $18. You're better off not investing in such a situation.

Compare this scenario to another one, where you limit your broker fees to 1% of your transaction. Same facts: your broker charges $6 per transaction and the stock you want to buy trades for $6 a share. But this time around, you have $606 to invest. You pay the broker his fee, leaving you with $600, which is enough for 100 shares. Since the broker will charge you another $6 to sell, your investment has to go up $12 in value for you to break even ($6 to buy plus $6 to sell). That means the stock has to go up 2%, or 12 cents, to $6.12 per share. I'm sure you would agree that that is a big difference—if the stock goes up to $18 a share, you will have almost tripled your money in this scenario whereas in the previous one you would just break even.

If you are buying individual stocks instead of an ETF, say because you'd rather have the ETF's top ten holdings instead of the entire thing, keep in mind that the total commission you pay for the stocks will be greater than what you would pay for the ETF (ten trades versus one). But note that this doesn't mean that you will save money by buying the ETF instead. Once you own the individual stocks, you don't pay any additional fees. With the ETF, however, an annual expense is deducted from your returns. As it is a percentage of the fund's net asset value, the better the fund does, the more you will pay. If you limit the broker fee on each individual stock purchase to one percent or less, you will end up saving money in the long run over the ETF, even though you spend more initially.

For example, suppose your broker charges $10 per trade and you have $10,000 to invest. If you buy the ETF (and you can buy fractional shares), you will spend $10 for the trade. This comes out to 0.1%. If you invest in the ETF's top ten holdings, say $1000 per stock, you'll end up paying $100 in commissions. That's 1%. The ETF seems like the better deal. It's ten times cheaper after all.

But suppose the ETF has a relatively cheap expense ratio of 0.18%. Here I'm looking at the Vanguard Dividend Appreciation ETF (VIG). Its 0.18% is far lower than the 1.13% average expense ratio of similar funds. If you hold the ten individual stocks for ten years, you will pay nothing more in fees. If you hold the ETF for ten years, however, you'll end up paying around $457 out of your returns. If we take the average expense ratio of 1.13%, this jumps to $2,751 according to Vanugard. So now we're comparing $457 and $2,751 to $100. Add to this the ETF's portfolio turnover, which can increase costs. As I've mentioned previously, buying all of an index's holdings is cheaper in the long run than buying an ETF that tracks the index. The more money you have to invest, the better it is to buy individual holdings to replicate an index than the ETF. After all, by doing so you are cutting out the middle man. The less money you have to invest, on the other hand, the better ETFs are because you save on commissions as a percentage of your total investment.

An obvious way to save on broker commissions, other than trading less frequently, is to use a broker or transfer agent that charges less per transaction. Don't just look at the cost to buy. See how much it costs to sell too. Most of the time these fees are the same, but sometimes they are not. If you are going to write calls or puts, check to see how much the broker charges per contract in addition to what the broker charges per trade. A broker that may seem cheaper may not be, depending on how many contracts or shares you trade. Brokers that allow you to do multi-leg trades (simultaneously buy or sell two different securities) are generally cheaper than those that do not.

Many brokers now offer no fee purchases and sales of certain ETFs. If these ETFs interest you, it's better to buy them through a broker that doesn't charge you for them than to buy them through a broker that does. This is most advantageous if you invest small amounts frequently.

One final thing about brokers. It may not always be best to pick the one that charges the cheapest fees. Sometimes brokers are cheap for a reason. Trades may be executed slowly or not at all. Customer service may be incompetent or nonexistent. Read reviews. Ask your friends about their experience. This will help you avoid brokers that seem cheap but will cost you a lot in terms of time, aggravation, and lost opportunity.

If you are thinking about buying a mutual fund in a taxable account, it is usually best to avoid doing so at the end of the year. This is when most mutual funds issue a distribution. Some of this distribution may be income, but most of the time it is capital gains. Thus, you are taxed for gains that you didn't receive. So, don't rush to buy a mutual fund for its end of year dividend. If you are thinking about buying an ETF at the end of the year, it is good to check its past end of year distributions too. You'll often get a better price on ex-dividend day.

Another way to avoid costs is to reduce bid/ask spreads. The bid/ask spread is the difference between the ask price of a security and its bid price. The ask price, as mentioned in the options chapter (but it applies to stocks and funds too), is the price at which a seller is offering to sell the security. The bid price is the price at which a buyer is offering to buy the security. The ask price is usually higher than the bid price, and in the normal course of things, when you are buying your trade is executed at the ask price, and when you are selling your trade is executed at the bid price. So, for example, if the bid price for a stock is $43.69 and the ask price is $43.75, the bid/ask spread is $0.06.

The bid/ask spread is how market makers get paid. They collect the difference between the bid and ask on each trade. For those securities that are heavily traded, the bid/ask spread is usually around one cent. For those securities that are thinly traded, however, the bid ask spread can be as much as 5% of the share price. If you buy such a security for the ask price and attempt to sell it right away for the bid price, you will lose 5%. In other words, where the bid/ask spread is very wide, you suffer an instant loss. The reason that the market maker charges you more for a thinly traded security than a heavily traded one is because it is far riskier for him. The longer he holds a security, the greater his risk. With heavily traded securities, his holding time is often seconds or fractions of a second. With a thinly traded security, where only a few thousand shares trade, his holding time can be hours.

Therefore, you can save a lot of money by buying or selling those securities that have bid/ask spreads of a few cents. For example, if you are choosing between two ETFs that track the same index but one of the ETFs has lower bid/ask spreads, all else being equal, the ETF with the lower spreads is better. Note that with options, the further out in time or the deeper in or out of the money you go, the greater the bid/ask spread.

Another cost is the time you spend on your investments. Can you be doing something else instead? Like spending time with your family, working another job, or doing something you enjoy? The less time you have to devote to your investments, the better off you will be investing in an index. If you enjoy doing research, reading financial reports, and so on, then by all means do so. Just keep in mind that there are costs to everything, and this includes the amount of time you spend trying to make your money work for you.

Finally, unless you are buying shares in a tax deferred account or have very good reasons to believe that the stock will go up significantly in the next few days, never rush to buy shares in order to get the dividend. Most of the time you will be better off buying the stock on ex-dividend day. All other things being equal, if you buy shares in a taxable account it is better to do so on ex-dividend day than the day before. There are two reasons for this. The first is that the dividend is a tax event. When you rush to get the dividend, you are rushing to pay taxes. The second reason is that the stock goes down by the dividend amount on ex-dividend day. Buying the stock at a lower price locks in a higher dividend yield.

For example, suppose stock XYZ trades at $40 a share and tomorrow is ex-dividend day for the dividend payment of $0.50 per share (this is a quarterly payment, and the annual payment is $2 a share). Suppose you buy the shares for $40 today in a taxable account, and the tax rate on dividends is 15%. First, your dividend yield will be 5% ($2 divided by 40 and expressed as a percentage). Second, on ex-dividend day the stock will drop to $39.50 a share. Third, on payable day you will receive $0.50 per share out of which the government will want $0.075 per share, leaving you with a dividend payment of $0.425 a share. Because the stock dropped by the dividend amount the day after you bought it, what really happened was you gave the government $0.075 a share.

Now, suppose that you buy the shares on ex-dividend day instead, for $39.50 apiece. First, you save the $0.075 a share you would have given to the government. Second, you've locked in a higher dividend yield (not much higher, but higher still), in our example 5.06%. Third, because you buy the shares at a lower price, depending on how large your investment was, you get more of them, which in turn increases your future dividend payments.

Stocks do not simply drop by the dividend amount on ex-dividend day. Sometimes they drop more, sometimes they stay flat, and sometimes they close above the previous day's price. The point is, simply, that unless the stock takes off or you are buying shares in a tax deferred account, there is no reason to rush to get that first dividend.

Chapter 31 - Have a Plan

Formulate a plan when you are calm and the markets are closed. Construct your own strategy or adopt one that someone else uses, and stick with it. Ask yourself what can go wrong, and what you will do about it if it does. Never let your emotions steer you away from your plan. Always remember that when it comes to investing, emotions are your enemy. According to the *Wall Street Journal*,

> people with an impaired ability to experience emotions could actually make better financial decisions than other people under certain circumstances....lack of emotional responsiveness actually gave them an advantage when they played a simple investment game. (Jane Spencer, "Lessons From The Brain-Damaged Investor," *Wall Street Journal*, July 21, 2005.)

Feelings get in the way of decision making. They make you rush to sell when you should be buying, and they push you to buy when you should be selling. Having a plan that you developed in a calm, rational state of mind, and sticking to it, will help you make more money and sleep better during turbulent times. So plan ahead. When will you buy? For what reasons? When will you sell? What will trigger your selling? What will you do if there's a market crash? What will you do if you lose your job? What will you do if the market rallies?

Whether your strategy is a sound one is a good question. My take is that you should evaluate your plan from time to time when the markets are closed and you are calm. Has something gone wrong that you hadn't accounted for? Has something gone right that you hadn't considered?

Does this put the entire strategy into question? If so, dump the plan and come up with a new one. Learn from your mistakes. You'll make plenty of them, but hopefully only once per mistake and at not too great a loss.

Remember, as long as you are still buying shares, whether through new purchases or dividend reinvestment, you are better off if the share price goes down. The lower the share price goes, the more shares you're able to buy, and the better your dividend yield will be. This is assuming that the dividend stays the same or rises.

Finally, there is usually no reason to rush to buy a stock that you've just discovered. Calm down and think about it rationally before you commit your money. If the investment is a good deal today, it will be tomorrow too (unless you're in it for a short term trade, but then you aren't investing. You're speculating). A portfolio can take a long time to build. Don't rush to buy everything at once. And once you do buy, don't fall in love with your investments. No emotions, remember? If a stock (or any holding, for that matter) isn't working for your strategy, dump it.

Chapter 32 - Diversify, Diversify, Diversify!

As I keep insisting, no one knows the future. One of the best ways to reduce risk is to spread it out. Just as it's less risky to invest in a number of stocks than it is to invest in one, it is less risky to invest in a number of industries and sectors than it is to invest in one. It is also less risky to invest in a number of asset classes than it is to invest in one asset class. So, invest in more than one company. Invest in companies in more than one industry. Invest in companies in more than one sector. Don't just invest in stocks. Look at other asset classes like cash, precious metals, bonds, and real estate.

Some of your investments will go down in value. Some will even be completely wiped out. The idea is to have the gains in your other investments compensate you for these losses and provide you with a solid overall return. Recall my example in Part One of buying the top ten yielding stocks in the Dow. Over the course of a decade one of the companies went bankrupt, while another almost did (and by the time your read this EK might be in bankruptcy court). Despite these losses, the total portfolio rose some 40%. Had one invested all of one's money in what turned out to be the best stock of the bunch, one would have a far greater return. On the other hand, had one invested in the company that went bankrupt, one would have lost everything. Diversification evens these out. You will never have the best possible return (e.g., some stock no one's ever heard of that rises from a few cents per share to tens of dollars) with a diversified portfolio, but neither will you have the worst.

Be aware that you are not done diversifying when you own a diversified portfolio of stocks, bonds, real estate, precious metals, and so on. Even if it is below the FDIC limit, do not keep all your cash at one bank. Keep it at several banks and keep some in a safe at home. Don't hold all your stocks with one broker or transfer agent. Keep your stock holdings in a few brokerages. Make sure none of these separate banks or brokers are owned by the same parent company. When financial institutions go out of business their customers' accounts are frozen. Even if records aren't lost, it can take a long time to get your money out.

Don't concentrate your investments in one region. If possible, have your cash and precious metals in a few countries. Don't rely on someone else to hold these for you. Keep some yourself. Don't rely on being always able to buy food and water in the store. Keep emergency supplies at home. (If you think about it, canned and dry food, bottled water, medical supplies, and precious metals are just another method of storing your cash.) Equally important, don't spread yourself too thin either. For example, if you have $1,000 to put in the bank, don't open 1,000 bank accounts. One will do just fine. If you have several hundred thousand dollars, on the other hand, banking with three or four different institutions might be a good idea.

Unless you own and work in a small business, do not invest significant amounts in your employer's stock. If your employer goes out of business, not only do you lose your job, you also lose your investment.

Asset Allocation

If there is ever a free lunch in investing, it is diversification, which enables you to get a rate of return with lower risk. Diversification is not, however, simply buying a whole bunch of different assets. Allocating these different assets (assigning a weighting for each class in your portfolio) is the single most important investment decision you can make.

In allocating your assets, you should limit your exposure to any individual risky asset class to a level that allows you to maintain that exposure even when the markets are down. In other words, the goal of asset allocation is to maximize returns while minimizing risk.

For example, small cap value stocks have outperformed all other asset classes since the 1920s. At first it might seem to be a good idea to have your entire portfolio composed of small cap stocks. But of course it's not, and not only because the future might be different from the past. Very few, if any, investors have been able to hold small cap stocks (or any other asset class) for a long time. Upheavals, crises, and other events make people sell. Small caps, for example, lost 90% of their value during the great depression. What did small cap investors do near the bottom? They sold, of course. If your portfolio consists entirely of one asset class and this asset class goes down significantly (which is likely to happen, especially when dealing with stocks), despite all your plans and preparations (e.g., "if it falls I'll buy more shares, and I'll never sell!") you will sell, and probably at the bottom too.

And it's not just individual investors that do this. After the 1987 stock market crash, university endowments increased their bond holdings and decreased their stock holdings, ending up selling low and buying high.

If your portfolio consists of a number of different asset classes, on the other hand, some of which will rise when others fall (for example, treasury bonds rose sharply in price during the Great Depression—so those who sold their small caps at the bottom were buying bonds at the top!), you will be less likely to sell. That is because your portfolio as a whole will not take as much of a hit. It might even rise. Once you set an asset allocation for yourself, stick with it. It will tell you the best places to put new money.

Before we get into the details, consider the following. There are three sources of portfolio return: asset allocation, market timing, and security selection. Asset allocation contributes more than 100% of a portfolio's return. Both market timing and security selection contribute negative returns. It makes sense if you think about it. Market timing and selection are not a zero sum game for the investing community as a whole. First, we have transaction costs. Second, our transactions have an impact on the market. This is what David Swenson, Yale University's endowment manager, calls "leakage." The leakage transforms market timing and security selection from a zero sum game to a negative sum game.

To repeat, *asset allocation contributes more than 100% of a portfolio's return.*

Asset Allocation Models

There are a number of standard allocation models. They are usually based on historical returns and risks (typically measured by standard deviation) of different asset classes, the portfolio's goal (retirement, home purchase, college tuition, etc) which factors in time, and the individual's risk tolerance. There is no perfect asset allocation. Every individual's situation is different and a one size fits all approach is rarely the best. That said, risk tolerance is a very important factor. You should think very carefully about how much pain you can take without selling your investments at a loss and calling it quits; then assume that you'll handle less pain than that. The problem with you thinking about it, no matter how carefully, is that you'll probably be wrong. Everyone is an aggressive, high risk tolerant investor

288

when the markets are up, and a low risk tolerant, conservative investor when the markets are down. Keep this in mind when thinking about your own risk tolerance, and adjust it down accordingly. Most people take their money out of equity funds after they go down, and put it in bond funds after they've gone up. The key is not to be one of these people.

So when you are looking at the standard asset allocation models below and in other publications (just Google "asset allocation" and you'll get hundreds of examples from reputable sources with historical return and risk data), which tell you the average annual returns of different asset allocations over some period, pay particular attention to the figures that tell you about the losses. In your decision making, put more weight on the declines in the worst years, than on the gains in the best years. Also think about when you are going to need the money. The sooner you need it, the less of the riskier assets (those that suffer the biggest declines) you should own. Also keep in mind that the future may be very different from the past. The past is but a guide, not foresight. See box 15.

Standard Asset Allocations Historical Returns 1926 through 2010

	Conservative Portfolio			Balanced Portfolio			Aggressive Portfolio		
Bonds	100.00%	80.00%	70.00%	60.00%	50.00%	40.00%	30.00%	20.00%	0.00%
Equities	0.00%	20.00%	30.00%	40.00%	50.00%	60.00%	70.00%	80.00%	100.00%
Average Annual Return	5.50%	6.70%	7.30%	7.80%	8.30%	8.70%	9.10%	9.40%	10.00%
Best Year	32.60%	29.80%	28.40%	27.90%	32.30%	36.70%	41.10%	45.40%	54.20%
Worst Year	-8.10%	-10.10%	-14.20%	-18.40%	-22.50%	-26.60%	-30.70%	-34.90%	-43.10%
Number of Years When Portfolio Declined	13	12	14	16	17	21	22	23	25

Box 15

Source: Vanguard

My method of allocating is somewhat different. I have a 70/30 mix in favor of equities over fixed income, but my approach, as outlined in the next chapter, is to make individual stock selections that are based on an index but do not include the entire index. My goal is to grow over time the income that my portfolio generates and not necessarily have high total returns (though the theory is that as my income grows, so should the total return). As such, I did not go all in when starting the portfolio. Rather, I accumulated positions gradually. This involved market timing—but not in the way you might think. I did not select assets that I thought would go up the most in price. Instead, I selected those assets (and particular stocks in the dividend paying stocks category) that paid the most income at the time or would pay the most over time (combination of current yield and historical dividend growth rate, as far as dividend paying stocks were concerned). The stocks, ETFs, and so on that I bought were the ones that reached their target prices on my shopping list. In theory, I was buying the most undervalued assets relative to my choices at the time.

See box 16 for my allocation. Note that in my portfolio commodities are not listed. I'm exposed to commodities through my basic materials stock holdings, upstream MLPs, and royalty trusts. I use small cap and growth stock ETFs to buttress the portfolio. Yes, dividend stocks tend to outperform over the long term, but you can have too much of a good thing (concentration risk). The stock portion of my portfolio is skewed toward dividends, but I want to diversify away some of the risk by owning growth stocks too. The rest, like gold, silver, and food, as mentioned, I consider part of my cash holdings (as these are hedges against the breakdown of the system, I keep them in my personal possession—not in the form of ETFs or in someone else's vault). Note also that I hold a number of CEFs (after spending a chapter talking about how much I hate them). There are certain asset classes (preferred shares, lower grade sovereign bonds, mortgage bonds) where I think professional gamblers can be useful because I lack the understanding and the time to do my own due diligence. Moreover, these funds hold assets that pay an income, and the funds' objective is to maximize that income. This objective discourages lots of trading. It is also an issue of access, especially with foreign bonds. With these assets, I look for fund managers that have long histories of solid performance (i.e., no terrible blunders and no bad kind of return of capital). I buy these CEFs when they are at a relative discount to NAV, and to spread the manager risk, I buy more than one CEF for each category.

With both the standard model and my model a beautiful thing happens once you are fully invested and are bringing in new money. Your portfolio will tell you the best place, in terms of relative value (not in terms of potential future gains), to put your new money (or accumulated income that you do not need). As asset prices change, some of your portfolio's holdings will grow and thus will take up a greater portion of the whole than your target. Other holdings will decline, stay the same, or grow less, and so will take up a smaller portion than your target. Your new money should go into these decliners and laggards, until the portfolio is, once again, at your target proportions. When you put money into the laggards, you are in theory buying low. In an income oriented portfolio, you are also, in theory, buying the greatest income producing assets available at the time. That is to say, your asset allocation helps you pick the best assets in terms of relative value and prevents you from investing with your emotions.

My Portfolio Target Allocations (Excluding Cash)

Equities 70%			Fixed Income 30%		
Type	Method of Holding	Weight in Portfolio	Type	Method of Holding	Weight in Portfolio
Dividend Achievers, Aristocrats, and Other Dividend Growers, Global small cap and growth funds	Individual stocks, ETFs	20.00%	US Treasury and Agency Bonds	Ladder of individual securities	5.00%
International Dividend Payers	ETF, individual ADRs	10.00%	International Investment Grade Sovereign Bonds	ETF	4.00%
MLPs	Individual stocks	15.00%	International Lower Grade Sovereign Bonds	CEF	2.00%
Global REITs	Individual stocks, ETF	5.00%	Investment Grade Corporate Bonds	ETF ladder, Individual bonds	5.00%
Preferreds & ETDS	CEFs, Individual Stocks	5.00%	Asset Backed Bonds	CEFs	4.00%
High Yield Bonds	ETF, CEF	10.00%	Certificates of Deposit	Ladder at bank	4.00%
			TIPS	ETF	4.00%
Royalty Trusts	Individual stocks	5.00%	Personal and Business Loans	Peer to Peer Lending Sites*	2.00%

*You can lend to people and businesses and trade these loans at websites like Prosper.com

Box 16

293

The more fine grained your asset allocations (e.g., you divide bonds into categories like sovereign, corporate, and so on, and divide stocks into international, domestic, large caps, small caps, etc), the more likely that you will put new money into undervalued assets). Make sure, though, that you do not increase your transaction and time costs by having your portfolio too finely grained.

Other Considerations

Your broker, investment websites, fund websites, and tons of publications have enormous amounts of information about asset allocation. There are even websites and brokers which suggest target asset allocations for you after giving you a quiz. Note that whatever type of investor you are (conservative, balanced, moderate, aggressive) you are probably less aggressive than you think. Taking the same quiz during bad times will yield a different result from the good times. People are usually more aggressive when their portfolio is up than when it is down. Keep that in mind when selecting your asset allocation.

Also keep in mind that your goals, and the time to reach your goals should be one of the top considerations for you. If you are retired, for example, you shouldn't have a large portion of your portfolio in assets that can decline substantially. In other words, don't stretch for gains or yield.

Finally, there is a debate about portfolio rebalancing. When you have little or no new money coming in, your portfolio's allocations will swing out of your target ranges. There is a school of thought that advocates an annual rebalancing—selling off your best performing assets (the ones now taking the largest part of your portfolio) and using the proceeds to buy more of the lagging assets so that your portfolio is reset to its target allocation. In theory, rebalancing makes you sell high and buy low. Another school of thought says this is nonsense and usually cites figures to show that over the long term portfolios that do not rebalance do better when you factor in rebalancing costs (buying and selling fees, taxes, time spent, etc). I am agnostic on the matter, as I still put new money in. Generally, I will rebalance when my portfolio is 10% out of whack. For example, I'll sell some shares of stock and buy bonds with the proceeds if stocks make up 80% of my portfolio. On the same note, if stocks go down and/or bonds rise so that bonds make up 40% of my portfolio, I'll sell some bonds and buy stocks with the proceeds so that my portfolio is once again at a 70/30 mix.

If your portfolio becomes seriously out of whack and your goal is only in a few years, however, rebalancing may be a good idea. For example, if you are about to retire and stocks make up 90% of your portfolio, you should consider selling a portion because of the risk of a market downturn and no time to make up your losses if it occurs. Similarly, if you have many years left to retirement and your portfolio, originally supposed to have a skew toward equities, now consists of 70% bonds, you should seriously consider trading the bonds for stocks. When your portfolio deviates significantly from your target weights, this is usually an indication that one category of assets is overvalued and is due for a decline and another category of assets is undervalued and due for a rise.

Finally, your target allocation should gradually change as you approach your goal from the riskier asset classes to the less risky.

Chapter 33 - My Approach to Dividend Stocks and Other Assets

Before I put in any money, I make a shopping list. The goal for the dividend stock portion of my portfolio is to eventually own the top two or three companies (basically the Coke and Pepsi) of every industry that I think will still be around when my heirs and their heirs die of old age.

To be on my shopping list, the companies should dominate industries that will not go away any time soon. For example, unless there is some major change, people will have to eat, drink, clothe, and clean up after themselves. People need places to live, and they will always need fuel (for transportation, moving goods and services, heating and cooling indoor areas, and for keeping the lights on). Furthermore, people will always need to communicate with each other for business as well as personal reasons. Finally, there will always be war. And if there isn't war, that will mean either that we are all dead or there's a one world government. If we're all dead, non of our investments matter. If there's a one world government, it will still need the implements of war (to quash rebellions, etc) to maintain its power. The aim of my dividend stock portfolio, therefore, is to own the dominant companies in these industries.

When I say that the company should dominate its industry, what I mean is that it tops its competitors in sales, name brand recognition, and financial heft. For example, Coca Kola (KO) and Pepsico (PEP) dominate the non-alcoholic beverage industry. With domination come certain perks, like pricing power. If some new competitor enters the market, the dominant company can lower its prices to drive the competitor out of business. If there is some innovative new start up that poses a danger, the dominant company can usually buy it out.

Also, you are probably aware that governments are corrupt—and if corrupt is too strong a word for you, you should be aware of the so called "revolving door policy" that exists between government regulators and the businesses they regulate. Oftentimes a corporate official is appointed to a government body that regulates his previous employer. A few years later, the official is back at the company. A few years after that, he's back at the government in a higher ranking position. And on it goes.

There is certainly a conflict of interest here. If you are a government regulator and you want to work in the future (even supposing you didn't work there in the past) for the company you are regulating, you will not give it a hard time. You will draft regulations that are favorable to the industry, if not the company. Most often, regulations serve not to benefit consumers, or the environment, or whatever cause the do-gooders promote when they ask for more regulations, but to keep competition out.

For dividend investors (putting ethics aside, because that's another debate entirely—if certain unethical conditions exist we can certainly strive to change them, but why not take advantage of them, or avoid the disadvantages of not taking advantage of them, in the meantime?) it's best to own shares of companies that use the government to keep their competition out of the marketplace than to own shares of a competitor that must force itself into the industry. Lobbyists for industry dominant companies, often former senators, congressmen, congressional staffers, or regulators, usually end up writing the regulations for the industry. Therefore, it pays to pick the big fish in the pond if you're going to invest for dividends in the industry.

Companies in my core holdings should not be in industries where innovation or the existence of outside risks is the norm. They can be great companies paying a generous dividend. But if they have to innovate just to survive (which means a misstep or two and they're out of business), they do not belong in my long term portfolio. They can make great investments and I might buy them— but not for my core holdings.

For example, even if Apple (AAPL) paid a generous dividend, I would not have it in my core dividend portfolio. The devices it sells are obsolete within a couple of years. The company has to innovate just to keep up. It has plenty of competitors, some of them big companies like Google (GOOG), that will take advantage of any misstep. If you're reading this book in 2025, is Apple still around? I wouldn't be surprised that it is. But I also wouldn't be surprised if it isn't. An industry leader that sells tapes, tape decks, video tapes, and VCRs goes out of business or is seriously hurt if it fails to adapt by changing its product line to CDs, CD players, DVDs, and DVD players, and then to MP3 players and so on. Eastman Kodak (EK) and Polaroid were industry leaders in the photography business. They failed to adapt quickly enough to digital photography and film. EK, a one time blue chip stock, lost over 98% of its share price since 1972. Polaroid went bankrupt (it was revived and is still an active business, but original shareholders didn't fare well at all).

Similarly, while there will always be a need for moving people and goods around the planet (and in the future possibly around the solar system and between stars), this does not mean that investing in companies in such industries is a good idea. It can be and you can make a lot of money with them—but how many airlines, railroads, and shipping companies have stayed in business for a long time? Transports are subject to large risks that are often beyond their concern. Fuel prices, interest rates, and economic downturns have brought many of these companies to an early grave.

No one knows the future, and it's hard to tell which companies will be innovative enough not just to survive but to thrive. But I know that companies that sell food, water, toilet paper, and other daily necessities, those that provide and transport the energy involved in moving these, and those that move these necessities will still be here years from now. Sure, some of the products or services they sell might be banned or become unpopular (for environmental, health, or other reasons), but not all of them. Unless humanity undergoes a dramatic change or there is a catastrophe, companies that manufacture, move, and provide the energy to move consumer staples will endure and prosper. And if there are world changes that are so major or catastrophic that even these companies do not survive, then either we will have a lot more to worry about than our investments, or we'll be living in a utopia.

Hey, maybe in the future we will have some sort of *Star Trek*-like communist society where we don't need money. Or maybe we'll all be dead. It might be that all businesses are nationalized. Aliens might land and eradicate us or transform our society into something we can't imagine. No one knows the future, as I keep saying. We can only guess what is more or less likely to happen. If I had to bet (and I am betting with my money by investing in dividend paying industry leaders in industries that are likely to always be around) which company will be around 100 years from now, Coca-Cola or Apple, I would choose Coca-Cola. Apple depends on new products to fuel its sales. Coca-Cola has sold pretty much the same thing since 1886. Can I be wrong? Sure. All investments carry risk, after all. That's what diversification is for!

Indexing is the best and most cost effective way to invest. I do not buy ETFs for my core portfolio if I can buy their individual constituents. The S&P 500 is a great index and few active investors, whether individuals or professionals, can consistently generate a better return. But many of its components do not pay a dividend. As such, the dividend aristocrats and dividend achievers indexes are more suitable for dividend investors. One way to use the indexing approach with individual stocks is to buy the top 20 or so components of one or both of these indexes. For example, the top 22 holdings of the S&P 1500 Dividend Aristocrats Index make up about 50% of the index's holdings, and the top 15 or so components of the Mergeant Dividend Achievers Index make up around 50% of that index. By owning the shares of these companies, instead of the ETFs that track them, you will track the index with about the same accuracy, but you will have a higher yield. You will also, as mentioned, save on costs from fund expenses and portfolio turnover if you hold the stocks over the long term.

I take a different approach. Perhaps it's a boneheaded thing to do, but I use the dividend indexes to narrow down stocks for my shopping list. That a company is a component of the index speaks to its quality. The index is a sort of a filter that gets rid of companies that have been inconsistent with their dividends.

300

Next, I shift through the index, finding the Pepsi and Coke of every industry I think will still be here hundreds of years from now. In focusing on companies that produce or derive their income from the staples of daily life, I'm looking for producers of beverages, food, toilet paper, and other things that people do not give up when times are tough unless they absolutely have to, utilities (this includes electric, water, gas, and telecomunications), energy companies, REITs, and MLPs. If there are more than two great companies in an industry, I apportion the amount I want to invest among all of them (e.g., if I planned to invest $2,000 each on two, I will spend $1,000 each on four).

Once I narrow my list down, I look to see the companies' past performance. How do they treat their shareholders? Do they have a lot of debt compared to their peers? Are they more or less efficient than their peers? Are earnings growing on par with or faster than dividends? How did they perform during the financial crisis? I don't mean share price performance. Rather, did earnings and dividends grow even after the economy fell off the cliff? If yes, these companies will survive almost anything.

Once I narrow down my list, I look to make sure that it is diversified geographically. Most of the consumer staples producers are multinational corporations, so this isn't as much a concern with them (but it does depend on how much currency hedging they do). However, natural resource transporters (MLPs), landlords (REITs), and utilities are often regionally based. For these, I make sure they are fairly well spread out. In the case of MLPs I also make sure that I'm diversified in what they transport—I don't want to own only those MLPs that transport natural gas, or only those that transport oil, or biofuels. I want to own them all.

301

Simply buying the Alerian MLP index's top ten to fifteen components does the trick.

When I'm satisfied that the list is diversified, it's time to decide when to initiate my investments. I'm a big fan of dollar cost averaging. I don't plan to buy a stock just once, so it's okay if I don't buy it at the bottom (the more frequently I buy it, the more likely I am to buy some shares at the bottom—but also at the top). That said, I do try to "time" the market. This has less to do with guessing when the market will turn up than it does with having a target price for each stock.

My target purchase prices are based on the dividend yield I want to lock in. For healthy dividend growers (those companies whose dividend growth rate is in the double digits), I look for a dividend yield between 3 and 4%. For the slower dividend growers, I look for a dividend yield between 4 and 8%. I will buy stocks that have higher dividends, but I will be cautious and do extra homework, because when a common stock dividend approaches 8% the market thinks it's unsustainable.

To find the target share price based on target dividend yield, divide the trailing annual (or forward, if you know it) dividend rate by your target yield. For example, suppose a stock pays $3 a share in dividends this year and you want to buy it when it yields 4%. Divide the $3 by 0.04 and you get $75. At $75 per share, a stock that pays an annual dividend of $3 per share will have a dividend yield of 4%.

I allocate the shares and units based on the riskiness of the companies' businesses. For example, I will put less money in an upstream MLP (and demand a higher yield) than in a midstream MLP.

I do not measure my performance by total return. Rather, I measure it by the amount of income my portfolio generates on an annual basis. So, for example, when I look at a stock yielding 4%, I do not think about it in terms of how much the position will be worth when I retire. Rather, I view it as, "this stock will give me an extra $40 per year for every $1,000 I put into it (provided that the dividend isn't cut)," and attempt to calculate how much this income will grow with reinvestment and dividend raises. I also think about how much risk I'm taking on for each additional dollar of annual income. Share prices do not concern me as long as the dividend stays the same or is rising. It's the income level that I care most about.

In other words, when I'm putting in new money (or old money from a position where the dividend was cut), I make my choice (which is what the shopping list is for) based on yield and risk. Which asset class the new money will go into, on the other hand, is made for me by my asset allocation model. The awesome thing about trying to maintain assets in a portfolio according to your preferred allocation, as mentioned, is that you know when one asset class is relatively under priced as compared to another.

Once I own the stocks, the goal is to hold them forever (the one exception is that I sell some shares occasionally to rebalance the portfolio). My plan is, however, to sell those stocks that I think are very likely to cut or suspend their dividend, and to sell those stocks that actually have cut or suspended their dividend. I monitor my holdings regularly (not everyday, but I at least skim news items about them). If a company has a couple of major customers (say another company or a government), I also monitor the customers' health. If there's trouble, I look to see whether it will result in a fundamental change for the worse. If I think that this is more likely than not, the plan is to sell the shares.

The financial crisis has soured forever my opinion of bank stocks. For this reason, I will never own their common shares again. I invest in banks through their preferred shares or bonds. My preference is to buy the preferred share ETF rather than reading through all the prospectuses, but I hold individual issues as well. Since the business of banks is lending money, investing in them is almost like investing in bond CEFs. The difference is lack of transparency and more risk (because of leverage, unbridled use of derivatives, fraud, and so on).

Shopping for Fixed Income Securities

When shopping for preferreds, exchange traded debt securities, and bonds my strategy is somewhat different. It is always better, all else being equal, to own the debt of companies that are leaders in industries that will be around forever. For they are less likely to default. But things are rarely equal. Industry leaders, especially in a defensive industries, usually have low bond and preferred share yields. Investors are willing to pay more for them (take a lower yield) because these issues are safer. In some cases the companies' preferred shares and bonds have lower yields than their common stocks. For example, at the time of writing Johnson & Johnson's (JNJ) common stock has a dividend yield of around 3.5%. Its longer term bonds, those expiring in 12 years, on the other hand, have a yield of 3.33%. The common share dividend is eligible for the qualified tax rate. The bond interest is not—so the common stock yield is even higher than it looks if you compare it with the bond yield. And don't forget that JNJ has been raising its dividend every year for decades. The common stock is clearly the better choice for income investors as long as the company's business remains stable.

So with bonds and preferreds, I don't go looking for competitive advantages, industry leadership, history of dividend raises, and so on. These are a bonus, but they're not necessary. What I look for instead is the company's ability to pay its obligations.

As with dividend paying common shares, my approach with bonds and preferreds is to add them to my shopping list with a target yield. That is, if a preferred share currently yields 7.5% and I want to buy it when it yields 8%, I will wait for its share price to drop until it yields 8% or more. In addition, my rule is to never buy a bond or preferred share over par—over the redemption amount. If a preferred can be redeemed by the company at $25 per share, for example, I will not buy it above $25 per share. Additionally, I try to go as far up the capital structure as possible without sacrificing yield. It's better to own a company's bonds than preferred shares if both yield around the same.

Oftentimes a company will have several different preferred share classes outstanding. They will have the same redemption value (as mentioned, usually $25 per share) and priority in the capital structure, but usually different redemption dates and dividend rates (because they were issued in different times). Because of the latter differences the different issues' share prices will be different.

For example, suppose company XYZ has two preferred share classes, XYZ-PA and XYZ-PB. Suppose that they are equal in the capital structure and have the same redemption value, $25 per share. Also suppose that XYZ-PA was issued one year ago with a dividend rate of $2 per share while XYZ-PB was just issued with a dividend rate of $2.25 per share. Suppose both shares currently trade with a yield of 9%. That means XYZ-PB is trading at par, at $25 per share. XYZ-PA, on the other hand, is trading below par, at $22.22 per share (dividend rate of $2 per share divided by $22.22 per share and expressed as a percentage is 9%). XYZ-PA is the better choice because if you hold it to maturity you will receive a capital gain of 12.5% in addition to the 9% per year in dividends. Holding XYZ-PB to maturity will give you an income of 9% per year, but you have no potential for capital gains (unless interest rates fall, XYZ-PB trades above par, and you sell it—but then you no longer get income, and if interest rates fall the XYZ-PA shares will also rise). Buying XYZ-PA instead of XYZ-PB and holding it to maturity gets you a capital gain that is equal to over a year's worth of dividends with no extra risk.

It's also often the case that the preferred shares (or bonds) of a company, that have equal priority in the capital structure, that mature at around the same time, are all trading under par, and so on, have different yields. When deciding between these, I consider how close to par each of them is and what they are yielding. Companies rarely call preferred shares that are well under par. Those close to par, on the other hand, are often called. That is because the company might be able to issue new debt at a lower interest rate to replace the current outstanding issue.

For example, suppose a company has three preferred share classes outstanding. They all have a par value of $25 per share, all are currently callable by the company (i.e., the company can buy the shares back any time it wants for $25 per share) and all mature in over 20 years. The A shares currently trade for $24.80 and have a yield of 8.9%. The B shares currently trade for $22.12 and have a yield of 8.1%. The C shares trade at $22.50 and have a yield of 8.4%. If you want to invest in the company's preferred shares, which would you choose?

The A shares are most likely to be called. That is because investors are willing to lend the company money as low as 8.1%. The company can therefore save on interest costs by calling back its A shares and issuing D shares that yield 8.1% at par. The company would lose only $0.20 per A share at the current market price in calling them back. It would save more than enough money on interest, however, by calling the A shares back and issuing D shares with a lower yield.

The B and C shares, on the other hand, have little danger of being called by the company, as they are well below par. If for some reason the shares are called, the B shareholders will get a 13.01% capital gain. The C shareholders will get an 11.11% capital gain. This might make the B shares look more appealing.

Nevertheless, I think the C shares are the better investment. They have as much chance of being called in the near future as the B shares. Given how far under par they're trading, the chances of them being called are very little. It will be a long time before these shares are called, if ever. Because the C shares have a higher yield, holding them to maturity will provide a better total return (and more current income) than the B shares.

In sum, although the A shares yield the most, in this example they are the worst choice. The difference between the B and C shares is debatable, but for the reasons stated above, I believe that C is the best choice.

With higher yielding preferreds and bonds (over 7%), my plan is to hold them forever. If I can get a relatively safe 7% plus gain per year, I don't want the security to be called (but in case it is, I only buy below par). To this end, if I own a preferred share or bond that's trading at or above par and is currently callable, if I can replace it with a similar credit quality security (with the same or higher priority in the capital structure) that is trading below par (or at par and isn't currently callable), and has the same or higher yield, I will.

For example, suppose a few years ago I bought ABC corporation's preferred stock at $22 per share for a yield of 8%. The stock has bounced around and is now trading at $25.50 per share. Let's say the shares are callable. Suppose also that company CBA has the same credit quality as ABC. Let's say CBA has preferred shares that currently yield 8% and trade for $24.50. I'll sell my ABC preferred shares and buy CBA preferred shares with the proceeds.

* * *

As mentioned in the chapter on preferred shares (this applies to bonds too), instead of hunting individual issues you can simply buy an ETF, CEF, or mutual fund. That is always an alternative, and I combine both owning funds and individual securities for maximum income and diversification.

* * *

I keep as many of my income generating investments in a tax deferred account as possible. Why pay taxes when you don't have to? When it makes more sense to hold the investment in a taxable account, as with MLPs, I do so. I also have a much smaller trading account, where I play with mining stocks, consumer discretionary companies, high flying tech businesses, options, and so on. This provides me with enough entertainment that I'm not tempted to gamble with my long term holdings. Guess where the great majority of my stock market losses are? That's right, the trading account.

So that's my plan. It may not work for everyone, but it works for me. Take the time to formulate a plan that will work best for you.

www.ingramcontent.com/pod-product-compliance
Lightning Source LLC
Chambersburg PA
CBHW051442170526
45166CB00001B/81